Delete previous word	Option-Delete
Kern by 5 em spaces	Option-⌘-→ or -←
Kern by 1 em space (finer kerning)	Option-⌘-Shift-→ or -←

FOOTNOTES

Insert Footnote	Shift-⌘-F
Override footnote preference	Option + select Insert Footnote command

FRAMES

Adjust baseline height of in-line frame	Option + drag frame border
Move graphic image within a frame	⌘ + drag graphic image
Move object one pixel (overriding grid)	⌘-←, -→, -↑ or -↓
Open Modify Frame dialog box	Option + double-click in frame
Open Scale Picture dialog box	Double-click on graphic image
Override Auto Grid preference	⌘ as frame is drawn
Resize contents with frame	Option + drag selection handle
Resize contents proportionally with frame	Shift-Option + drag selection handle

For every kind of computer user,
there is a SYBEX book.

All computer users learn in their own way. Some need straightforward and methodical explanations. Others are just too busy for this approach. But no matter what camp you fall into, SYBEX has a book that can help you get the most out of your computer and computer software while learning at your own pace.

Beginners generally want to start at the beginning. The **ABC's** series, with its step-by-step lessons in plain language, helps you build basic skills quickly. Or you might try our **Quick & Easy** series, the friendly, full-color guide.

The **Mastering** and **Understanding** series will tell you everything you need to know about a subject. They're perfect for intermediate and advanced computer users, yet they don't make the mistake of leaving beginners behind.

If you're a busy person and are already comfortable with computers, you can choose from two SYBEX series—**Up & Running** and **Running Start**. The **Up & Running** series gets you started in just 20 lessons. Or you can get two books in one, a step-by-step tutorial and an alphabetical reference, with our **Running Start** series.

Everyone who uses computer software can also use a computer software reference. SYBEX offers the gamut—from portable **Instant References** to comprehensive **Encyclopedias**, **Desktop References**, and **Bibles**.

SYBEX even offers special titles on subjects that don't neatly fit a category—like **Tips & Tricks**, the **Shareware Treasure Chests**, and a wide range of books for Macintosh computers and software.

SYBEX books are written by authors who are expert in their subjects. In fact, many make their living as professionals, consultants or teachers in the field of computer software. And their manuscripts are thoroughly reviewed by our technical and editorial staff for accuracy and ease-of-use.

So when you want answers about computers or any popular software package, just help yourself to SYBEX.

For a complete catalog of our publications, please write:

SYBEX Inc.
2021 Challenger Drive
Alameda, CA 94501
Tel: (510) 523-8233/(800) 277-2346 Telex: 336311
Fax: (510) 523-2373

SYBEX is committed to using natural resources wisely to preserve and improve our environment. As a leader in the computer book publishing industry, we are aware that over 40% of America's solid waste is paper. This is why we have been printing the text of books like this one on recycled paper since 1982.

This year our use of recycled paper will result in the saving of more than 15,300 trees. We will lower air pollution effluents by 54,000 pounds, save 6,300,000 gallons of water, and reduce landfill by 2,700 cubic yards.

In choosing a SYBEX book you are not only making a choice for the best in skills and information, you are also choosing to enhance the quality of life for all of us.

THE
MacWrite Pro Book

THE **M** ac**Write Pro Book**

MARVIN BRYAN

SYBEX ®

San Francisco • Paris • Düsseldorf • Soest

Acquisitions Editor: *Dave Clark*
Developmental Editor: *Kenyon Brown*
Editor: *Guy Hart-Davis*
Technical Editor: *Martin Ilian*
Book Designer and Chapter Art: *Lisa Jaffe*
Screen Graphics: *John Corrigan*
Page Layout and Typesetter: *Stephanie Hollier*
Production Assistant: *Lisa Haden*
Indexer: *Matthew Spence*
Cover Designer: *Ingalls + Associates*
Cover Illustrator: *Tom McKeith*
SYBEX is a registered trademark of SYBEX Inc.

TRADEMARKS: SYBEX has attempted throughout this book to distinguish proprietary trademarks from descriptive terms by following the capitalization style used by the manufacturer.

SYBEX is not affiliated with any manufacturer.

Every effort has been made to supply complete and accurate information. However, SYBEX assumes no responsibility for its use, nor for any infringement of the intellectual property rights of third parties which would result from such use.

Library of Congress Card Number: 92-62323
ISBN: 0-7821-1084-3

Manufactured in the United States of America

10 9 8 7 6 5 4 3 2 1

TO NORB SKULAN,

a good friend through the years,
though we last met when
we worked together at Radio Tokyo
some time before the dawn of history.

•   •   •

•   •   •

•   •   •

ACKNOWLEDGMENTS

My thanks to Keri Walker of Apple and to Jonathan Weinstein of Claris for their help.

Computer artist Erin Bryan created original drawings used in this book.

At SYBEX, I'm indebted to Dave Clark for recommending the project, Ken Brown for some great suggestions, and Guy Hart-Davis for careful editing.

A T A GLANCE

C ONTENTS

Chapter 3:
PLACING PAGE ELEMENTS IN FRAMES 58

Chapter 8:
USING SHARED DATA AND FILES 172

Chapter 9:
CUSTOMIZING THE PROGRAM 202

I NTRODUCTION

When you buy this book, you also get a coupon for a free disk that contains professional typefaces and clip art worth several times the price of the book itself. There's even more on this disk. It includes a series of time-saving templates (called stationery files) that you can use "as is" or modify to print envelopes or produce your own newsletters, reports, invitations, and announcements. So *The MacWrite Pro Book* is a smart purchase even before you consider the content of the book.

The book will teach you everything you need to know about MacWrite Pro, an exciting program that adds sophisticated desktop-publishing capabilities to the features already enjoyed by more than a million MacWrite users. For example, with this successor to the original, classic Macintosh word-processing program, you can make text flow automatically around drawings and other graphic images, even when these objects are irregular in shape. You need to learn how to use options like these so you can use the full power of the program as soon as possible.

If you haven't purchased MacWrite Pro yet, reading this book will provide you with the facts you need to make an informed decision.

The MacWrite Pro Book was written by Marvin Bryan, an authority on typefaces, desktop publishing, and word-processing applications. He is also a Macintosh expert and the author of numerous other computer books, including the best seller *Introduction to Macintosh System 7*, published by SYBEX. He has written this book in a simple, straightforward style so you can understand the meaning of every word and sentence, even if you're new to the Macintosh and have never used a word-processing program before. Step-by-step instructions and tutorials are included to make even complicated procedures seem easy. On the other hand, if you're a Macintosh veteran and a long-time user of MacWrite, you'll find that you can skip the tutorial material and use the book as a reference, quickly finding the answers to your questions and tips for power users.

All major points are demonstrated in hundreds of screen shots, printed samples, and labeled illustrations and tables—so you can understand all of the chapters without using a computer as you read them.

H OW THE BOOK IS ORGANIZED

This book is divided into 14 chapters, plus two appendices. Each chapter begins with a quick-reference list of the subjects covered and ends with a summary that either reviews the features presented or gives some final pointers on using them. Frequent tips—highlighted in each chapter—provide shortcuts and additional options not mentioned in the main text. In addition, you're warned about actions you could take that might create problems.

Occasionally, the author mentions other products that may help you in using MacWrite Pro. For your convenience, Appendix B lists the manufacturers of these products alphabetically, along with their addresses and phone numbers.

Appendix A provides information on installing the program.

M ETHODS AND CONVENTIONS USED

Throughout the chapters, the words you should type to perform a task or complete an exercise are presented in boldface. New or unfamiliar terms or phrases are shown in *italics*.

Illustrations are numbered as *Figures* for each chapter and are explained both in the text and in captions accompanying each figure.

W HAT'S IN EACH CHAPTER

Here's a brief summary of what you'll find in each chapter:

Chapter 1: Learning the Basics. Starts with a tour of the MacWrite Pro desktop and shows how easy it is to create and print a simple document without even using the menus. Explains how to accomplish such tasks as setting tabs and line spacing, changing the number of columns, and zooming in on a page for a closer look or zooming out for an overall view.

Chapter 2: Using Menus, Palettes, and Styles. Describes the commands and other items on each menu, including the spell checker and thesaurus. Also tells how to use the program's *palettes* (small windows which can display some program options and tools continuously for easy access) and *styles* (settings you can name and save in order to reuse special combinations of fonts, borders, backgrounds, margins, and other formatting).

Chapter 3: Placing Page Elements in Frames. The creation and manipulation of *frames*, which are used to display drawings and other graphic images, tables of numbers and other data, notes, and special text that you want to set apart from the rest of a document. You can move material in frames anywhere you like on a page, change the formatting, place one frame in front of another, and make text flow around a frame.

Chapter 4: Handling Graphic Images. The graphic formats used on the Macintosh. How to integrate text and graphics in MacWrite Pro. Importing spreadsheet charts. Using clip-art libraries. Scanning graphic images.

Chapter 5: Using Multiple Columns. Preparing text for multiple-column documents. Selecting the right column width to display various kinds of text properly. How to separate a heading from multiple-column text. Using columns with different widths on the same page. Examples of single- and multiple-column pages.

Chapter 6: Making the Most of Typefaces. Why it's better to use only a few typefaces in most documents. How typefaces differ from one another. Definitions of typeface components. How typefaces are named. *Kerning* text (adjusting the space between two or more characters). Locating and using special characters from your keyboard. Installing and managing typefaces. Creating special effects.

Chapter 7: Creating and Using Tables. The advantages of using a data table within a frame. Options on the special Table menu. Step-by-step instructions on creating a sample table.

Chapter 8: Using Shared Data and Files. Using System 7's Publish and Subscribe features supported by MacWrite Pro. How to set up the necessary control panels and specify user privileges and restrictions, plus how to access files on other Macs from your computer.

Chapter 9: Customizing the Program. Changing how MacWrite Pro normally works, including picking your own typeface, display, measurement, and operational preferences.

Chapter 10: Creating Form Letters with Mail Merge. Merging a data file with a form letter to print "personalized" correspondence. How to select the symbols (*delimiters*) to mark insertion points for the data. Creating the data file and letter. Using conditional statements that will insert data based on circumstances. Printing a document with merged data.

Chapter 11: Designing Your Documents. How to manage design elements. Using basic kinds of layouts. Making the design enhance the message.

Chapter 12: Using Stationery Files and the Free Disk. How to use, create, and edit *stationery files*—special files you can open again and again, then modify and save under new names—without the danger of changing the original. Stationery files can be reports, invitations, newsletters, or any other kind of document you may want to change or reuse frequently. This chapter also tells you how to use the complete stationery files included on the free disk offered with this book.

Chapter 13: Building a Typeface Library. Making one typeface look like many. Learning category names that can provide clues to typeface characteristics. Help from free typeface utilities. Free fonts you don't know you have. Using the standard LaserWriter typefaces. How to find new typefaces in your library.

Chapter 14: Creating Your Own Typefaces. How to use the new multiple master typefaces. Creating new typefaces with the Kernus utility. Designing typefaces with Fontographer, FontStudio, and Ikarus. How to convert a typeface to a different format.

Appendix A: Installing MacWrite Pro. Installing the program, including how to select a partial installation if your hard-disk space is limited and how to adjust the amount of memory allocated by the operating system to MacWrite Pro.

Appendix B: Product Sources. An alphabetical list of sources for products mentioned in the book, including addresses and phone numbers.

T HE BOTTOM LINE

The MacWrite Pro Book offers everything you need for learning the program quickly and efficiently, whether you're a beginner or a Macintosh expert. In addition, the free disk provides you with a ready-to-use file for printing envelopes and producing professional-looking documents ranging from reports to newsletters. If that's not enough, the disk also includes free typefaces and clip art that you can use for any of your own projects; these extras alone would normally cost far more than the price of the book.

Learning the Basics

CHAPTER 1

FEATURING

Touring the MacWrite Pro desktop

Setting tabs and line spacing

Selecting and justifying multiple columns

Zooming in and out on a document

Creating and printing a memo

You can write simple letters, memos, and reports in any word-processing program. With MacWrite Pro, you can do much more. You can create tables, convert single-column text into multiple-column pages by a click of your mouse button, use irregularly shaped graphic images and wrap text around them automatically, and save special formatting as style sheets—to mention only a few of the powerful capabilities. Yet, like the original MacWrite, MacWrite Pro is easy to learn and use. In fact, if you've used other Claris products such as MacDraw Pro or FileMaker Pro, you'll find that you already know how to use some of the features.

In this first chapter, we'll get you started in a hurry. You'll learn the location of important elements and how to access on-screen tools with a mouse click. Then you'll create and print a brief memo to experience how effortlessly you can do basic word processing. Incidentally, MacWrite Pro is so user-friendly that you won't even need to look at any of its menus until Chapter 2.

Before you continue, install the program if you haven't done so already, following the instructions in Appendix A.

 OURING THE MACWRITE PRO DESKTOP

MacWrite Pro

To start MacWrite Pro, double-click your MacWrite Pro folder to open it, then double-click the MacWrite Pro program icon shown above.

N O T E

 If you're a new Macintosh user, note that to double-click an object, you place the mouse pointer on the object, then depress the mouse button twice in quick succession. A double click opens a selected folder or program; a single click merely selects the item so you can perform some other operation with it. An icon is a small

graphic image used in the Macintosh environment to represent a folder, document, program, command, or tool. Icons come in many shapes, designs, and colors.

When you double-click the program icon, MacWrite Pro will load by first displaying an opening screen containing the name and the version number of your copy of the software, as well as other related information and the name of the individual or department and company (if any) that were entered during the installation process.

This screen will be followed by the main screen, which displays the pull-down menu bar above a new document window ready for use. The first new document window you open in a session will always be named Document1 until you save the file and give it a permanent name.

Figure 1.1 shows the MacWrite Pro desktop, with its major features labeled.

FIGURE 1.1

The MacWrite Pro desktop, with major features labeled

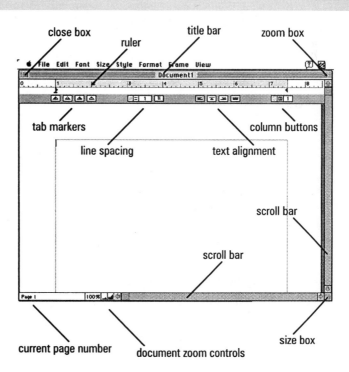

The menus operate in the standard Macintosh fashion: to display a menu, you place the mouse pointer on the menu name and press the mouse button. The menu will drop down, displaying its options. To select an item from the menu, continue to hold down the mouse button, then move the pointer down the menu until the item you want is highlighted, and release the button. The area where the menus are located is called the *menu bar*.

As shortcuts, you can select many menu options by holding down the ⌘ key and pressing a designated letter of the alphabet. For example, if you use the key combination ⌘-P, you'll bypass the Print... command on the File menu and bring up the Print dialog box, which would otherwise be displayed by selecting the Print... command.

N O T E

New Macintosh users should know that the ellipsis (the three dots) in the Print... command indicates that issuing the command will display a dialog box rather than immediately execute the command. A dialog box is a small window containing options you can choose before a command is executed.

STANDARD MACINTOSH FEATURES ON THE DESKTOP

Some of the features of the MacWrite Pro desktop are standard Macintosh features that you'll find in any Mac application. Others are specific to this program. The standard features include the following items that are labeled in Figure 1.1:

title bar This shows the name of the active document. To *drag* the window displaying a document to a new location on your screen, place the mouse pointer on the title bar, and hold down the mouse button while you move the mouse to a new position. The window will move in response to the mouse movement.

close box Click here to close the window.

zoom box Click here to zoom the window to its full size or restore it to its previous size.

size box   Press here and drag this corner of the window to resize the window manually.

scroll bars   Click an arrow within a scroll bar or drag its square *scroll box* along the bar to display another portion of a document that is too large to be shown in its entirety on your screen.

SPECIAL MACWRITE PRO DESKTOP FEATURES

The remaining labeled items in Figure 1.1 are features that pertain to MacWrite Pro itself rather than to Mac applications in general. Most of these items are located on the *ruler*, described next.

Using the Ruler

The top half of the ruler looks like a small version of the conventional yardstick and, like a yardstick, is marked in inches. Here you can drag *indent markers*—small inward-facing black triangles—to indent your paragraphs from either their left or right margins.

The *first line indent marker* looks like an upside-down capital T and, by default, is displayed at the same position as the left indent marker, so that only the horizontal line of the inverted T is visible below the marker triangle. (A *default*, in Macintosh terminology, is the way an element appears or functions if you don't change the setting.)

As illustrated in Figure 1.2, if you drag to move the first line indent marker to the left of the left indent marker, you'll create a *hanging indent*; the first line will extend to the left of the other lines in each of the paragraphs that follow.

TIP

By default, both the left indent marker and the first line indent marker are located against the left margin, so you must move the left indent marker to the right of the first line indent marker in order to create the typical hanging indent. To move the left indent marker without dragging the first line indent marker along with it, hold down the Option key as you drag to the right.

FIGURE 1.2

Dragging the first
line indent marker
left to create a
hanging indent

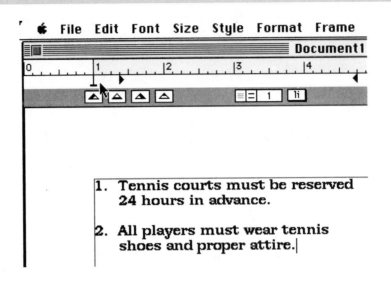

If you double-click anywhere in the portion of the ruler that resembles a yardstick, you'll display the Document dialog box shown in Figure 1.3, from which you can change margin settings and specify how you want any footnotes displayed.

FIGURE 1.3

The Document
dialog box

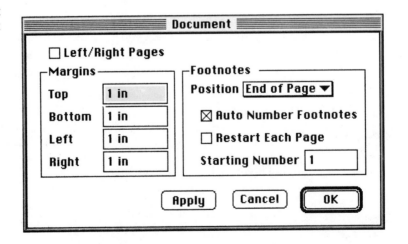

In the Footnotes area of the dialog box, you can press the downward-facing arrow beside the Position option to reveal a list of options for placing footnotes somewhere other than at the default End of Page. The other options are End of Text, End of Section, and End of Document.

In this portion of the dialog box you can also select these numbering options: to number the footnotes automatically, to start with new footnote numbers on each page, and to start with a number you specify.

If you click the Left/Right Pages box to activate it, you can make margin and footnote settings different for left and right pages; for example, you could increase the right margin of the left-hand page and the left margin of the right-hand page to create a larger gutter for binding purposes. (The *gutter* is the space between the contents of two facing pages.) If the box is not selected, margins and footnotes will be handled the same on both left and right pages.

T I P

You can change margin settings right on the screen, without using the Document dialog box, by holding down the Option key and dragging a page guide—*one of the four lines making up the rectangle marking the boundaries of each page.*

By using the Preferences... command on the Edit menu—explained in Chapter 2—you can change the measurement standard used on the ruler from inches to inches decimal (inches divided in tenths rather than eighths), picas, points, millimeters, or centimeters.

The bottom half of the ruler contains icons representing options you can select directly, without using the regular MacWrite Pro pull-down menus. You can compress the ruler to hide this bottom half by double-clicking just below the "yardstick" that constitutes the top half. Double-click in the same location again to restore the display of the bottom half. You might want to hide the bottom half to provide more room to show text on a small screen.

You can also hide the entire ruler by issuing the Hide Ruler command located on the View menu. When you issue this command, it is replaced on the menu by a Show Ruler command that lets you restore the display of the ruler.

While some word-processing programs use multiple rulers, in MacWrite Pro you see only one ruler, always located at the top of the screen (unless you've hidden the ruler).

If you change ruler settings somewhere in the middle of a document, the new settings (margins, tabs, and so on) will affect what you type below the location of the pointer at that time but will not affect previously completed parts of the document.

You can also copy ruler settings from one area to another by clicking within a paragraph containing the settings and then issuing the Format menu's Copy Ruler command. Follow this command by repositioning the pointer and clicking or dragging to select a portion of the text to receive the new ruler settings, then issue the Format menu's Apply Ruler command. This command will apply the selected ruler settings to the new location.

Setting Tab Stops

Starting from the left end of the bottom half of the ruler, the first four icons (shown below) are the tab marker icons that control the placement of tab stops. MacWrite Pro comes with tab stops automatically set at .5-inch intervals—a default you can change through the Preferences... command on the Edit menu. However, you can drag one of these tab marker icons to any position you like on the ruler to insert a custom tab stop.

You can also double-click any of the icons to display the Tab dialog box shown in Figure 1.4, in which you can enter a precise position for a tab and specify a Fill Character. You can use this option to fill the spaces between tabs with some character from your keyboard. This option is useful in tables, particularly tables of contents.

As shown in Figure 1.4, the four tab varieties are Left, Center, Right, and Align On. A left tab stop behaves in the same way as a standard tab on a typewriter: the left side of text you type following the tab stop will be aligned against the stop.

If you select the Right option, text you type after pressing the Tab key will align with its right edge against the stop. With the Center option selected, text you type afterward will be centered on the stop position (with half of the text on each side of the stop).

By default, the Align On option aligns text or numbers to each side of a period or decimal point. This option is most useful for aligning rows of numbers

FIGURE 1.4

The Tab dialog box

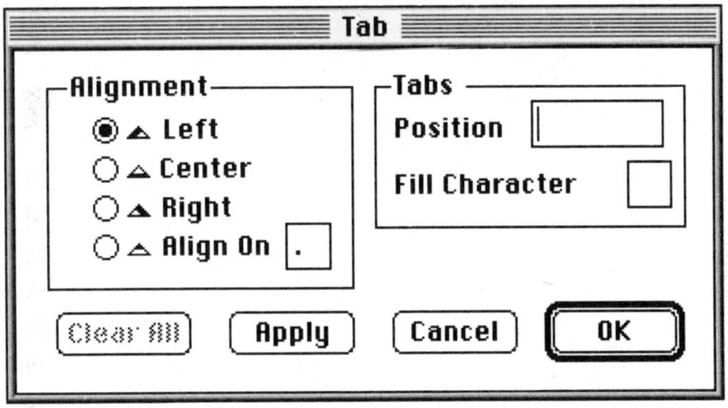

```
╔═══════════════════════════════════════════════╗
║                      Tab                        ║
╠═══════════════════════════════════════════════╣
║  ┌─Alignment──────────┐  ┌─Tabs ────────────┐  ║
║  │  ⦿ ▲ Left          │  │ Position  [      ]│  ║
║  │  ○ △ Center        │  │                   │  ║
║  │  ○ ▲ Right         │  │ Fill Character [ ]│  ║
║  │  ○ △ Align On  [.] │  └───────────────────┘  ║
║  └────────────────────┘                         ║
║                                                 ║
║  [ Clear All ]  [ Apply ]  [ Cancel ]  [ OK ]   ║
╚═══════════════════════════════════════════════╝
```

that contain decimal points, including dollars-and-cents figures. For special purposes, however, you can change the alignment character in the Tab dialog box to any other character you may prefer. To do this, double-click the tab marker icon to display the Tab dialog box, click the check box next to Align On, and type in your chosen alignment character.

As Figure 1.5 demonstrates, you can hold down the ⌘ key while this dialog box is displayed to reveal shortcut key combinations you can also use with the ⌘ key to select some of the options. In fact, by holding down the ⌘ key, you can view shortcut combinations in this manner in several of the other MacWrite Pro dialog boxes.

FIGURE 1.5

Shortcut key combinations for the Tab dialog box are revealed by holding down the ⌘ key

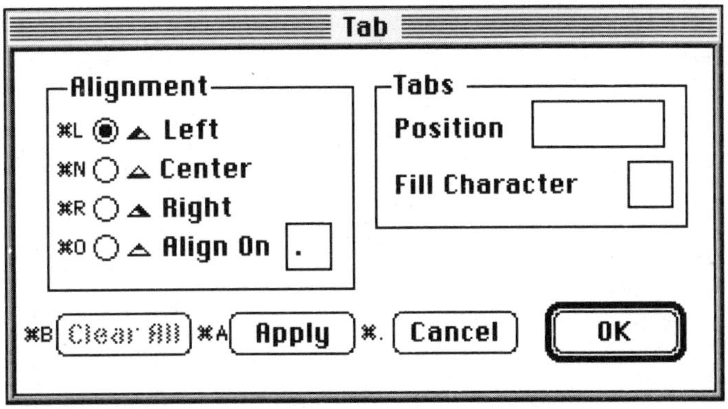

```
╔═══════════════════════════════════════════════╗
║                      Tab                        ║
╠═══════════════════════════════════════════════╣
║  ┌─Alignment──────────┐  ┌─Tabs ────────────┐  ║
║  │ ⌘L ⦿ ▲ Left        │  │ Position  [      ]│  ║
║  │ ⌘N ○ △ Center      │  │                   │  ║
║  │ ⌘R ○ ▲ Right       │  │ Fill Character [ ]│  ║
║  │ ⌘O ○ △ Align On [.]│  └───────────────────┘  ║
║  └────────────────────┘                         ║
║                                                 ║
║ ⌘B[Clear All] ⌘A[Apply] ⌘.[Cancel]  [ OK ]      ║
╚═══════════════════════════════════════════════╝
```

T I P

If you insert two custom tab stops into a document, the standard tab stops between those two stops will no longer function. So if you want to retain those standard tabs as well as added tabs, you must specify all of the tab stops manually in this part of the line.

Specifying Line Spacing

To the right of the tab markers are two buttons you can click to increase or decrease the line spacing of the document. The default line spacing is single-spaced, which is as close together as the lines can be.

Click the second button (which displays lines drawn widely spaced) to increase the line spacing in half-line increments: the first click converts single-spaced lines so that each line is separated by spacing equivalent to half a line, and the second click increases the spacing to standard double-spacing, with an entire blank line between each line of text.

You can increase line spacing until there are 20 or more blank lines between your lines of text, although it's doubtful that you would ever want to use this capability.

Click the first button (which shows lines drawn closely together) to decrease the line spacing in half-line decrements.

Immediately to the right of the two line-spacing buttons is a small box that shows the current line spacing. To the right of this box is another box displaying the characters *li*, indicating that line spacing is being measured *in lines*. You can press this box (by placing the pointer on it and depressing the mouse button) to reveal four alternate scales for measuring line spacing: these scales are in points (a point is approximately $1/72$ of an inch), inches, millimeters, or centimeters.

Figure 1.6 shows the line-spacing buttons, the box indicating the current spacing, and the unit measurement options. (This sort of list is often called a *pop-up menu.*)

FIGURE 1.6

The MacWrite Pro
line spacing and
measurement
options

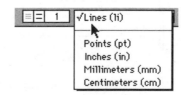

Aligning Text

The next group of buttons on the ruler aligns text. You can click one of these buttons to align text yet to be typed or to align completed text that you've highlighted by dragging the mouse pointer. Your alignment choices are left, centered, right, or justified. Here's what these terms mean:

left-aligned (also known as left-justified, flush left, or ragged right) Text aligned against its left margin, to create a straight left margin and an irregular right margin (the normal result of using a typewriter).

centered Text in which the words on each line are centered.

right-aligned (also known as right-justified or flush right) Text aligned against its right margin, to create a straight right margin and an irregular left margin.

justified (also known as fully justified or full justification) Text aligned so that both margins are straight. This alignment usually requires the hyphenation of some words (especially in short lines) in order to avoid large, unsightly gaps caused by the increased spacing between words used to make both margins straight.

The four alignment buttons are shown below. The lines on each button indicate the alignment that button will produce: for example, the second button, which will produce centered text, shows centered lines.

Figure 1.7 demonstrates the results of using each of the four alignment choices on a sentence. Note that the *justified* option creates large spaces in the second line because the word *soon* is too long (by one character) to fit onto the second line and cannot be hyphenated.

Incidentally, the typeface family used in the examples in Figure 1.7 is Stone Serif. Throughout this book, we'll identify typefaces used so you can become familiar with the effect achieved by different choices. (Chapter 6 is devoted to the subject of typefaces.)

FIGURE 1.7

Examples of the four alignment options

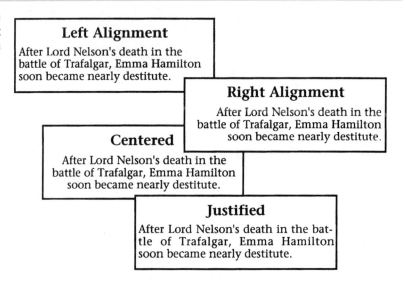

Changing the Number of Columns

When you write a letter or memo, you want the text to appear in a single column, with the margins set to your specifications. However, in MacWrite Pro, you can create documents with as many columns as you like—a real advantage if you want to produce newsletters or reports that incorporate a large amount of information on very few pages.

Why is it an advantage to use multiple columns in such instances? The main reason newspapers, magazines, and many other types of publications are printed in multiple columns is that reading text becomes difficult for the human eye when there are too many words on a single line.

The relatively small type sizes in which professional publications are printed place many more words on each line than a typical typewriter does. Furthermore, the proportional typefaces usually used by these publications can increase the number of characters on a line by up to a third. In a proportional typeface, each character on a line takes up only as much space as it needs, whereas in a *fixed-pitch* typeface the thin i occupies exactly as much space as the wide *m*.

You can easily convert single-column text into multiple columns (or vice versa) by clicking the column buttons at the right end of the ruler. As shown below, the left column button (used to reduce the number of columns) depicts a single-column page; the right column button (used to increase the number of columns) depicts a two-column page. The box to the right of these buttons indicates the number of columns currently selected.

Each time you click the right column button, the number of columns increases by one. Each time you click the left column button, the number of columns decreases by one—unless the page already has only one column, in which case the number of columns is unchanged.

Identifying the Numbers of Displayed Pages

At the lower-left corner of the window you'll see listed the page numbers of the pages currently displayed. "Pages"? Yes—in MacWrite Pro you can display more than one page at a time, either by reducing the size of the document as viewed (see the next section of this chapter) or by viewing the document on a two-page monitor.

The ability to view facing pages simultaneously (pages that will face each other in the printed document) is a big help in the design process, since facing pages should harmonize in design.

Magnifying or Reducing the Document View

As in MacDraw Pro and FileMaker Pro, you can magnify or reduce the displayed size of pages you're viewing by using the zoom buttons at the bottom of the window, shown below.

Click the left button, which shows distant mountains, to see more of a document, reducing its size so you can judge its overall effect. Click the right button, which shows the same mountains magnified, to enlarge the document so you can concentrate on a portion of it.

To the left of these two buttons is the zoom percentage box, which shows how much you've enlarged or reduced the view of the document from the default 100 percent. You can click this percentage box once to restore the normal 100-percent view.

You can also double-click the zoom percentage box to display the small View dialog box shown in Figure 1.8, where you can enter a specific percentage by which you want the view enlarged or reduced.

Changes that you make in this area affect only the size of the display—they do not affect the actual size of a document in any way.

CREATING AND PRINTING A MEMO

Now that you've become familiar with the icons and buttons displayed as part of the MacWrite Pro desktop, you can easily create simple letters, reports, and other documents without pulling down any of the menus. Try this capability now by creating and printing a short interoffice memorandum.

Imagine that you work in the research department of a major television network. A Mr. Walsh with the network is producing a special program that will deal with famous rock groups of the '60s, and he needs some basic background information on the Steppenwolf group. You send him the memo shown in Figure 1.9.

Follow these steps to create the memo:

1. Start MacWrite Pro, if you haven't already done so.

2. Click the Center text alignment button to center the first line you're about to type.

3. Press ⌘-B, the shortcut key combination that will make the text you're about to type appear in boldface.

FIGURE 1.8

The View
dialog box

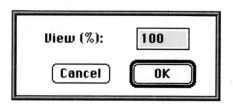

FIGURE 1.9

An interoffice
memo produced in
MacWrite Pro

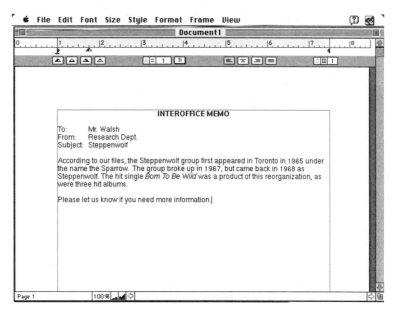

4️⃣ Type **INTEROFFICE MEMO.** Because of the choices you've made, these words should appear centered and in boldface. They will appear in a Helvetica font in a 12-point size because 12-point Helvetica is the standard MacWrite Pro typeface, and you haven't used either the Font or Size menus to change this default.

5️⃣ Press ⌘-B again to discontinue the boldface attribute and continue in plain text.

6️⃣ Add a new tab stop by dragging the left indent marker to the ruler at the 3/4-inch mark.

7️⃣ Press Return to insert a blank line after the heading you've typed.

8️⃣ Click the left text alignment button. The pointer will move to the left page guide.

9 Type the remainder of the memo as shown in Figure 1.9. If you make a mistake, simply press the Delete key to backspace and erase the error so you can correct it. Turn italics on and off by pressing ⌘-I.

After typing the memo, you can quickly save and print it—again without using the menus. Of course, in order to print this memo, you must have a printer attached to your Macintosh (or available through a network) and selected as your current printer (see Appendix A), and the printer must be turned on.

Follow these steps to save and print the memo:

1 Press ⌘-S, the shortcut key combination for saving a document. The Save As dialog box will appear.

2 Give the document the name **Steppenwolf**, and click the Save button to complete the saving procedure and close the dialog box. The name on the document title bar will change from Document1 to Steppenwolf.

3 Press ⌘-P, the shortcut key combination for printing a document. The Print dialog box will appear and should resemble Figure 1.10, which shows the MacWrite Pro Print dialog box for an Apple LaserWriter IIg printer.

FIGURE 1.10

The Print dialog box for a LaserWriter IIg printer

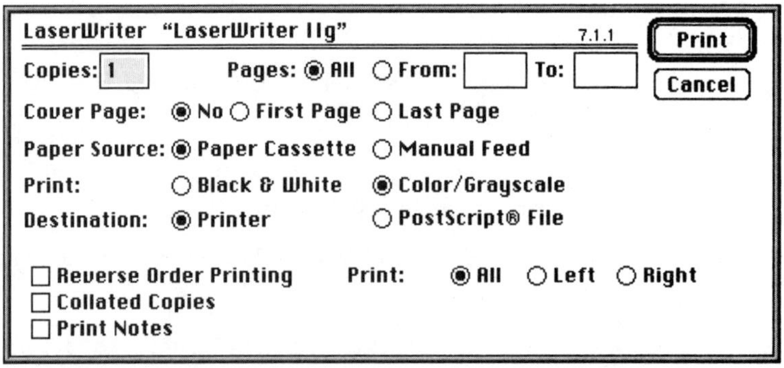

4 Because you don't need to make any changes in the default settings for this dialog box, simply click the Print button, and the document will be printed. (If your Mac is running under a version of the operating system created prior to System 7, you won't see a Print button; click the OK button.)

SUMMARY

In this first chapter you've learned how easy it is to perform basic word-processing tasks in MacWrite Pro, without using a single menu. For example, you can change margins, insert tab stops, change line spacing, align text, change the number of columns, zoom in and out on the document, and switch to a bold font—all right from the active window.

In the next chapter you'll investigate the menus and also learn how to set up and use special palettes and paragraph and section styles.

Using Menus,
Palettes, and Styles

CHAPTER 2

FEATURING

The MacWrite Pro menus contain options that range from selecting simple file-management commands to customizing the way the program works and specifying how a photo will be displayed in relation to the text on a page.

You can also display three palettes that help you modify documents without using the menus, and you can save and re-use *styles*, which preserve formatting combinations that you can assign to documents on a regular basis. These features are the subject matter of this chapter.

USING THE FILE MENU

As shown in Figure 2.1, the File menu contains the usual commands placed on all Macintosh File menus for:

- starting a new file;

- opening an existing file;

- closing a file;

FIGURE 2.1

The File menu

File	
New	⌘N
Open...	⌘O
Insert...	⇧⌘I
Close	⌘W
Save	⌘S
Save As...	⇧⌘S
Auto Save...	
Revert to Saved	
Mail Merge...	⌘M
Page Setup...	
Print...	⌘P
Quit	⌘Q

- saving a file;

- adjusting page-setup specifications;

- printing; and

- quitting the program.

MacWrite Pro also has four commands specific to the program: Insert...,
Auto Save..., Revert to Saved, and Mail Merge...

Insert... imports an external file into your current document. Auto Save...
lets you automatically save the current document as you work. When you select
the command by clicking the check box, you'll bring up the dialog box shown in
Figure 2.2, from which you can select a box to save your current document at intervals you specify. (The default interval is 10 minutes.)

Using the Auto Save option will protect you against power failures (except
for work completed since the file was last saved). You can also click the Keep session backups check box to make a backup of each session, retaining the number
of previous versions of the document you specify (the default is four).

Click the Set Folder... button if you want to specify a special folder for storing backup files. When you've finished selecting backup options, click OK to save
your choices.

If you issue the Revert to Saved command, any changes will be discarded
that you've made to the current document since it was last saved. You'll be asked
to confirm this decision.

FIGURE 2.2

The Automatic
Save/Backup
dialog box

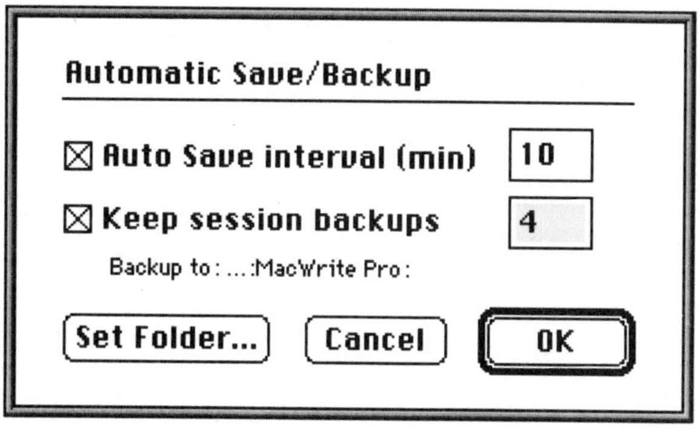

Automatic Save/Backup

☒ **Auto Save interval (min)** `10`

☒ **Keep session backups** `4`

Backup to : ... :MacWrite Pro :

[Set Folder...] [Cancel] [OK]

You select the Mail Merge… command to display a dialog box from which you can choose a file to merge with the current document for creating customized form letters. We discuss MacWrite Pro's mail merge capability in Chapter 10.

SING THE EDIT MENU

The Edit menu is headed by a series of commands that you'll find on the Edit menus of most other Macintosh applications too. The first command is Undo, which is dimmed if you've just opened the program and/or haven't performed any action or selected any command that can be undone. (On any Macintosh, a dimmed menu item is one that is not currently available for selection.)

As you can see in Figure 2.3, the wording of the Undo command differs according to what can be undone. Usually, you can undo something only if you issue the Undo command immediately after completing the action or command you want to retract or reverse—once you've performed some other action, it's too late.

FIGURE 2.3

The Edit menu

Edit	
Undo Typing	⌘Z
Cut	⌘X
Copy	⌘C
Paste	⌘U
Clear	
Select All	⌘A
Publishing	▶
Spelling	▶
Find	▶
Insert Variable	▶
Sort Paragraphs…	
Preferences…	
Show Clipboard	

Below the Undo command, you'll find the Cut command, which removes a selected item from its position in the current document and stores it in the Clipboard.

NOTE

The Clipboard is an area of Macintosh memory used for the temporary storage of items to be moved or copied to another location. For example, when you issue the Cut command, a selected item is transferred to the Clipboard. You can then use the Paste command to place it in a different location—even in a different document or application. The Clipboard can store only one item at a time: the next time you cut or copy an item, the item previously stored in the Clipboard is deleted.

The Copy command copies a selected item in the document to the Clipboard without disturbing the original.

The Paste command copies the material stored in the Clipboard to the pointer location in the current document.

The Clear command erases a selected item, without copying it to the Clipboard or another location.

The Select All command selects all of the current document for moving, copying, or deletion.

If your Mac is running under System 7, you'll also see a Publishing command on the Edit menu, which lets you access the Publish and Subscribe features of this version of the operating system, explained in Chapter 8.

The commands that follow these standard Macintosh commands are specific to MacWrite Pro.

USING SPELLING COMMAND OPTIONS

When you press the Spelling command, you'll see the pop-up submenu shown in Figure 2.4. Here you can choose to check the spelling of all words in the current document or only a selected portion of the text.

In addition, if you've selected the Spell As You Type option, the program will either beep or flash the menu bar when it questions the spelling of a word. You can then select Spell Word... from the Edit menu's spelling submenu to view the information on this word or, as a shortcut, press ⌘-Y. (To select Spell As You Type, choose Preferences from the Edit menu, then select the Spelling/Hyphenation icon in the scroll box. In the Spelling dialog box, click the check box for Spell As You Type, then click OK to close the dialog box.)

FIGURE 2.4

The Spelling
pop-up submenu

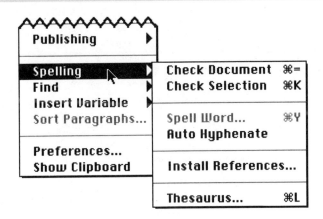

The spelling utility consults two dictionaries to determine misspellings: a main dictionary in the language of your choice (provided you've purchased more than the default dictionary sold with MacWrite Pro) and a user dictionary that consists of words you've chosen to add. You cannot add words to a main dictionary.

Running a Spell Check

Figure 2.5 demonstrates how a spell check works. A word that is *questionable* (meaning that it's neither in the spelling utility's currently selected main dictionary nor in the current user dictionary) is displayed in the Word text box at the top of the Spelling dialog box.

If the Show Suggestions box is selected (as it is by default), the spellchecker will display a list of words that you might have intended to use instead of the word questioned. If no alternative words are shown, the dictionaries don't contain a word that the utility considers a reasonable substitute.

Remember that a spellchecker is no substitute for a thinking human being. It may suggest another word for a word you've misspelled that is actually a different word entirely—with a completely different meaning. It's a good idea to use a dictionary with definitions to check the meaning of any suggested word with which you're unfamiliar.

Figure 2.5 shows a misspelling of the word *cauterize*; the correct spelling is offered as the sixth suggestion. You could insert the correct spelling in two different ways: either by highlighting the correct spelling and then clicking the Replace button, or by pressing ⌘-6, the shortcut key combination.

You can use shortcuts to start a spell check too: press ⌘-= to check the entire document or ⌘-K to check a selected part of the document.

You can type an alternate spelling yourself for a questioned word, then click the Check button to have the spellchecker search for the alternate spelling in its dictionaries.

If you know a questioned word is spelled correctly but you won't be using it enough to warrant adding it to the user dictionary, click the Skip button.

Click the Learn button to add the word to the user dictionary.

Click Cancel to end the spell check without replacing the word currently highlighted.

At the bottom of the Spelling dialog box, a small horizontal bar will show the percentage of a document or selection that has been checked, as well as how many words have been checked. If you click the small upward-pointing lever to the right of *100%* in the dialog box, thereby turning the lever downward, you'll expand the dialog box to reveal more information: the number of words checked, the number of words questioned and replaced, the name of the main dictionary in use, and a text box that will show a questioned word in context within the sentence in which it appears.

FIGURE 2.5

The Spelling
dialog box

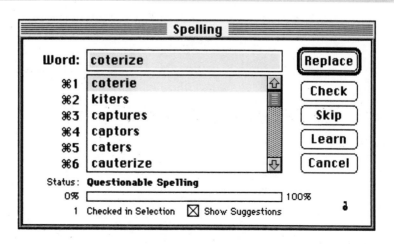

If the Auto Hyphenate option on the Spelling submenu is selected, Mac-Write Pro will automatically insert a hyphen at a suitable point when the word is too long to fit at the end of a line.

Installing a Dictionary

When you select the Install References... command from the Edit menu, you bring up the Install References dialog box (see Figure 2.6), which shows the names of the main dictionaries currently installed.

You can press the downward-pointing arrow beside the words Main Dictionary in the Type box to see a list of other kinds of installed dictionaries whose names you can display: user, hyphenation, and thesaurus.

To add a dictionary to the currently displayed category, click the Add... button, select the file in the Find Reference dialog box that will appear, and click the Open button in that dialog box.

To add a new user dictionary, first select the User Dictionary category in the Install References dialog box, click the Add... button, then in the Find Reference dialog box click the New... button and enter a name for the new dictionary. Then press Save. The Install References dialog box will reappear, displaying the name of your new dictionary as a User dictionary.

Editing a User Dictionary

To edit the contents of a user dictionary, select the name of the dictionary in the Install References dialog box and click the Edit... button. You'll see a small dialog

FIGURE 2.6

The Install References dialog box

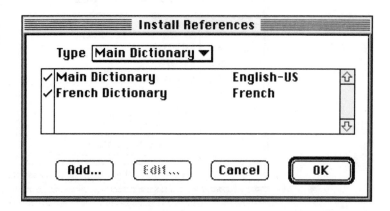

box in which you can scroll through a list of all the words in the dictionary, edit the spelling of any entry or remove the word, or type new words you wish to add.

Using the Thesaurus

Through the Edit menu's Spelling submenu Thesaurus... command (shortcut: ⌘-L), you can search for synonyms either for a highlighted word or for a word you type in the Thesaurus dialog box.

Figure 2.7 shows the words the thesaurus suggests for *wind*; note that these suggestions are separated into nouns and verbs. At any time you can type a new word or highlight a displayed synonym, then click the Lookup button to see another list of words for the new selection. For example, if you select *meander* from the *wind* synonyms, then click Lookup, you'll see a list that includes *promenade*, *ramble*, and *stray*.

If you find a suitable word, click Replace. The new word will appear in your text, replacing the highlighted word if there was one.

If the thesaurus can't find your word, it will present a selection of similar words. You can then click one of the words and click Lookup.

Working in a Foreign Language

MacWrite Pro considers a foreign language a style. If you want to check words in a foreign language for which you have a main dictionary installed, follow these steps:

1 Select the words or section to be checked.

2 Pull down the Style menu and highlight the Language command. A submenu will appear listing the languages available.

FIGURE 2.7

Synonyms offered in the Thesaurus dialog box for the word *wind*

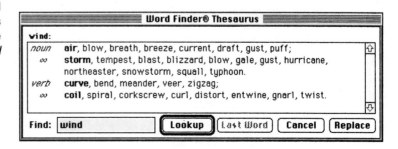

③ Still holding down the mouse button, move the highlighting to the language you want, then release the button. MacWrite Pro will now look upon the selected words or section as having the particular foreign-language style applied to them.

④ Pull down the Edit menu, select Spelling, and then the Check Selection option (or press ⌘-K). MacWrite Pro will proceed to check the selected words using the foreign-language dictionary instead of the default main dictionary.

USING THE FIND COMMAND

Selecting the Find command on the Edit menu displays a pop-up submenu from which you can choose Find/Change..., Find Selection, Find Next, or Change.

Find/Change... displays the Find/Change dialog box. Figure 2.8 gives an example of a typical use for the command. If you found that you'd misspelled the last name of a customer throughout a document, you could quickly rectify the blunder by entering the incorrect name (Johnson) in the Find box and the correct name (Jensen) in the Change box.

Since you would interested only in whole words and would want to maintain the same capitalization, you would also check the boxes labeled Whole Word and Case Sensitive.

Clicking the *Find Next* button would start the search. You would then click the *Change, Find* button to change each occurrence found of the error and then search for the next occurrence.

If you saw no reason to look at each instance, you could instead click the Change All button to find and change all occurrences of the mistake without having each one displayed for your approval. Note that when you select Change

---

FIGURE 2.8

The Find/Change
dialog box

Find/Change

Find:

`Johnson`

Change:

`Jensen`

☒ Whole Word   ☒ Case Sensitive   ☐ Use Attributes ♪

[**Change All**]   [Change]   [Change, Find]   [**Find Next**]

All, a dialog box will warn you that you can't undo the edit. Click OK to continue. Upon completion, a dialog box will tally the changes.

Sometimes you may want to conduct a more sophisticated search. Let's say you've written a book, and each chapter starts with the word *Chapter* in 18-point Helvetica bold, followed by the chapter number in another font.

You want to replace these occurrences of the word Chapter with the same word displayed in small capital letters, using the Perpetua typeface family instead of Helvetica and a 24-point size instead of 18-point. Of course, you don't want to change any occurrences of the word Chapter that may occur in the main body of each chapter—only in the headings for the chapters.

First, select the Use Attributes box in the Find/Change dialog box (accessed from the Edit menu's Find command). This will automatically turn the small lever beside the selection box to a downward position, expanding the dialog box downward to reveal the many additional options shown in Figure 2.9.

As you can see, the dialog box in Figure 2.9 has been set up to make all of the changes mentioned in the previous paragraph, without making any other un-wanted changes. For example, occurrences of the word Chapter within each chap-ter won't be affected because these occurrences won't match the specifications: the text will be in a smaller size font, probably without boldface, and could even be displayed in a different typeface family.

After setting your changes, click Change All. A dialog box will appear, warn-ing you that the changes cannot be undone. Click OK to continue. A dialog box will tally the changes.

The Find Selection option on the Find submenu starts a search for additional occurrences of a highlighted word or phrase.

The Find Next (shortcut: ⌘-E) option resumes the search for another occur-rence of the text or attributes you want to find and/or change, after you've already found one occurrence.

The Change option (shortcut: ⌘-R) gives the program the okay to change an occurrence that has been located but not yet replaced.

You can use the shortcuts for the Find Next and Change options (⌘-E and ⌘-R) to look for and change text and attributes according to specifications pre-viously established in the Find/Change dialog box, even when you've closed the dialog box.

To find text including any single unknown character, type /?; to find a group of unknown characters, type /*.

FIGURE 2.9

Finding and
replacing text by
searching for
attributes in the
expanded
Find/Change
dialog box

```
▣  ▦▦▦▦▦▦▦▦▦▦▦  Find/Change  ▦▦▦▦▦▦▦▦▦▦▦
Find:         ☒ Text          Change:      ☒ Text
┌──────────────────────┐      ┌──────────────────────┐
│ Chapter              │      │ CHAPTER              │
└──────────────────────┘      └──────────────────────┘
☒ Whole Word  ☒ Case Sensitive  ☒ Use Attributes ?

☒ Helvetica  ▼  ☒ 18 pt ▼      ☒ Perpetua SC ▼  ☒ 24 pt ▼
☒ Style                        ☒ Style
  □ Plain     □ Strike Thru      ☒ Plain     □ Strike Thru
  ☒ Bold      □ Underline  ▼      □ Bold      □ Underline  ▼
  □ Italic    □ Superior   ▼      □ Italic    □ Superior   ▼
  □ Outline   □ Small Caps ▼      □ Outline   □ Small Caps ▼
  □ Shadow                        □ Shadow
☒ English-US ▼  ☒ 0  ☒ ■        ☒ English-US ▼  ☒ 0  ☒ ■

┌──────────┐  ┌──────────┐  ┌───────────────┐  ┌──────────┐
│Change All│  │  Change  │  │ Change, Find  │  │Find Next │
└──────────┘  └──────────┘  └───────────────┘  └──────────┘
```

INSERTING VARIABLES

You use the Insert Variable command to add a *variable* at the pointer position in your document. By a variable, MacWrite Pro means the current date, time, page number, section number, revision number, or the document name. These options are revealed on a pop-up submenu when you highlight the command, as shown in Figure 2.10. Of course, the date and time are picked up from the settings of your Macintosh's system clock.

SORTING PARAGRAPHS

The Sort Paragraphs... command on the Edit menu displays a dialog box that lets you sort selected paragraphs either in ascending or descending order. (*Ascending order* means in alphabetical order, and *descending order* means in reverse alphabetical order; in either case, non-alphabetic characters such as numbers and symbols are sorted first.)

You can also select a box to have these sorts conducted according to the ASCII values of the characters. (*ASCII* stands for the American Standard Code for Information Exchange. According to this code, numeric values are assigned to each letter, number, and symbol—and to control codes as well, such as a return or a tab. A capital letter has a different ASCII value than the same lowercase character.)

FIGURE 2.10

Options for the
Insert Variable
command

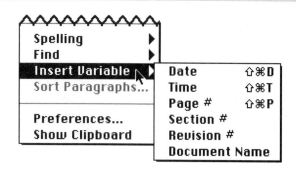

OTHER EDIT MENU OPTIONS

Selecting the Preferences… command brings up a dialog box from which you can choose a series of screens where you can set new defaults for the way MacWrite Pro operates, including such subjects as the handling of variables and spelling/hyphenation preferences. These options are discussed in Chapter 9.

The final command on the Edit menu is Show Clipboard, which lets you examine the current contents (if any) of the Clipboard.

U SING THE FONT MENU

As in all Macintosh applications that let you change the typefaces used in a document, the MacWrite Pro Font menu is where you make these changes.

First, let's clarify some of the terms we're using. A *typeface family* is type that is joined together by a common design concept; when you use different type in the same family, the reader can usually perceive that there is a family relationship.

A *typeface* is a specific portion of a family—all of the sizes with the same attributes. For example, 10-pt. (point) Times Roman bold and 12-pt. Times Roman bold both represent the same typeface; however, 10-pt. Times Roman italic is a different typeface.

A *font* is one size of a typeface; 10-pt Times Roman bold is one font, and 12-pt Times Roman bold is a different font. Some people use the words typeface family, typeface, and font interchangeably; as you can see, however, their meanings are actually quite different.

The Macintosh Font menu would be more correctly called the Typeface menu, since typeface sizes and attributes such as boldface and italics are shown on the separate Size and Style menus.

The MacWrite Pro Font menu is different from most Macintosh font menus in that, by default, all typefaces are shown as they will appear when printed—a big help in selecting the right typeface for a job.

Figure 2.11 shows a minimum MacWrite Pro Font menu that displays only the Chicago, Geneva, Monaco, and New York typefaces that come with the Mac operating system. On the other hand, Figure 2.12 shows a portion of the same menu with the typefaces installed that are typically provided with a LaserWriter printer.

Note that these typefaces too are displayed as they will appear when printed. However, all of the bold typefaces are shown together (prefaced by the letter B), all of the bold italic typefaces (prefaced by the letters BI), and so on. This arrangement can make it difficult to select exactly the typeface you want from a particular family, since you can't always tell how many variations are available.

If you plan to use many different typefaces, you may want to purchase Adobe Type Reunion, a utility which unites the members of each typeface family, as shown in Figure 2.13. The disadvantage of this display is that you don't see the actual design of the typefaces on the menu. However, if you have Adobe Type Reunion installed and you want to see how a particular typeface will appear, you can hold down the Shift key as you select the Font menu to disable Type Reunion temporarily and show the menu choices in their actual typefaces again.

In Chapter 6, you can read about other utilities that will help you in working with typefaces.

FIGURE 2.11

The Font menu can display typefaces as printed.

FIGURE 2.12

The same Font
menu with the
usual LaserWriter
typefaces installed

Font
Avant Garde
B Avant Garde Demi
B Bookman Demi
B Courier Bold
B Helvetica Bold
B New Century Schlbk Bold
B Palatino Bold
B Times Bold
BI Avant Garde DemiOblique
BI Bookman DemiItalic
BI Courier BoldOblique
BI Helvetica BoldOblique
BI New Century Schlbk BoldIt
BI Palatino BoldItalic
BI Times BoldItalic
Bookman
Chicago
Courier
Geneva
✓Helvetica
I Avant Garde BookOblique
I Bookman LightItalic
I Courier Oblique
I Helvetica Oblique
I New Century Schlbk Italic
I Palatino Italic
▼

SING THE SIZE MENU

The Size menu is where you select the font size for any typeface you're using (unless you want to accept the default 12-pt. size often used for text). The sizes you actually have installed as bitmapped fonts (explained further in Chapter 6) are shown on this menu in an outline typeface.

FIGURE 2.13

Typeface family
members reunited
through Adobe
Type Reunion

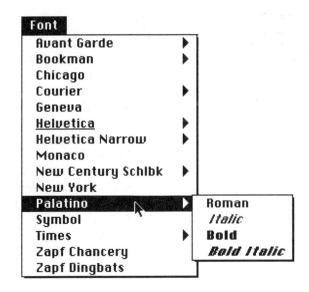

You can see a typical Size menu in Figure 2.14, showing sizes for the currently selected typeface. Bitmapped fonts for the typeface currently active in this figure are installed only for the 10- and 12-pt. sizes, so those sizes are outlined.

Size menus show you which sizes are available as bitmaps to help you get good printing quality. Most bitmapped typefaces these days are accompanied by printer files that will print the typeface with excellent quality in any size desired. However, if the typeface exists only in the bitmapped form, you will obtain good printing quality only when you select a size actually installed, since this kind of typeface actually consists of a fixed pattern of tiny dots. Sizes not installed are approximated by the operating system.

If you want to use a typeface in a size not shown on the menu, select the Other... option from the Size menu and enter the size you want in the dialog box that will appear. You may want to use this option often. For example, if a heading doesn't quite fit on one line in a 24-pt. size, you could try it in 22-pt.

FIGURE 2.14

The Size menu,
with a typeface
selected for which
bitmapped fonts
are installed
only in 10- and
12-pt. sizes

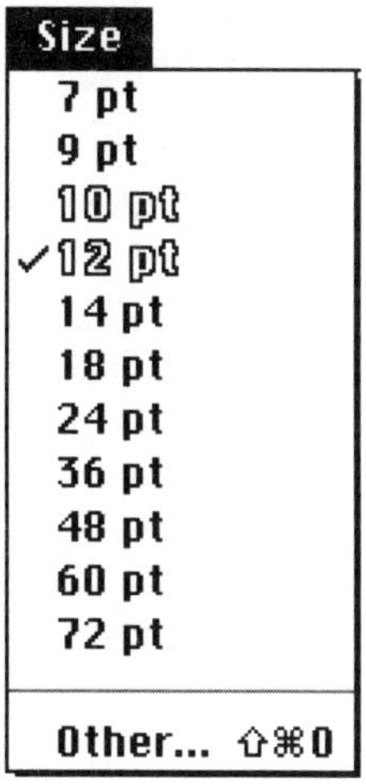

Size
7 pt
9 pt
10 pt
✓12 pt
14 pt
18 pt
24 pt
36 pt
48 pt
60 pt
72 pt
Other... ⇧⌘0

Ⓤ SING THE STYLE MENU

The first six commands on the Style menu add the following attributes either to selected text or to text typed after issuing the command: plain text, bold, italic, underline, outline, and shadow.

You can use keyboard shortcuts instead of the menu to add (or terminate) any of the first four commands. For example, as mentioned in Chapter 1, you can press ⌘-B to make text subsequently typed appear in boldface, then press ⌘-B again to continue typing text without the bold attribute.

The keyboard shortcuts are:

- ⌘-B for boldface
- ⌘-T for plain text
- ⌘-I for italic
- ⌘-U for underline

Directly under the Outline and Shadow commands, you'll find the word Other. When you select this item, you'll see the pop-up submenu shown in Figure 2.15, which presents style options that are less frequently used.

The Style menu,
also showing the
Other submenu

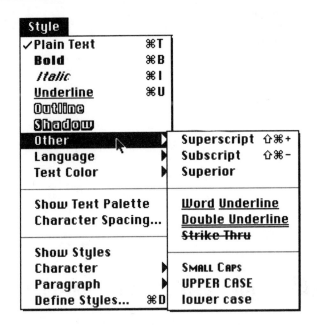

The Superscript option raises characters above the line that are typed after the command is issued.

The Subscript option places characters below the line that are typed after the command is issued.

The Superior option raises characters above the line that are typed after the command is issued and also enters the characters in a smaller font size, such as you would see in a text reference to a footnote.

As illustrated in Figure 2.15, the Word Underline option places a single underline under text, Double Underline places a double underline instead, and Strike Thru draws a line through the text—an option used in law offices to show which sections of a contract have been deleted.

The Small Caps option displays characters in small capital letters that would otherwise be in lowercase.

The UPPER CASE option converts the selected text to all capital letters, and the lower case option converts the selected text to all lowercase letters.

Highlight the Language item on the Style menu to pop up a submenu where you can assign a foreign language to selected text. When a language has been added as a style, you can run a spell check using dictionaries in that language.

When you select Text Color, you display a palette of colors from which you can select a color to replace the default black.

Choose Show Text Palette or Show Styles to display helpful palettes you can show continuously to manage the selection of text options and styles. After one of these commands has been selected, the wording of the command on the menu changes to start with the word Hide rather than Show. Palettes and styles are explained in later sections of this chapter.

The Character Spacing... command brings up a small dialog box in which you can adjust the spacing between characters in selected text. You might want to increase the default spacing to create a special effect for a heading.

The final choices on the Style menu let you assign styles to characters and paragraphs, or define new styles. These commands are covered later in the chapter.

U SING THE FORMAT MENU

The first commands on the Format menu bring up the dialog boxes that let you modify or select formatting for an entire document, a section, or paragraphs. You can also adjust tab settings.

As you learned in Chapter 1, you can double-click in the ruler and tab marker areas to produce the Document and Tab dialog boxes respectively. You'll read about the Section and Paragraph dialog boxes later in this chapter.

INSERTING BREAKS

The Insert Break command, shown in Figure 2.16, has three options for starting a new page, column, or section at the pointer position in your document.

COPYING THE RULER

As explained in Chapter 1, when the pointer is positioned within a paragraph, you can issue the Copy Ruler command to copy the ruler settings from that paragraph to a special area of memory (not the Clipboard). After issuing this command, you can then reposition the pointer and issue the Apply Ruler command to paste those ruler settings into the new location.

FIGURE 2.16

The Format menu,
also showing
the Insert Break
submenu

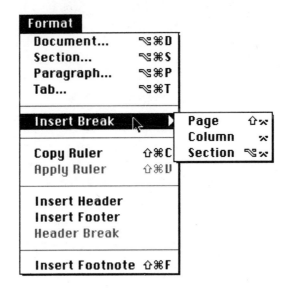

INSERTING HEADERS AND FOOTERS

The Insert Header and Insert Footer commands create an oblong box to contain a header or footer. This box runs the width of the document and is one line deep, but can be dragged by a center handle to expand the box to two lines or more; pressing Return within the box also expands it.

A *header* is an area at the top of a page that will be reproduced on each page of a document or section of a document; a *footer* is the same, except that it appears at the bottom of each page. Headers and footers are useful for displaying the name of the document, the page number, the time and/or date, and other variables controlled through the Edit menu.

If you've previously activated the Left/Right Pages box in the Document dialog box, as discussed in Chapter 1, the Insert Header and Insert Footer commands will each have a submenu, from which you can choose to place the header or footer on both left and right pages or only on left or right pages.

As illustrated in Figure 2.17, one of these three header and footer placement options will always be dimmed. For example, if the pointer is currently on a left page, your choices are to create a header that will appear on that page and other left pages to follow, or to create a header that will appear on both left and right pages. To create a header for right pages only, you would first click the first right page where you want the header to appear.

Using Header Breaks

The Header Break command on the Format menu is available only at the beginning of a new section. This command allows you to change the content and nature of a header for the new section without disturbing the headers for previous sections. Sections are explained later in this chapter.

ENTERING FOOTNOTES

The Insert Footnote command inserts a small superior number into your text at the current pointer position, to indicate to a reader that there is a footnote on the subject.

At the same time, a box is opened in which you enter the footnote itself. The number that is inserted and the position of the footnote in the document are determined by the current settings in the Document dialog box.

By default, footnote numbers in a document start with 1 and footnotes are numbered consecutively throughout the document, but you can change this default to start with some other number. You could use this option to produce a book in which each chapter is a separate document but in which the footnote numbers are consecutive for the entire book. You can also elect to restart footnote numbering with each page.

As far as the position of the footnotes is concerned, you can choose to place them at the bottom of the page to which they refer, at the end of the text, at the end of the section, or at the end of the document.

FIGURE 2.17

Header options when the Left/Right Pages box has been activated in the document dailog box

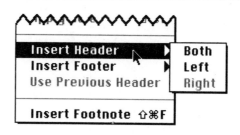

To return to the main body of your text from a header, footer, or footnote, press ⌘-Return.

SING THE FRAME MENU

The first item on the Frame menu displays the Tool Palette, which contains tools primarily used in working with *frames*. Frames are areas you define on your pages that can contain special text, notes, tables, or graphic images; you can add custom backgrounds and borders to frames, resize them, and move them wherever you like on your pages. We'll examine Frames in detail in Chapter 3.

As illustrated in Figure 2.18, the second command on the menu, Modify Frame…, is dimmed unless a frame has been created and is currently selected. Modify Frame… brings up a dialog box from which you can make adjustments to a frame and how it works. We'll explain this too in Chapter 3.

The Insert Table… command is used to create a table in a frame and is the subject of Chapter 7.

USING NOTES

Insert Note creates a small note window which appears at the current pointer position. This window resembles self-stick removable notes, as demonstrated in Figure 2.19.

FIGURE 2.18

The Frame menu

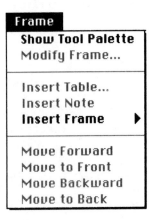

FIGURE 2.19

A note super-
imposed over the
text of a document

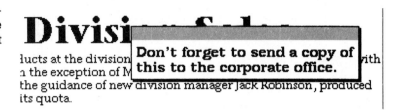

In writing a note, you can use any typeface available in your system, in any size you like. You can drag a corner to resize a note and drag within the note area to move the note to another position on your screen. These notes are intended primarily for storing and displaying comments regarding the document in which they appear.

You can hide a note using the Hide Notes command on the View menu. (We'll discuss this menu later in the chapter.) You can also choose to print a document with or without its notes, by selecting or deselecting a box in the Print dialog box.

Don't confuse these notes with footers or footnotes, which we looked at earlier in this chapter.

Whenever a note is selected on the screen, it is framed by four selection handles at its corners, like other selected objects in the Macintosh environment, and the special Notes menu appears that is shown in Figure 2.20. (This menu disappears again when no note is selected.)

FIGURE 2.20

The Notes menu,
seen only when a
note is selected

Notes
Delete All Notes
Collapse All Notes
Collapse Note
Record
Stop
Play
Erase
Show Note Palette

As the Notes menu indicates, it has options that let you delete all notes, collapse all notes, or collapse only a note currently selected. Collapsed notes are reduced to small icons and take up much less space on the screen.

The note icons can take different forms (see below). On the left is an icon representing a text note. The icon in the center was drawn to represent sound emitting from a loudspeaker and indicates that the note is not text, but consists of spoken comments recorded on a Mac that has a microphone. The icon on the right represents a note consisting of both text and sound.

To expand a collapsed note again to its full size, you choose either the Expand All Notes or Expand Note command from the Notes menu. These commands replace the Collapse All Notes and Collapse Note commands when a note is currently selected that has been previously collapsed.

TIP

 You can use shortcuts to collapse or expand a note. Simply double-click the note to collapse it, and double-click it again to expand it.

Below the commands on the Notes menu that relate to collapsing or expanding notes, there are four commands relating to recording notes: Record, Stop, Play, and Erase. Their meanings are self-evident.

The final command on this menu is either Show Note Palette or Hide Note Palette, depending upon whether or not the Note palette is currently displayed.

The Note palette (shown below) contains icons (starting from the left) that you can click to start a recording, stop it, pause it, or play it. During a recording, the bar underneath the icon shows how much recording time remains.

Options in the Preferences dialog box (accessed through the Edit menu) let you choose the maximum length allowed for a recording and the sound quality you want. High sound quality and long recordings require more disk storage space.

You can click the small lever at the lower-right corner of the Note palette to expand the palette to reveal the source of the note (the name assigned to the Mac on which the note was recorded) and the date and time of the recording.

Palettes are explained in more detail later in the chapter.

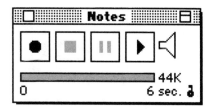

Both text and sound notes function as frames and can be modified in the same manner as other types of frames.

The next Frame menu option, Insert Frame, brings up a submenu that lets you create text and picture frames (see Chapter 3).

MOVING FRAMES

The final four commands on the Frame menu are easy to understand: Move Forward moves an existing frame forward in relation to other objects that are also displayed in frames; Move to Front moves a frame all the way to the front; Move Backward moves a frame backward; and Move to Back moves a frame all the way to the back.

U SING THE VIEW MENU

If you need more space on a small screen, you may want to use the Hide Ruler command to remove the ruler temporarily. This command is the first option on the View menu, shown in Figure 2.21. Once the ruler is hidden, the command changes to read Show Ruler.

SHOWING INVISIBLES

The Show Invisibles command displays normally hidden symbols that indicate where you've inserted formatting such as spaces between words, tabs, and returns. You can see these particular symbols in Figure 2.22. The symbol at the bottom of the figure indicates that a page break was inserted at that point. As you might expect, after this command is issued, it's replaced on the menu by a Hide Invisibles command.

FIGURE 2.21

The View menu

```
┌─────────────────────────────┐
│ View                        │
├─────────────────────────────┤
│ Hide Ruler           ⌘H     │
│                             │
│ Show Invisibles      ⌘;     │
│ Hide Page Guides     ⌘G     │
│ Hide Pictures               │
│ Hide Notes                  │
│                             │
│ Side By Side                │
│ Fit To Window       ⇧⌘R     │
│ Arrange Windows          ▶  │
│                             │
│ Go To Page #...     ⇧⌘G     │
│ Document Info...            │
├─────────────────────────────┤
│ ✓Document1                  │
└─────────────────────────────┘
```

FIGURE 2.22

The result of issuing the Show Invisibles command

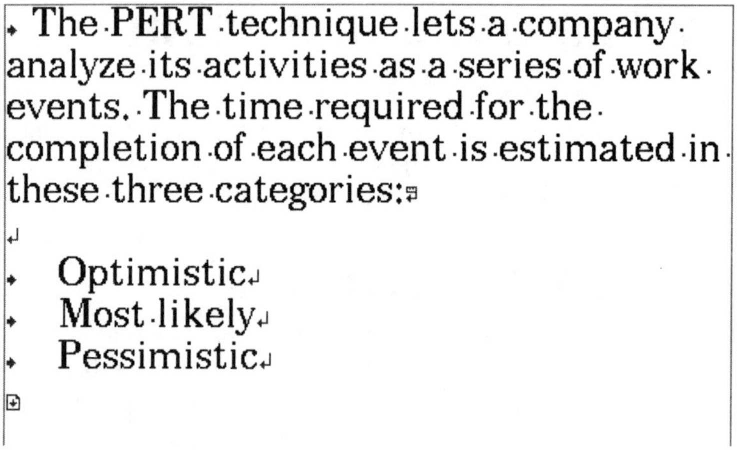

The·PERT·technique·lets·a·company·
analyze·its·activities·as·a·series·of·work·
events.·The·time·required·for·the·
completion·of·each·event·is·estimated·in·
these·three·categories:¶

↵

◆   Optimistic↵
◆   Most·likely↵
◆   Pessimistic↵

HIDING PAGE GUIDES, PICTURES, AND NOTES

The Hide Page Guides command hides not only the non-printing border that appears on-screen outlining each page but also hides non-printing column and frame borders. Issuing this command reduces the clutter on the screen and lets you see your pages in a form that more closely resembles how they'll look when printed.

The Hide Pictures command hides any graphic images you're using and displays only their frames. If you have a slow computer, you can use this command to speed up the redrawing of the screen during periods when you're not working with the images themselves.

The Hide Notes command, mentioned before, temporarily hides any notes you've created in a document.

After any of the three preceding Hide commands has been issued, it is replaced on the menu by a Show command that will restore the hidden element.

VIEWING YOUR DOCUMENT

The Side By Side command displays pages side by side that will face each other when printed (such as pages 2 and 3). By default, all pages are displayed one below another. Even if you have a Macintosh with a small screen, you can look at facing pages side by side to judge how well their layouts complement each other— simply use the zoom controls to reduce the size at which the pages are displayed.

The Fit To Window command reduces the size of a page just enough that all of it can be seen on your screen.

The Arrange Windows command lets you rearrange the display of your open documents. Each document appears in its own window, but through the Arrange Windows submenu you can change the way those windows are seen.

Tile   This option displays the open windows one under another, with each window overlapping the one above it, like the tiles on a roof.

Stack   This option displays all of the windows in a single offset stack, with a large portion visible of the window in front (space permitting) and only the left and top edges of the other windows revealed; this arrangement lets you see which windows are open and easily click on an inactive window to select it. Figure 2.23 illustrates the manner in which the Stack option overlaps windows.

Zoom   This option enlarges the currently selected window so that it occupies the full screen.

FIGURE 2.23

How windows are arranged with the Stack option

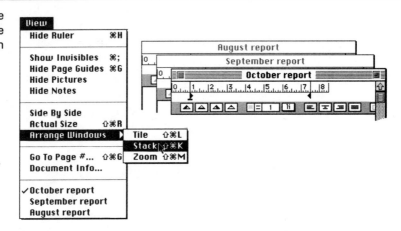

USING THE GO TO PAGE # COMMAND

The Go To Page # command is useful primarily in a large document. For example, if you've printed out a 50-page report and suddenly discover a typographical error on page 28 that must be corrected, you can easily locate the page you want in MacWrite Pro with this command, eliminating the need to scroll page by page looking for the error.

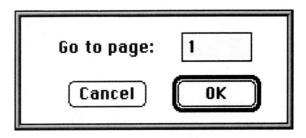

To use the small Go to page dialog box (shown below), simply enter the page number you want and click OK; the page will be located and displayed.

TIP

You can double-click on the page number in the lower-left corner of the screen to bring up the Go to page dialog box.

GETTING INFORMATION ON YOUR DOCUMENTS

The Document Info... command brings up a window in which you can click selection boxes to obtain a count of the number of characters, words, lines, and/or paragraphs in a selected portion of the text and/or in all of the main body of text in the document (excluding text in frames). Click Count to see these tallies, and click Done to close the dialog box.

This window also contains statistics on the author of the document (actually, the name assigned to the computer on which it was written), the date it was written, the date of the last revision, the number of pages, the number of sections, the total time spent in creating or revising the document (as of the current moment), and the size of the file on disk. Click the Copy button if you wish to copy the contents of this window to the Clipboard.

Below this command you'll see a list of the documents that are open in MacWrite Pro. You can select any of the document names to activate and display the contents of that file.

U SING THE PICTURE MENU

The Picture menu (shown below) is displayed only when a picture frame is selected. Through this menu you can scale a picture with or without the frame, vertically and/or horizontally, using percentages you specify. You can automatically change the boundaries of the frame to fit its contents—for example, enlarge the frame to display all of a large drawing or photo, or change the dimensions of the contents to fit the frame. You can also center the contents within the frame. You'll learn more about these commands in Chapter 3.

Picture

Scale...
Fit Frame To Contents
Fit Contents To Frame
Center Contents

USING THE TEXT, TOOL, AND STYLE PALETTES

This section explains how to use the Text, Tool, and Style palettes and how to manipulate the palettes on your screen.

First of all, display one of the palettes. To display the Text palette, pull down the Style menu and select Show Text palette; to display the Tools palette, pull down the Frame menu and select Show Tool palette; and to display the Style palette, pull down the Styles menu and select Show Styles.

Then take a look at the title bar of any of these palettes with the palette selected. In the left corner, you'll see the usual Macintosh close box. As with all windows, clicking the close box will close the palette, making it disappear from your screen.

You'll also see the dock box, a small box at the right end of each palette title bar. When you click the dock box, the palette will be reduced to a small horizontal icon, as shown below. (Claris refers to this configuration as a *docked palette*.)

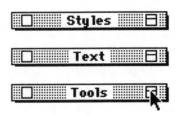

Click the dock box again, and the palette will expand once more to its full size. If you're working on a small screen, it can be helpful to dock any palette you're not using at the moment.

If you hold down the Option key while dragging to move a palette, you'll also set the *gravity point* for the palette: a permanent position for the palette to which it'll return whenever it's displayed on your screen. Hold down the Option key as you open or close any palette, and all palettes will be opened or closed simultaneously.

THE TEXT PALETTE

Look at the Text palette in Figure 2.24, or pull down the Style menu and select Show Text palette. As you can see, this palette provides a convenient method of changing the typeface currently in use, its size, and the attributes assigned to it, including bold, italic, and all of the other variations you would otherwise have to select from the Style menu.

The only style attribute not available from the palette is the ability to flag selected text for the spellchecker as having been written in a foreign language.

As demonstrated in Figure 2.24, you can also press the small black box to the right of the displayed point size to pop up a sub-palette of colors that you can apply to selected text or text subsequently typed. When you change the color, the black box will change too, to display the color you've selected as the current text color.

FIGURE 2.24

The Text palette, with text color choices displayed

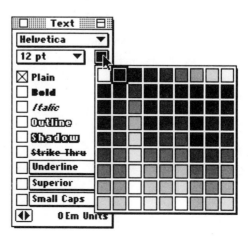

T I P

It's difficult or impossible in some word processors to obtain reversed text (white characters on a black background). This task is simple in MacWrite Pro. Just create a text frame with a black background, then use the Style menu or the Text palette to make the text white that you enter inside the frame. You can try this technique in Chapter 3.

At the bottom of the Text palette are small arrows pointing left and right. You can click one of these arrows to *kern* selected characters, meaning to move them closer together or further apart for a more pleasing appearance. See Chapter 6 for more information about kerning.

THE TOOL PALETTE

The Tool palette (accessed from the Frame menu) can be confusing at first glance, because it consists entirely of icons to be clicked rather than labeled options, so we've labeled all of the elements for you in Figure 2.25. Let's start at the upper-left corner.

The Selection arrow returns the shape and function of the pointer from a previously selected configuration to the standard Macintosh selection arrow, used when you select items on your screen.

FIGURE 2.25

The Tool palette, with its icons labeled and the line types displayed that can be used in frame borders

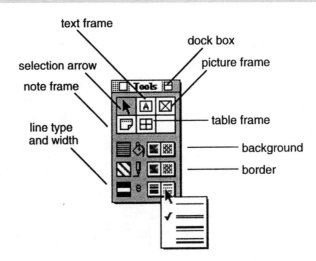

When you choose one of the next four icons (moving to the right, then down), the pointer is converted into a crosshair shape so you can draw a text, picture, note, or table frame.

Below the four frame icons, the Tool palette contains sections with pop-up sub-palettes for selecting frame background and border colors and/or patterns and for choosing the line type and width to be used in a frame border. The bottom three icons at the left side of the palette show the current choices in these categories.

THE STYLE PALETTE

The Style palette, accessed from the Style menu, lets you select currently defined paragraph and character styles that you can apply to portions of your work.

By default, no character styles are defined; the standard paragraph settings are included in the paragraph style named Default. As illustrated in Figure 2.26, you can press the small paragraph-symbol icon, then select a view, to switch the list of styles displayed between paragraph and character.

The concluding section of this chapter explains styles and *sections*—divisions you can create in your documents.

Ⓤ SING STYLES AND SECTIONS

You can define a named paragraph style with special line indentations, spacing, and alignment, and re-use it as often as you like.

By default, each document consists of one section. However, you can divide a document into multiple sections in order to apply different styles to the individual sections. Each section can also have its own header.

FIGURE 2.26

The Styles menu,
with view choices
displayed

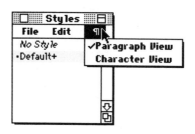

CREATING CUSTOM STYLES

One way to create a custom paragraph style is to change existing paragraphs so they have the features you want, then select those paragraphs, and choose the New Paragraph Style... command from the File menu on the Style palette. Figure 2.27 shows this menu, on which you can also choose or list existing custom styles. Figure 2.28 shows the Custom Paragraph Style dialog box, which is displayed when you select the New Paragraph Style... command.

If you have the Style palette set to show Character styles, you'll see options displayed on the File menu that relate to character rather than paragraph styles and a Character Custom Style dialog box instead of its paragraph equivalent.

The other way of defining styles is to use the Style menu. This method is the easiest if you want to create a custom style that's different from any style you currently have, because you can specify each element of the style and create the style in a single operation.

FIGURE 2.27

The Style palette,
with the File menu
displayed

FIGURE 2.28

The Custom
Paragraph Style
dialog box

Custom Paragraph Style

Create style based on current selection?

Name: New 1

Cancel   OK

To use this method, select the Define Styles… command from the Style menu to display the Define Styles dialog box (see Figure 2.29). From this dialog box you can select a base character or paragraph style on which to base a new style (the Base option), then click either the Character… or Paragraph… button to display a dialog box from which you can select elements for the new style.

The Next option lets you select a style to follow this style. For example, if you were defining a character style for sub-headings, you might want this style to be followed at all times by the style you're using for the main body of your text.

Select the Use Character Info box to incorporate a character style within a paragraph style.

Click the Paragraph… button in the Define Styles dialog box to display the Paragraph dialog box (see Figure 2.30).

Note that here you can stipulate the exact settings you want for the positions of the left indent, first line, and right indent markers.

You can adjust the line spacing within a paragraph and the spacing before and after each paragraph, measuring in lines, points, inches, millimeters, or centimeters.

You can preset the text alignment in paragraphs using this style so that the alignment will be flush left or right, centered, or fully justified (with the text flush against both the left and right boundaries of the column).

Note the two check boxes in the lower-left corner of the Paragraph dialog box. Click the Keep With Next ¶ check box to make sure MacWrite Pro places the

FIGURE 2.29

The Define Styles
dialog box

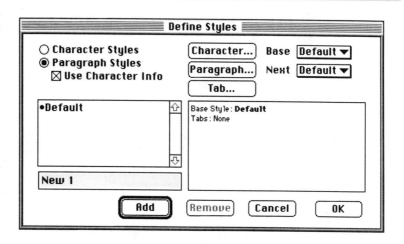

FIGURE 2.30

The Paragraph
dialog box

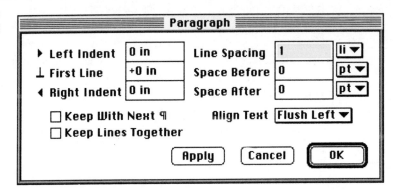

current paragraph assigned to this style on the same page as the paragraph that follows it. You can click the Keep Lines Together check box to keep all of the lines of a paragraph in this style on the same page.

The Apply button lets you observe the result of your choices on currently selected paragraphs without saving the new style. If you like the result, you can then click OK to save the style and close the dialog box.

Figure 2.31 shows the Character dialog box. Here you can select character style preferences, including the typeface, size, and style; the language dictionary

FIGURE 2.31

The Character
dialog box

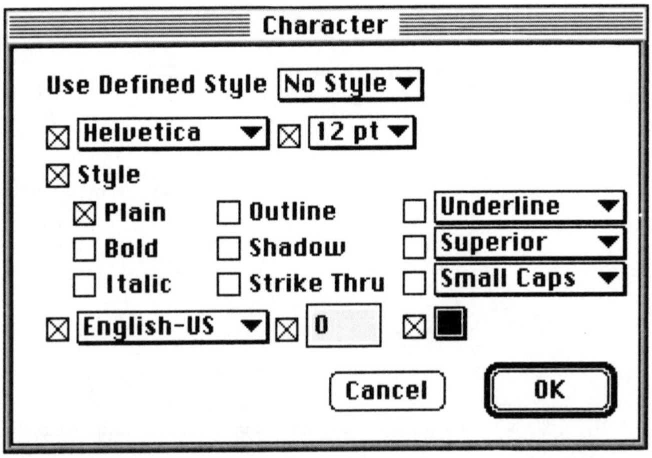

to be used; and a color to be assigned to text in this style. The selection box with a zero displayed next to it changes character spacing. Enter a positive number here (1, 2, 3, and so on) to spread characters further apart than normal spacing, or a negative number (−1, −2, −3, and so on) to squeeze characters closer together than normal spacing.

After you finish defining and naming a new style and click OK to close the Define Style dialog box, your new style will be listed on the Style palette. From this palette, you can easily add a style to selected text merely by clicking the name of the style.

TIP

To modify an existing style, change any paragraph that has had that style applied to it, then choose Redefine Paragraph Style from the Edit menu in the Style palette, and click OK in the alert box that will appear. All paragraphs formatted in that style will be updated.

DIVIDING A DOCUMENT INTO SECTIONS

To create a new section, select the Section... command from the Format menu. You'll see the Section dialog box displayed in Figure 2.32, where you can make several choices regarding the layout and appearance of a section. For example, the

FIGURE 2.32

The Section
dialog box

Section: 1

┌─Section Start──────────┐   ┌─Columns──────────┐
│ New Page ▼   │   │ ◉ Equal Width   │
│   │   │ ○ Variable Width │
├─Page Number───────────┤   │   ☐ Mirror Facing Pages │
│ ☐ Restart Page #   │   │ Number of   [1] │
│ Start at 1   │   │ Column Width   6.5 in │
│ Format [1, 2, 3 ▼]   │   │ Space Between 0.167 in │

☐ Section Title Page   ☐ Include Endnotes in Section

[Apply]   [Cancel]   [**OK**]

Section Start area lets you start the new section on a new line, a new page, or, specifically, a new left or right page.

You can continue the same page numbering sequence established at the beginning of the document or restart the numbering with a specific number. You can even change the format of the numbering so that pages in the new section are numbered according to capital or lowercase Roman numerals or listed alphabetically, beginning with the letter of your choice.

You can specify the number of columns and make them equal in width if you like. If you choose to make columns variable in width, you can specify that facing pages will mirror the same column widths; for example, if the outer column on the left page is wider than the other columns on that page, the outer column on the right facing page will also be wider than its companions.

You can specify exact columns widths, as well as the space between columns, and even include a special section title page if you wish. If endnotes have been selected for the document, you can specify that the notes for this section will be placed at the end of the section rather than the end of the document.

Once you've started a new section, a special marker will be included in the document at that point to indicate the beginning of the section. This marker can be seen only when Show Invisibles has been selected from the View menu.

The difference in appearance between this section-break marker and the page-break marker is shown below; the page-break marker is displayed on top.

Using Section Headers

You can make the header for a new section different from the header for the preceding section by issuing the Header Break command on the Format menu. Once you've issued the command, the header-break symbol shown in Figure 2.33 will be displayed above the header at any time the pointer is in the header.

FIGURE 2.33

The header-break
symbol displayed
above the header
for a new section

You can remove the special header for the new section by clicking this
header-break symbol. As soon as you click the symbol, you'll see the alert box
shown in Figure 2.34, warning that if you replace the header with the header of
the previous section, you can't change your mind and use the Undo command to
restore the deleted section header.

ⓈUMMARY

In this chapter, you took a quick tour of the MacWrite Pro menus and were introduced
to the palettes. You learned how to create and use custom paragraph and character
styles and how to divide a document into sections with specialized formatting.

In the following chapters, you'll explore menu options in depth that were
only mentioned for orientation purposes here in Chapter 2, and you'll have the
opportunity to put your new knowledge to work in producing sample documents.

FIGURE 2.34

The Alert box seen
if you click a
header-break
symbol

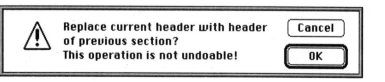

Placing Page
Elements in Frames

CHAPTER 3

F EATURING

How frames are used

Drawing and sizing frames

Creating special effects

Using multiple frames

Trying out frame techniques

If you write only letters or reports without illustrations or special typographic effects, you can work in MacWrite Pro very productively without using frames. However, as soon as you need to include a graph depicting sales records, a photo of the company chairman, or a list of items set off by a border and a shaded background, you'll need the versatility that frames provide.

When you copy a graphic image into a MacWrite Pro document through the Clipboard, the program will automatically create a picture frame the same size to contain it. In this chapter you will learn more about how and when to use frames and the results you can obtain.

D RAWING AND SIZING FRAMES

Notes and tables are specialized types of frames. (We looked at notes in Chapter 2, and Chapter 7 explains tables.) However, the remaining frame types—text and picture—are features you're likely to use every day.

INSERTING FRAMES

You can create text and picture frames in two ways. One method is to select the Insert Frame command from the Frame menu and then choose Text or Picture from the submenu for the command. The other method is to click the Text or Picture tool on the Tool palette and then draw a frame of the approximate size you want.

SIZING FRAMES

As you can see in Figure 3.1, the Insert Frame menu method produces text and picture frames with small default sizes. The text frame, shown as selected at the upper left intersection of the page guide lines, is one and a half inches wide and about a quarter of an inch in height—adequate for the display of one line of text consisting of a few words.

The picture frame—marked with a large x and shown directly underneath the text frame—is one inch square. However, you can easily change the size and proportions of these frames in several ways.

FIGURE 3.1

FIGURE 3.1

The default text
and picture frames
(reproduced
actual size)

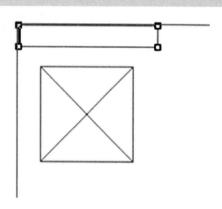

MOVING FRAMES

You can also move a frame and its contents to a new location simply by dragging the frame, unless the frame is configured as *anchored*—meaning attached to adjacent text. (You'll learn more about frame configuration later in the chapter.)

Figure 3.2 shows a frame move in progress. To move a frame, first make sure that it's not anchored. Select the Frame menu's Modify Frame... command, and click Frame Anchor NONE in the dialog box. Then pass the pointer over the frame slowly until the pointer changes its shape to appear as a small cross with its lines terminating in arrows pointing in four directions (as shown in Figure 3.2). Hold down the mouse button and drag to move the frame to its new position.

FIGURE 3.2

Dragging to move
a text frame

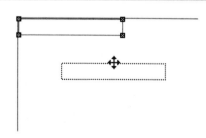

T I P

If you want to make very fine adjustments in the position of a frame, you can select the frame, click one of the corner section handles to make the handles black instead of white, then nudge the frame sideways or up or down by tapping one of the arrow keys.

To move the frame in even smaller increments with each tap of an arrow key, turn off the Auto Grid in the Preferences dialog box, accessed through the Edit menu's Preferences... command. (The Auto-Grid provides an invisible gridwork to which objects attach themselves for alignment; the selections in the Preferences dialog box are explained in detail in Chapter 9.)

USING AUTO-RESIZE

Unless the *Auto-resize Frame* box has been deselected in the Modify Frame dialog box (discussed later), a text frame will adjust in size to display all of the words you type. If you type more words than will fit within the left and right boundaries of the frame, the frame will expand downward automatically, with the text wrapping from line to line within the original left and right limits of the frame, as shown below.

> This text wraps
> from line to line
> within the left
> and right frame
> boundaries.

Resizing a Text Frame

You can also resize a text frame by dragging one of its corners, as shown below; the text within the frame will be adjusted automatically.

> This text wraps from line to line within
> the left and right frame boundaries.

RESIZING PICTURE FRAMES

You can resize a picture frame by dragging a corner, but the alternatives offered through the Picture menu are often more useful. As explained in Chapter 2, this menu appears only when a picture frame is selected that contains a graphic image; the menu does not appear when a frame is empty.

INSERTING A GRAPHIC IMAGE

You can insert a graphic image (for example, a drawing, a photo, or a chart) into an existing picture frame in two ways:

- paste it into the selected frame through the Clipboard
- use the Insert... command on the File menu

As demonstrated in Figure 3.3, you will probably find that only a portion of your chosen graphic image will be visible inside the default one-inch-by-one-inch

FIGURE 3.3

Initially, a picture
frame may display
only a portion of
a graphic image

FIGURE 3.4

A drawing
displayed in its
entirety by using
the Fit Frame To
Contents command

picture frame. To correct this problem, all you have to do is pull down the Picture menu and select the Fit Frame To Contents command. As shown in Figure 3.4, the frame will expand automatically to exactly the size required to display the entire image.

The Fit Contents To Frame command on the Picture menu performs the opposite function: it enlarges or reduces the size of an image to fit its frame.

Use this command with caution; it will display the entire image within the frame, filling the frame completely, regardless of the proportions of the frame. This means that the image may be severely distorted. Figure 3.5 shows the same image reproduced in Figures 3.3 and 3.4 (a drawing of a circus ringmaster), lengthened so that it is hardly recognizable.

FIGURE 3.5

The same drawing
distorted through
use of the Fit
Contents To Frame
command

TIP

To find out the size of a frame, position the pointer on its border and hold down the mouse button. The height and width will display in the lower-left corner of your screen.

Resizing a Graphic Image

You can use the Scale... command on the Picture menu to resize the horizontal and/or vertical dimensions of a graphic image by percentages of their current sizes. Issuing this command displays the Scale Picture dialog box shown in Figure 3.6.

As you can see in Figure 3.6, both the horizontal and vertical scale percentages are initially set at 100%. If the Scale Frame selection box is selected (as it is by default), the frame will be resized with the image.

TIP

There's a quick way to display the Scale Picture dialog box: double-click within the frame.

Using the Center Contents Command

The Center Contents command on the Picture menu centers the graphic image within a selected frame (provided you make the frame larger than the image). You can use this command to place white space around an image, since the frame normally does not print.

You can also use the Center Contents command to create the illusion of a framed picture with a matte, as shown in Figure 3.7. The effect in this figure was created with the Tool palette, by selecting a wide, patterned pen size (or line) to serve as a border for the MacWrite Pro frame and then selecting a gray background to represent the matte. On your screen the background will fill the entire frame, but when the document is printed, the area around the drawing will print as a white rectangle, thereby creating the matte effect.

FIGURE 3.6

The Scale Picture
dialog box,
showing its default
settings

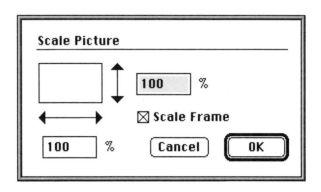

FIGURE 3.7

A framed drawing with a matte, created with the Center Contents command and a border and background chosen through the Tool palette. Note that the pattern stops at the edge of the printed graphic.

Ⓜ ODIFYING FRAMES FOR SPECIAL EFFECTS

When you create a new text or picture frame through the Frame menu, the frame is anchored by default to the text in the document—meaning that the frame will move only when the text moves.

In addition, the text wrap is *in-line*, meaning that the frame functions as if it were a character on a line in the main body of the document, moving when the text around it moves. If the frame is larger than the characters around it, the line spacing will increase at that point to accommodate the frame, creating a large gap within the paragraph.

When you create the same frame through the Tool palette, however, by default the frame is not anchored, and the main body of text in the document will wrap around it.

Whichever method you use to create the frame, the frame will be opaque. You can make the frame transparent instead, so that objects underneath the frame will show through.

You can click the *Move with Page* box to make an anchored frame move with the page on which it was created, if text wrap is off.

USING THE MODIFY FRAME... COMMAND

If you want to change the defaults for a frame you've created, select the frame, then pull down the Frame menu and select the Modify Frame... command. You'll see the Modify Frame dialog box. Figure 3.8 shows this dialog box with the default settings that are in place when a picture frame is created through this menu rather than through the Tool palette.

TIP

 You can also display the Modify Frame dialog box by double-clicking a frame border or Option-double-clicking inside the frame.

Note that—in addition to the items already mentioned—the Modify Frame dialog box also shows the position and size of the frame. The Auto-resize Frame selection box is dimmed and unavailable for picture frames, but is active and selected by default for text frames. When this box is selected, a text frame expands downward automatically when typing fills the existing frame, as mentioned previously. The Off-set is the amount of space that will separate the frame from the surrounding text, measured in points.

Figures 3.9 through 3.12 show the effect of various picture frame settings on the appearance of a document. These examples use the same drawing of a circus

FIGURE 3.8

The Modify Frame dialog box with its default settings for a picture frame created through the Frame menu's Insert Frame command

---

Modify Frame

Frame Anchor
- ○ None
- ◉ To Text   ☐ Move with Page

Text Wrap

◇ ◈ ◈
Wrap None In-line

◉ Opaque
○ Transparent

Offset 4 pt

Position
Top   1.014 in
Left   1.014 in

Height | 1 in |
Width | 1 in |
Baseline | 0 in |

☐ Auto-resize Frame   [Apply] [Cancel] [OK]

FIGURE 3.9

The effect of
anchoring a picture
frame in-line to text

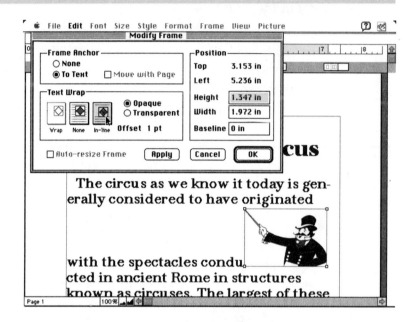

ringmaster that you've already seen in previous figures. By the way, the drawing
is a piece of *clip art*—meaning that it's included in one of many libraries of drawings that you can purchase for use in your own documents. (We'll discuss clip art
in more detail in Chapter 4.) This particular drawing is from the Dynamic
Graphics library.

Using the Text Wrap Feature

Figure 3.9 shows the result of the default picture frame settings provided through
the Frame menu: the frame is anchored to text, and is opaque, with the text wrap
in-line. The in-line wrap creates a large hole at the point where the line spacing
has changed automatically to make room for the picture frame, which MacWrite
Pro considers a giant "character."

In Figure 3.10, the picture frame is not anchored, has no text wrap, and is
opaque. As a result, the text continues all the way to the right margin, behind the
lines involving the picture, so several words are hidden and impossible to read.

FIGURE 3.10

A picture frame hides text because the frame is not anchored, has no text wrap, and is opaque

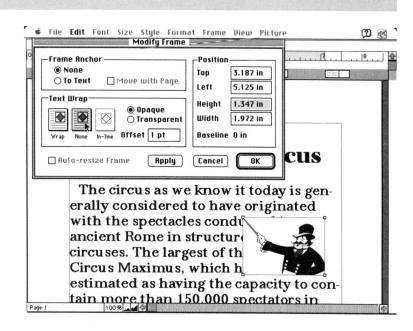

As you can see, these settings aren't much good for creating text intended for reading, but they would be just right for superimposing a text frame containing the words TOP SECRET or CENSORED to hide part of the main text.

What if you don't want to censor your document? Simply activate text wrap by selecting the Text Wrap icon at the far left of the Modify Frame dialog box. The text will wrap around the picture frame, and the effect is professional and usable, as you can see in Figure 3.11.

Change one other setting—making the frame transparent rather than opaque—and the text wraps around the irregularly shaped drawing rather than its frame (see Figure 3.12). This is called a *runaround*.

Printing Text Wrapped around Irregular Objects

You can create highly impressive documents with MacWrite Pro's ability to wrap text automatically around an irregularly shaped object. At the time of writing, however, there are limitations caused only by the available printer drivers.

FIGURE 3.11

The same picture
frame with text
wrap added

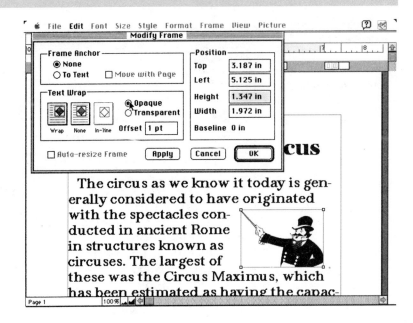

The Apple LaserWriter driver is unable to handle transparent pixels in color, so if you're using a printer that works with the LaserWriter driver, you can see text wrapping around an irregularly shaped drawing or photo on your screen; but if you print the document with Color/Grayscale selected in the Print dialog box, the frame around the object will be visible, covering up characters in the text that are inside the frame area.

There are three solutions for this problem:

- Print the document with Black & White selected in the Print dialog box. This method works fine with line art, but if the graphic is a photo or a drawing with shades of gray or a range of colors, the image may print as a black blob.

- To reproduce a photo or a drawing with shades of gray or a range of colors properly, print the document on a QuickDraw printer such as the ImageWriter or the StyleWriter. (The print quality of a StyleWriter compares favorably to that of some LaserWriters.)

FIGURE 3.12

The same picture
frame made
transparent

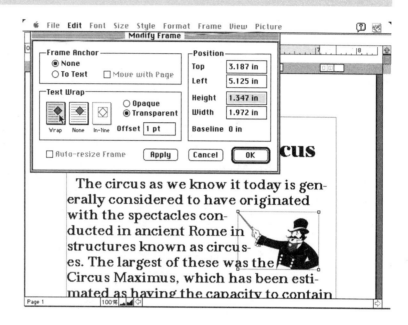

- Print with Color/Grayscale selected on a LaserWriter, but make
the picture frame opaque so that the text will wrap around the
frame instead of the image. This solution makes all of the text
visible while still achieving maximum print quality for photos
or grayscale drawings.

USING MULTIPLE FRAMES

Often you can achieve exactly the effect you want in a document by using multiple
frames. Figure 3.13 illustrates a different way in which you could use the ringmaster
drawing with the circus text—positioning the drawing as a sort of watermark behind
the text.

To accomplish this watermark effect, place the text in a text frame. Then you
can use the Move to Back command on the Frame menu to move the drawing behind the text; of course, the text frame must be configured as transparent to permit
the drawing to show through behind the text.

FIGURE 3.13

The ringmaster drawing used as a background for text about the origins of the circus

Origins of the Circus

The circus as we know it today is generally considered to have originated with the spectacles conducted in ancient Rome in structures known as circuses. The largest of these was the Circus Maximus, which has been estimated as having the capacity to contain more than 150,000 spectators in the era of Julius Caesar; it was enlarged under later emperors.

Roman circus entertainment included chariot races and gruesome contests pitting men against wild animals.

In modern times, a Royal Circus was established in England in 1782 by Charles Hughes. This circus featured trick horse riding. Hughes also took a circus to Russia in 1793.

Make the drawing gray rather than black so the drawing won't interfere with the reading of the text. See the Tip below for suggestions on how to make a drawing gray.

TIP

You can use several different techniques to make a drawing gray. One method uses MacDraw Pro. Display the colors or grays in a drawing through the Image Colors command on the Color palette's Special menu, and select the range of grays to be made lighter by holding down the

Shift key and clicking the first and last cells in the range. Select the Colors... command from the Layout menu to display the Color Editor, then use the Color Editor to make the selected range a light gray.

Another method requires Adobe Photoshop. Use the Adjust Levels command on the Image menu to display the Levels dialog box, then drag the left Output Level marker to the right to eliminate black and dark grays from the image.

ADDING HEADINGS OVER MULTIPLE-COLUMN TEXT

If you want to divide your main text into two or more columns and you still want to display a heading above the text, you'll need to place the heading in a text frame. Otherwise, when you issue the command to divide the text into multiple columns, the heading will automatically become a part of the first column.

Placing the heading in a separate text frame has an additional advantage. As demonstrated in Figure 3.14, you can also mount the heading on an eye-catching background surrounded with a border.

FIGURE 3.14

To keep a heading above text in multiple columns, you can place the heading in a text frame

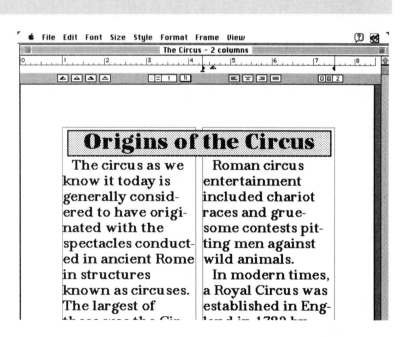

The typeface family used in these examples dealing with the circus is URW Antiqua, available from Digital Typeface Corporation, or directly from URW.

Ⓡ EMOVING FRAMES AND THEIR CONTENTS

To delete the contents of a text frame, select the text, then press the Delete key, or select the Clear command from the Edit menu. To delete the contents of a picture frame, select the frame, then press the Delete key, or select the Clear command from the Edit menu. In both instances, the empty frame will remain.

To undo the deletion, select the Undo Delete Frame command immediately from the Edit menu. (Shortcut: ⌘-Z.)

To delete a frame *and* its contents (if any), select the frame, then click one of the white corner selection handles; the white handles will turn black. With the handles black, you can delete the frame by pressing the Delete key or by selecting the Clear command from the Edit menu.

Ⓣ RYING OUT FRAME TECHNIQUES

Now that you know the basics of MacWrite Pro's frames, try creating and using frames for yourself. Figure 3.15 shows a heading you can reproduce that might appear in a newspaper advertising a special sale.

The heading consists of two frames: the smaller frame (containing the words Ends Saturday) is superimposed over the contents of the larger frame. For this example, we used the Barmeno Extra Bold typeface, released by Germany's Berthold foundry and available from Adobe. However, you can use any bold typeface in your system.

Follow these steps to duplicate the example:

① Start MacWrite Pro if necessary, or close any open documents and select New from the File menu (shortcut: ⌘-N) to open a new document.

② With a new document active, pull down the Frame menu and select the Show Tool Palette command. (If the Tool palette is already displayed, skip this step.)

A heading composed of two text frames

3 On the Tool palette, click the text frame tool (the middle icon in the top row, displaying a capital A). The pointer will become crosshairs.

4 Draw a text frame approximately the size shown in Figure 3.15. Next you'll make this frame black.

5 In the background section of the Tool palette (the first section under the tool icons), press the colored square to drop down a palette of colors, then select the black cell, as demonstrated in Figure 3.16. If need be, you can undo any move by selecting the Edit menu's Undo Frame Formatting command. (Although the color palette appears in this figure next to the pen section, it has actually dropped down from the background section just above.) As soon as you release the mouse button, the sample box at the left side of the background section will change to show black, and the color palette will close. Now you must make the text white.

FIGURE 3.16

Making the frame
background black

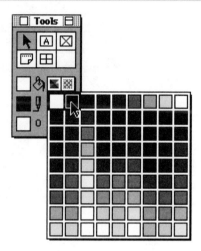

6 Pull down the Style menu, and select the Show Text Palette command. The Text palette will appear.

7 Press the small black square to the right of the point size to drop down the color palette, from which you can assign a color to the words you type, then select the white cell, as demonstrated in Figure 3.17. As soon as you release the mouse button, the square you pressed will change to display white, and the color palette will close.

8 In the Text palette, pull down the Size menu, and select a large point size for the white text you're about to type. (The word SALE! in Figure 3.15 is 125 pt., a special size obtained by selecting the Other... command on the Size menu and entering that specific point size in the Size dialog box.)

9 Select the typeface you want from the Font menu. If necessary, also select the bold attribute from the Style menu.

10 Click the Center alignment button on the ruler to center the text to be typed.

11 Type **SALE!** Congratulations! You've now completed the contents of the first frame.

FIGURE 3.17

Making the text to
be typed white

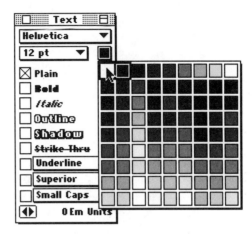

If you prefer, you can select the typeface, size, and bold attribute from the Text palette rather than from menus. You can also display and select colors for text by using the Text Color command from the Style menu rather than the Text palette.

In completing the steps above, be sure you select the correct items. For example, the pen section of the Tool palette changes the color of a frame border, not the text color.

You're almost finished. Now create and fill the smaller text frame:

1 Select the text frame tool on the Tool palette, and draw the smaller frame over the lower-left portion of the completed frame.

2 Following the steps provided for the first frame, change the typeface size to a smaller font (we used 24 pt.), the type color to black, and the frame background to white.

3 Click the Center alignment button on the ruler to center the text for this frame, and type **Ends Saturday**. Your screen should now resemble the example.

TIP

Use the patterns palette on the Tool palette (to the right of the palette of colors in both the background and pen sections) to add a pattern to a frame background or border. If you'll be printing in color, you may want to combine a color with a pattern, by making selections from both color and patterns palettes. Note that the Text palette does not contain a patterns palette; the reason is that you cannot apply a pattern to text you type.

S UMMARY

Now you've seen some of the professional effects you can obtain by using and modifying frames with a little creativity. A frame and its contents become an object that you can move and reshape to achieve exactly the result you want.

You can make the main text of the document wrap around the frame or not, as you wish. You can place frames in front of or behind other frames and make them transparent or opaque, with clear or white backgrounds or enhanced with colored patterns and borders.

In Chapter 4 you'll learn more about how to obtain and use graphics in your picture frames.

Handling Graphic Images

CHAPTER 4

FEATURING

Learning graphic formats

Integrating text and graphics

Importing spreadsheet charts

Using clip-art libraries

Scanning graphic images

Now that you know you can incorporate artwork into your documents by using picture frames, it's time to learn more about graphic formats, how to print drawings and photos with top quality, and tricks you can use to combine text and graphics. In the next few pages, we'll also discuss how to find and use clip art and how to turn images on paper into graphic files with a scanner.

LEARNING GRAPHIC FORMATS

Whether you create Macintosh artwork in a drawing program such as MacDraw Pro, purchase the art from a library, or import scanned images, the format of the graphic file produced will affect what you can do with the image. The format will also determine what precautions you must take to ensure that you get the best reproduction possible when you print the document containing the image. You should be familiar with the features and limitations of these basic graphic formats: MacPaint, PICT and PICT2, TIFF, and EPSF.

MACPAINT

MacPaint is the original Macintosh graphic format. Artists have done excellent work in this medium, achieving subtle shading and gradations that are admirable. However, you don't want to enlarge one of these images; if you do, you'll find that a MacPaint file actually consists of a series of small black and white dots, arranged in patterns to produce the effect of various shades of gray. This format is defined as a *bitmapped* image, with its resolution fixed at 72 dots per inch—the resolution of the Macintosh screen. Furthermore, the maximum picture size is 8 inches wide by 10 inches high.

Figure 4.1 shows a charming MacPaint picture of a group of children dancing in a circle. Superimposed over the upper right corner of this picture is an enlargement of the head of the boy dancer at the right. As you can see from this enlargement, his head is indeed nothing more than a pattern of dots (square dots, at that!).

Actually, this MacPaint file is a piece of clip art from Dubl-Click Software's WetPaint collection. Although a laser printer can smooth many of the dots in a MacPaint file into lines as it prints, we turned off this option to show both the

FIGURE 4.1

A bitmapped illustration, with a portion enlarged to show the dot patterns with which it was created

original file and the enlargement in their raw form, with all dots intact. You can expect better print quality if you use this clip art yourself.

Most Mac applications print their files to a laser printer using Apple's Laser-Writer print driver, and most manufacturers of these printers rely on the driver as well. Therefore, whatever brand of laser printer you use, you'll probably see the same LaserWriter Page Setup dialog box (shown in Figure 4.2) when you select Page Setup… from the MacWrite Pro File menu.

FIGURE 4.2

The LaserWriter Page Setup dialog box, with options set in the Printer Effects section for printing MacPaint files with maximum quality

```
LaserWriter Page Setup                              7.1.1      [   OK   ]
Paper: ● US Letter  ○ A4 Letter                             [ Cancel ]
       ○ US Legal   ○ B5 Letter   ○ [ Tabloid     ▼ ]
Reduce or [ 100 ]%        Printer Effects:                  [ Options ]
Enlarge:                  ⊠ Font Substitution?
Orientation               ⊠ Text Smoothing?
                          ⊠ Graphics Smoothing?
[ ↑👤 ][ ↑📄 ]             ☐ Faster Bitmap Printing?
```

The Page Setup dialog box is where you can turn Graphics Smoothing on or off. (It's on, by default.) For maximum quality in printing a bitmapped image, you want Graphics Smoothing on and Faster Bitmap Printing off. (The Faster Bitmap Printing option takes a few shortcuts technically in order to print the file faster.)

Using the Precision Bitmap Alignment Option

Another way to enhance a MacPaint file is to select Precision Bitmap Alignment in the LaserWriter Options submenu, accessed by clicking the Option button in the Page Setup dialog box. This option reduces the image by four percent, so that exactly four dots will be created by the laser printer for each dot in the original file, giving higher fidelity. You can see this Options submenu in Figure 4.3.

T I P

If you have one of the newer laser printers that can produce a resolution of 600 dpi or even 1000 dpi, don't bother with the Precision Bitmap Alignment option—selecting the option will result in no noticeable improvement.

Reducing an Image Further

If a four percent reduction in size can make a MacPaint file look sharper, will a greater reduction make the image look even better? Not if you reduce the image size within MacWrite Pro—further reduction will move the dots of the bitmapped image closer together in such a way that dots will merge with one another and produce a fuzzy, muddy appearance.

To reduce the size of a MacPaint file with maximum quality, reduce it in a graphics program such as Adobe Photoshop. Import the image into the program

FIGURE 4.3

The Options submenu for the LaserWriter Page Setup dialog box, with Precision Bitmap Alignment selected

> **LaserWriter Options**　　　　　　　　7.1.1　　　**OK**
>
> ☐ **Flip Horizontal**　　　　　　　　　　**Cancel**
> ☐ **Flip Vertical**
> ☐ **Invert Image**
> ☒ **Precision Bitmap Alignment (4% reduction)**
> ☐ **Larger Print Area (Fewer Downloadable Fonts)**
> ☐ **Unlimited Downloadable Fonts in a Document**

full-size, then convert it to another format that will permit you to reduce the individual dots in size, not merely move them closer together.

T I P

If your printer is an ImageWriter or a StyleWriter and you want first-class output (regardless of the format in which your graphic images were created), be sure you print with the Best quality button selected in the Print dialog box. This setting gives you the highest resolution. On an ImageWriter LQ, this means 216 dpi. On a StyleWriter, you can obtain 360 dpi. This is impressive performance for such relatively inexpensive products.

TIFF

TIFF stands for Tagged Image File Format. This bitmapped format is widely used (especially for scanned images) and has few of the drawbacks of a MacPaint file. TIFF files can have any desired resolution and can store both color and grayscale information.

You can adjust the grayscale output of some laser printers. For example, the LaserWriter IIf and IIg offer PhotoGrade, a feature you can adjust through the Utility menu of Apple's LaserWriter Utility. When you select the Set PhotoGrade... command from that menu, you'll see the small dialog box shown in Figure 4.4. (You

FIGURE 4.4

The PhotoGrade control dialog box, showing its default setting

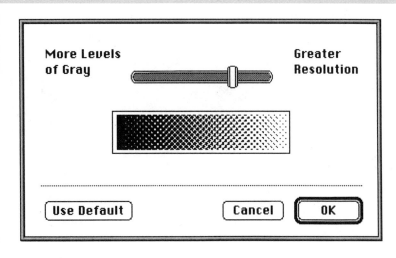

can use PhotoGrade on the LaserWriter IIf only if you have at least five megabytes of RAM installed; the LaserWriter IIg is shipped with this minimum RAM configuration.) In this dialog box, you drag the slider to the left to increase the levels of gray that will be printed; however, the more levels of gray shown, the less resolution you'll get. In the typical MacWrite Pro document that combines text and graphics, make sure you don't increase the number of grays to the point that type will appear jagged. If necessary, you can click the Use Default button to restore the setting to the default shown in Figure 4.4.

The LaserMaster Unity 1000 printer, which provides a resolution of 1000 by 1000 dpi (equivalent to the output of some professional imagesetters) has a feature called TurboGray, which smoothes the contours of grayscale images and is controlled through the TurboGray dialog box shown in Figure 4.5.

You access this dialog box through the TurboGray... command on the Setup menu of the LaserMaster Printer Utility. After you click the Contour Smoothing On button to activate this feature, you should evaluate the subsequent printer output carefully to see if the result is better than the output with the feature turned off. For example, if your MacWrite Pro documents include graphic files showing captured Macintosh screen displays, occasionally TurboGray may print the background of a window or dialog box as a shade of gray rather than white—undesirable. On the other hand, TurboGray can greatly enhance some photos and grayscale illustrations.

FIGURE 4.5

The LaserMaster
TurboGray
dialog box

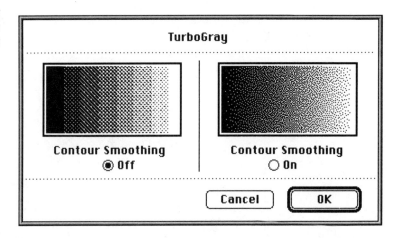

If you don't have a LaserWriter IIf or IIg or a LaserMaster, but do have access to a different, recently manufactured laser, check the manual to see if that printer has a grayscale-modification feature. You can use PhotoGrade with a LaserWriter Pro, but not at its maximum 600 dpi resolution.

PICT AND PICT2

PICT files are not bitmaps. They're actually small computer routines stored in the Mac QuickDraw language—the same language that's used to create the display on your Macintosh screen. These files handle artwork as a series of objects that can be redrawn and printed in any size specified, at the maximum resolution of the printing device.

The original PICT format is still supported by the Mac operating system, but rarely used, because its successor—the PICT2 format—is much more versatile. If your available disk-storage space and memory are at absolute minimums, you may want to use files in the PICT format simply because they're small; they store much less information than comparable PICT2 files. The PICT2 format can handle 32-bit color and grayscale data: it can discriminate between millions of colors and shades of gray.

A PICT2 file is not limited in size like the MacPaint format; the size of a drawing is limited only by how much RAM and disk space you have.

EPSF

Files in the EPSF format (for Encapsulated PostScript) contain two complete descriptions of a graphic image.

One description is in the PICT2 format and is used to display the image on your screen in the QuickDraw language the Macintosh uses to draw all screens. The other branch of the file is written in Adobe's PostScript language and describes the graphic image in terms understood by a PostScript printer such those in as Apple's LaserWriter line. EPSF files—like PICT2—can be printed at the maximum resolution of the printer.

Unfortunately, the QuickDraw and PostScript languages don't always agree perfectly on how to describe the placement of an object or character. Therefore, occasionally when you use a PostScript printer to print a MacWrite Pro document that looks exactly the way you want it on the screen, you may find that the spacing of elements will be slightly different in the printout. You may have to adjust the screen version and reprint the file three or four times to obtain the correct spacing in the printout. However, many users of PostScript printers never notice any difference between the appearance of their documents on the screen and on paper.

TIP

You can use the Insert... command on the File menu to import graphic files stored in any of the formats described. You must create a picture frame to receive the graphic image and have the frame selected before you issue the command.

INTEGRATING TEXT AND GRAPHICS

Ideally, when you use text and graphics together in your MacWrite Pro documents, these two elements should appear as if they belong together. If you're using clip art to accompany your ideas or data, the artwork should match the content and mood of the text so perfectly that your readers will think the drawings were specially created for the occasion.

For the match to be perfect, it helps to have many drawings and typefaces from which to choose, but you can often substitute a little ingenuity. For example, if you've been given the job of preparing and printing a notice announcing a new company retirement plan, you don't need to show a happy employee being awarded a gold watch by his grateful boss. With a drawing of a sailboat handy, you could suggest that the retirees will have "smooth sailing" in the future, thanks to the generous benefits they'll receive. If you have a drawing of a palm tree available, you could imply that life can be one long vacation in Florida or Hawaii, again thanks to those generous benefits.

But you get the idea. Tailoring the message to match the available artwork can make a limited clip-art library stretch a lot further.

POSITIONING TEXT WITH GRAPHICS

Figure 4.6 shows how the careful positioning of text in relation to graphics can also add to the illusion that they belong together. Here we combined text in an eye-catching typeface (Adobe's Juniper, based on wooden display fonts used during the last century) with a clip-art drawing from the Dubl-Click WetPaint library to give the impression that the type is actually part of a billboard being pasted on a wall by the man at the left.

FIGURE 4.6

Text and clip art
combined to create
a billboard

To accomplish this, the type should fit the period of the artwork—here an
ultra-modern font would be completely out of place. Furthermore, the text must
be positioned so that it appears to be part of the billboard.

The document shown in Figure 4.6 consists of three frames: a picture frame
containing the illustration, a text frame containing all of the text except the word
BIG, and a second text frame containing only the word BIG.

The basic reason for placing text within a frame rather than just typing it as the main body of the document is that you have more flexibility: you can move both the text and picture frames to align elements the way you want them. However, with the typeface used, the line spacing was such that the word BIG was too far above the word RACE for good composition.

The solution was to place BIG in its own frame and drag it closer to RACE. In order for this trick to work, the frame containing BIG was configured as transparent; otherwise, after being dragged to its new position, the frame would have overlapped and hidden the upper part of the word RACE.

Of course, we had to place the *picture* frame in a transparent mode too. If we hadn't, the picture frame would have hidden all of the text when the document was printed.

Figure 4.7 shows another example of integrating text and graphics, again using artwork from the Dubl-Click WetPaint library. In this case, each word was placed in a separate transparent text frame. The frames were then dragged carefully to positions that would not hide the underlying artwork.

The typeface is Adobe's Mesquite, with the shadow attribute added so the words would stand out from their background.

IMPORTING SPREADSHEET CHARTS

You can easily place charts from spreadsheet programs in picture frames by pasting them in from the Clipboard, as Figure 4.8 illustrates.

The chart was created in Microsoft Excel, then selected and copied to the Clipboard. When brought into MacWrite Pro, the chart retained its formatting and typefaces. Not only that, when we dragged a corner of the picture frame to reduce its size, then issued the Picture menu's Fit Contents to Frame command to match the chart size to the new frame size, all of the text in the chart was automatically reduced in size proportionally as well.

The document heading was printed in Berthold's AG Old Face Shaded typeface, available from Adobe. The chart heading is in Monotype Script Bold, available either from Monotype or Adobe, and was added from within Excel. The body copy is Goudy, from Digital Typeface Corporation.

The picture frame was configured in the Modify Frame dialog box as not anchored, opaque, and with text wrap activated. We changed the Offset (the white space to be maintained around the frame) from the default 4 pt. to 1 pt. to eliminate awkward spaces above and below the frame.

FIGURE 4.7

Words positioned
in individual
frames over a
picture frame so
that artwork details
are not hidden

These unwanted spaces occur because MacWrite Pro ends a line of text at the edge of the offset area on the wrap side of the frame any time even a tiny horizontal segment of the line would otherwise intrude into the area. So a smaller offset can reduce the number of lines that will be shortened to wrap around the area.

Ⓤ SING CLIP-ART LIBRARIES

You can download free clip-art files from some Macintosh bulletin boards. However, buying art from commercial clip-art libraries is usually well worth the modest price. First, the art is nearly always displayed according to subject matter

An Excel chart imported into MacWrite Pro

Fashion Division Tops Expectations

The marketing department reports that sales in the Women's Fashion Division have exceeded projections by 20%. Division manager Sheila Prentiss credits two factors for this success: the innovation embodied in the new line and hard work by the field sales force. Judging by current advance orders, she expects sales to continue at this level for at least the next six months.

in convenient printed catalogs, making the right drawing easy to locate and use. Second, most of these illustrations are by professional artists and are produced to high technical standards. Third, the subject matter has been chosen not according to the whims of the artist, but in response to market research as to the most useful kinds of drawings for the average computer user.

USING UNSTUFFIT

Graphic files can be very large, particularly if grayscale or color information is stored in them, so libraries frequently provide their art files in a compressed form, to save space on floppy disks. The files must be expanded (decompressed) before you can use them.

Figure 4.9 shows the method used to expand files by purchasers of art from the Metro ImageBase library.

1 Copy the contents of a clip-art floppy to your hard disk.

2 Use the UnStuffit utility provided to restore the files to their original size.

- You can highlight a group of files that you wish to expand and even select an Options menu item that permits background operations during the decompression process (see Figure 4.9).

- A message at the bottom of the UnStuffit window shows the total size of the selected files in their compressed, "archived"

FIGURE 4.9

Decompressing Metro ImageBase clip-art files

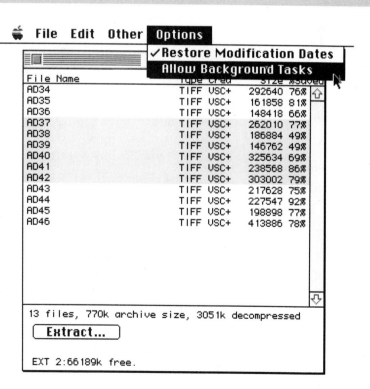

form, plus the amount of disk space the files will occupy after being expanded. By looking at this message, you can easily see if you have room to store expanded files before starting the decompression process.

3 Click the Extract... button to expand the selected files.

4 Choose a destination disk and folder for the files in the dialog box that will appear. You can rename each file that is expanded. Obviously, renaming a file such as AD34 is a good idea; you can use the illustration of the file in the company's catalog as a help in giving the drawing an appropriate name.

ADVANTAGES OF CD-ROM DISKS

Some firms offer their entire clip-art libraries on CD-ROM disks. If you have a CD-ROM drive to play these disks, you may wish to take advantage of this highly efficient storage method to have a large selection of graphic images just a mouse-click away.

In most instances, you'll have the choice of buying the entire library at one time—at a substantial discount—or of purchasing just the art you need by making a phone call with your credit card handy. When you buy only selected files, the company sends you the entire library in "locked" form on their CD-ROM disk with your first order. Then, each time you make a subsequent purchase, you're provided with a code number you can use to "unlock" the files on the disk already in your possession—instant delivery of your order!

There are many clip-art libraries, so there's room in this section to showcase only a few.

DYNAMIC GRAPHICS

Dynamic Graphics, Inc., offers clip-art services called Electronic Clipper and Designer's Club. Electronic Clipper provides subscribers with approximately 70 clip-art drawings a month in TIFF and EPSF formats; Designer's Club offers approximately 50 EPSF images monthly.

This art is also available in CD-ROM collections. The subscriptions include Image Quest, a utility that indexes the art for easy reference.

Figure 4.10 shows typical illustrations from these libraries: a stylized sailing ship, an abstract pattern, marching holiday toys, and an ethnic drawing. The

FIGURE 4.10

Samples of clip art
by Dynamic
Graphics

ringmaster in Chapter 3 is also from this source, and you'll see other examples later in the book.

Since this company offers primarily subscription services, its files can be helpful to anyone who must produce regular publications. However, many home computer users who need clip art only occasionally and who don't have a CD-ROM drive may find this professional source beyond their current requirements.

IMAGE CLUB DIGITART

Image Club has been producing clip art since 1985 for use on the Macintosh. All of the art is created in Adobe Illustrator and saved in the EPSF format and is available in volumes on floppy disks, arranged by subject matter. The entire library is also furnished on a CD-ROM disk.

The Image Club DigitArt collection includes many cartoons, such as the Mac with a virus shown in Figure 4.11; caricatures of celebrities such as Oprah Winfrey, as well as historical personages; and full-page drawings of many types that can be used as backgrounds for your MacWrite Pro documents.

As you'll find by looking at examples in later chapters, the Image Club library has great variety—except in the category of serious, realistic drawings. The DigitArt volumes include more than 5,000 inexpensive images.

METRO IMAGEBASE

Metro ImageBase provides clip art in the TIFF format, based on the company's print clip-art service, which has operated so long that some of its electronic volumes include authentic drawings and cartoons from the 1920s.

Figure 4.12 shows an example from this period (at the right), plus a holiday food display and a montage integrating the skyscrapers of a large city with a modern industrial site and a suburban home.

Other subjects in this large library include sports, medicine, and family life. Many drawings are lifelike portraits of people engaged in their daily activities.

As discussed previously, this company provides compressed files that you expand to their original size with the UnStuffit utility.

WETPAINT BY DUBL-CLICK SOFTWARE

Although Dubl-Click Software's WetPaint library consists entirely of black-and-white paint files, fans of this clip-art source hardly notice this limitation. Nowhere else can you find some of the subject matter in this conglomeration of electronic images from many eras, ranging from the hieroglyphics of ancient Egypt to the U.S. space program.

You'll find weather symbols, rare plants, King Kamehameha of Hawaii, a turn-of-the century guest house in Tasmania, a steam fire engine, and the Marx Brothers. You can see other examples in Figure 4.13, where the cavalry mingles with a Gibson girl, a Renaissance dandy, and a surprised schoolmaster who just sat on a tack.

The WetPaint collection is modestly priced and is also available on CD-ROM. All of these paint images are provided as full-page files. Most of the pages contain several pictures. No file compression is involved.

FIGURE 4.11

Samples of Image
Club's DigitArt
clip art

To use an image, you select it on its page through the ArtRoundup utility
provided free with each purchase of a volume from the library, copy the image to the

FIGURE 4.12

Samples of Metro
ImageBase clip art

Clipboard, and then paste it into a MacWrite Pro picture frame (or, of course, paste it into some other application if you wish).

Figure 4.14 illustrates the process of using a lasso tool to select an ambulance within ArtRoundup. Figure 4.15 shows the ArtRoundup menu, from which you can choose to copy a selected drawing as an opaque or transparent image, scale the image, invert it (switching black and white), flip it horizontally or vertically, or rotate it 90 degrees.

You can also draw on a copy of an image or erase any portion of it before you copy it to the Clipboard. In addition, you can run a "slide show," displaying pages in sequence while you look for an image you want to use.

TIP

If you have a paint or drawing program and a little artistic ability, try modifying or combining clip-art images to produce graphics that look very different and suit your special purposes. In MacDraw Pro, you can even

change grayscale art or photos into color images by converting ranges of grays into specific colors. (Use the Color palette's Image Color command and the Color Editor, as described in the Tip in Chapter 3.)

FIGURE 4.13

Samples
of Dubl-Click
Software's
WetPaint clip art

FIGURE 4.14

Using the lasso
tool to copy an
image from a
WetPaint page

FIGURE 4.15

The menu for
Dubl-Click
Software's
ArtRoundup utility

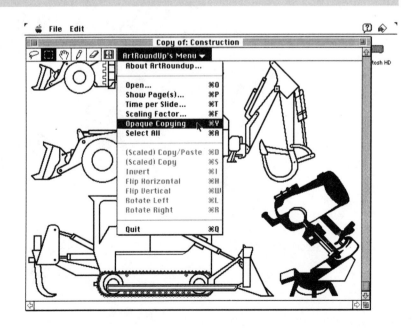

Ⓢ CANNING GRAPHIC IMAGES

If you have access to a scanner, you can create your own clip art by scanning pictures from old books and magazines. Good sources are garage sales and your local library. You can also use a scanner to add photos of employees to a company newsletter.

Scanners can convert images on paper into computer files in standard graphics formats such as TIFF, EPSF, and PICT2.

DANGER

If you're thinking of copying an image you find on paper, be sure that the image is not protected by the copyright laws. It's illegal to copy a picture from a book unless any copyright on the book has expired and has not been renewed.

For as little as $300 you can buy a hand scanner suitable for scanning small black and white images. Flatbed, full-page scanners cost more, but are well worth the investment if you have regular scanning to do.

Many scanners work through graphics programs such as Adobe Photoshop, using special "plug-in" modules provided by the scanner manufacturer. Figure 4.16 shows the window for the scanning software supplied with the Epson ES-300C color scanner, which can operate through Photoshop.

In the figure, a preview scan has been made of a photo. The resulting image appears in the upper left corner of the window. The left side of the window shows the entire 8.5-by-11-inch area that can be scanned. Once the preview scan appears on your screen, you can use your mouse to draw a selection box around a smaller area of the image for the final scan, as demonstrated in the figure.

Note that an option in the window let you choose whether or not you want a color preview. You can also pick the resolution in dots-per-inch, scale the image during the scan to any percentage between 50 percent and 200 percent of its actual size, and make other choices that affect the technical quality of the image. You can set the scan for color, grayscale, line art, or halftoning (with which you can choose between various dot patterns specifically designed to approximate colors or grays for black and white printing).

Make sure you have enough disk space to store the file produced in a scan. Color scans take up more file space than black and white scans, and large scanning areas and high resolution also require more storage space. These requirements can be alleviated to some extent by storing the file in a compressed form, provided the software you have available makes this possible.

FIGURE 4.16

The scanning
window for the
software provided
with the Epson
ES-300C color
scanner

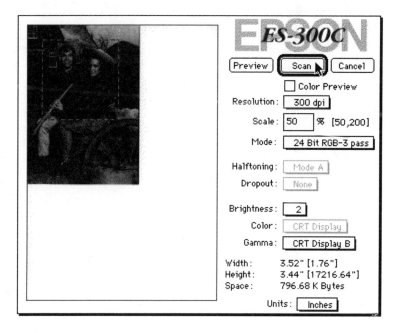

Figure 4.17 shows the result of the final scan of the photo previewed in Figure 4.16. The photo now appears in Adobe Photoshop, where you can modify such characteristics of the image as color balance (illustrated in the figure), contrast, and the degree of sharpness.

At this point, the image is stored only in the program's memory; you decide within Photoshop in which graphic format you want to save the image. If you pick TIFF, for example, Photoshop will let you choose to compress the file to save disk space, by using the LZW compression technology.

USING MAC SCREENS AS GRAPHIC IMAGES

There are times when you might want to capture all or part of a screen display on your Macintosh and use it as a graphic image in a document. An example would

FIGURE 4.17

You can adjust a
scanned image in
Adobe Photoshop
before saving the
image to disk

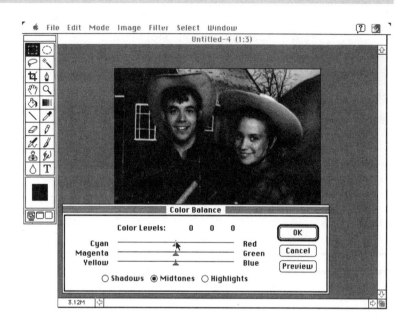

be the creation of a memo showing employees how to use certain features of a
software program.

CAPTURING AN ENTIRE SCREEN

To capture an entire screen as a PICT2 file, simply arrange the screen display the
way you want it, then press ⌘-Shift-3 (hold down all three keys at once). A new
file icon will appear in the window of your startup disk; the file will be named Picture 1 and will contain the screen image.

If you continue to capture screens without renaming the resulting files, suc-
ceeding screens will be named Picture 2, Picture 3, and so on. Obviously, you
should rename screens captured in this manner as soon as possible, before you
forget what each contains.

EDITING SCREEN CAPTURES

If you want to capture only part of screens, or erase or add elements, you may want to purchase Exposure Pro, an amazing utility from Baseline Publishing. With Exposure Pro, you can freeze a screen and then modify it in almost any way you like before saving it to disk in your choice of several graphics formats, including color PICT2. You can even add special effects, use draw and paint tools, and write new text on the screen you've captured, selecting any font installed in your system. You can name a captured screen before you save it, thus eliminating any confusion as to the file contents.

Although any key or key combination can be assigned as the "hot key" to start Exposure Pro, most purchasers who have an extended keyboard use the F13 function key, which can otherwise be used to print the contents of the current screen. Apple used Exposure Pro to capture screens for their System 7 manual.

T I P

You can use the system software's Scrapbook (accessed through the Apple menu) as a convenient storage area for any graphic images you use frequently. Just draw a selection box around the image on your screen (or any part of your screen, including text), copy your selection to the Clipboard, then choose Scrapbook from the Apple menu and issue the Paste command. The image will be stored in the Scrapbook until you delete it.

To use an image stored in the Scrapbook, open Scrapbook through the Apple menu, and click the Scrapbook scroll bar until you see the image you want. Copy the image to the Clipboard using the Copy command on the Scrapbook's Edit menu and paste it into a picture frame in your MacWrite Pro document.

Portfolio Systems publishes SmartScrap, a substitute for the Scrapbook that offers several additional features. For example, you can use multiple scrapbook files and copy only a selected portion of a scrapbook image into your document.

Ⓢ UMMARY

You now know the basic features of the most popular Mac graphics formats and have been provided with some tips on how to integrate graphics with your Mac-Write Pro text. In addition, you've had a look at some popular clip-art libraries and received an introduction to the procedures involved in a typical scanning operation. Finally, you learned how to capture and store Mac screen displays as graphic images.

Armed with this knowledge, you're ready to use graphics in multiple-column layouts—one of the subjects covered in Chapter 5, which is devoted to the fine points of how and when to split your text into two or more columns.

Using Multiple Columns

CHAPTER 5

FEATURING

Try your hand now at creating some multiple-column documents. As you proceed, we'll provide tips that can make jobs of this sort easier to complete and more professional in appearance. At the end of the chapter, we'll also show you some more advanced examples and explain how they were produced.

PREPARING TEXT FOR A MULTIPLE-COLUMN DOCUMENT

This section will brief you on some general rules that you should follow when you use multiple columns.

ENTERING ONE SPACE BETWEEN SENTENCES

Back in the days before computers, students in high-school typing classes learned that you enter one space after a comma or semicolon, but two spaces at the end of a sentence. Many instructors in today's word-processing classes still follow this rule. But if you pick up a professionally-printed book or magazine, you'll find only one space at the end of each sentence. Closing up the gap accomplishes two purposes: it makes the text seem to flow more smoothly for the reader, and it saves valuable space for the printed characters, particularly when the text is divided into narrow columns.

We recommend that you too hit the spacebar only once at the end of a sentence intended for use in a multiple-column document, particularly if you're using a *proportional* typeface (defined in Chapter 1 as a typeface in which each character takes up only as much room as it needs on a line). A two-space gap in a paragraph of proportional text can appear huge and awkward.

HYPHENATING WORDS

The hyphenation of words becomes a major consideration when you're working with narrow columns. If long words at the ends of lines are not hyphenated (and thereby divided into two segments), you may end up with only one or two words on some lines, which can make the affected columns unattractive and hard to read.

Although MacWrite Pro offers automatic hyphenation, probably this feature will not be adequate for all of your needs. You'll find that the program has divided some words in the wrong places, particularly if the words are not in its hyphenation dictionary. Therefore, for the exercises in this chapter, turn off the Auto Hyphenate feature (if it's on); you'll enter necessary hyphens manually, a skill you need to master.

Turning Off Automatic Hyphenation

Follow these steps to turn off automatic hyphenation:

1. Pull down the Edit menu, and highlight the Spelling option. The Spelling submenu will appear, containing the Auto Hyphenate command.

2. If you don't see a check mark before the Auto Hyphenate command, simply release the mouse button without selecting the command, thereby closing the menu. The automatic hyphenation feature is already off.

3. If there is a check mark before the Auto Hyphenate command, the feature is active, and you need to turn it off. Highlight the command, as demonstrated in Figure 5.1, then release the mouse button. The check mark will disappear, the Edit menu will close, and automatic hyphenation will be turned off.

To hyphenate a word manually, you'll probably want to look it up in a dictionary that shows how each word is correctly hyphenated; you don't want to break a word in the wrong place.

Once you know where a word should be split, you could click the pointer at that position in the word, type a hyphen, then tap the spacebar. MacWrite Pro would then automatically leave part of the word at the end of one line and move the remainder of the word to the beginning of the following line. This technique will work, but it's not a good idea.

The reason you shouldn't use this technique is that hyphens of this type will remain in the positions where you entered them, even if you change the width of a column or decide that you want to use three columns instead of two. In other words, you can end up with both of those word parts together on one line, as illustrated in Figure 5.2.

FIGURE 5.1

Turning off the
automatic
hyphenation
feature

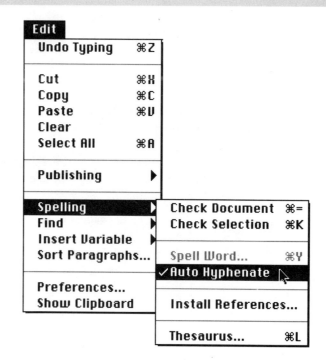

FIGURE 5.2

A manually
entered hyphen
remains, even
when not wanted

The quick
brown fox
jumps o- ver
the lazy dog.

Using Discretionary Hyphens

The solution to this problem is to enter a *discretionary* hyphen—a hyphen that appears and breaks a word only when the word won't fit in its entirety at the end of a line. To enter a discretionary hyphen, simply hold down the ⌘ key as you type the hyphen.

T I P

Even if you hyphenate expertly, narrow columns often look terrible if the text is formatted as fully justified. The reason is that this setting requires that the program make the text on each line touch both the left and right margins of the columns. As a result, even with proper hyphenation, you're likely to see ugly gaps between words on most lines, gaps required to keep those margins straight. It's usually wiser to format narrow columns with left justification only. See Figure 1.7 in Chapter 1, which illustrates different justification settings.

CHANGING THE DEFAULT INDENTATION

Since typewriters made their first appearance during the last century, the tradition has been to indent new paragraphs five spaces—or approximately half an inch. Computer word-processing programs usually adhere to this tradition today, and MacWrite Pro is no exception. By default, when you press the Tab key, the pointer will move half an inch to the right.

This deep indentation looks fine if you're typing a one-column document in Courier or some other fixed-pitch typeface (wherein each character occupies the same amount of space on a line, regardless of the actual width of the characters). But when you're using a proportional typeface, particularly in narrow columns, a half-inch indentation looks terrible.

In preparation for the document you're about to create, open a new document and add a new tab stop a quarter of an inch from the left margin. (The default tab stops at half-inch intervals are not shown on the ruler.) To add the tab stop, drag the left tab marker to the quarter-inch position on the ruler. A copy of the tab marker will move with your pointer; when you release the mouse button, the new marker will remain displayed at the quarter-inch tick mark, as shown in Figure 5.3.

A new tab stop
set one quarter
of an inch from the
left margin

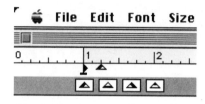

ENTERING THE TEXT

Before you start working with columns, you'll need some text to manipulate, so type the short "news story" shown in Figure 5.4. If you make a mistake, just press the Delete key to backspace and remove the error, and type your correction. Press the Tab key for a quarter-inch indent at the beginning of each paragraph.

Choosing Suitable Fonts

In Figure 5.4, the headline is in Helvetica Bold, and the *body copy* (as the main text is often called in the printing and advertising industries) is in Times Roman. We made the two-line headline fill both of its lines by entering it in a 33-pt. size. You won't find this size listed on the Size menu, but you can obtain it by selecting Other... from the bottom of that menu, typing the size in the tiny dialog box that will appear and clicking OK. (You can enter any size here that you like—even 150-pt. if you want to emphasize one or two characters. The printed samples in this chapter are reproduced smaller than their actual sizes.)

The size for the remainder of the text is 18 pt., which we used to be sure that you could read the words easily for copying. You can use any size you wish for this main text, since you'll soon be changing its size anyway. However, try to make your heading fill its two lines by picking an appropriate size, because you'll use the heading in this configuration throughout some later sections of the chapter.

If you want to use typefaces other than Helvetica Bold and Times Roman, feel free to do so. Don't bother to hyphenate any words at this time; long lines of text that are left-justified usually look good even when displayed only as whole words.

FIGURE 5.4

Type this text for use in the exercise that follows

ANGRY DOG SUPPORTERS QUESTION Q. B. FOX CLAIM

Supporters of L. Dog today demanded a formal investigation of the claim by Quick Brown Fox that he "jumped over the lazy Dog." The Dog backers pointed out that there were no known witnesses to the jumping event and that Fox's veracity has been questioned on previous occasions, particularly regarding his account of the death of an acquaintance to whom he offered a ride across the river.

Furthermore, the Dog organization stated that Fox is "barking up the wrong tree" when he calls Dog lazy. Dog has stated repeatedly that his regular morning and afternoon naps are taken on doctor's orders and that he personally would prefer to chase cars all day.

Fox replied to the charges by saying, "If the case comes to trial, I will produce my witnesses at the proper time. I consider it a vile slur on my reputation when these animals allege that I'm lying about this jump and have no verification. In fact, I'm considering filing a suit for slander."

USING LINES THAT ARE TOO LONG

In Figure 5.4, you can easily read the main text of the article because we made the font size large enough that there are relatively few words on each line. However, to experience for yourself the difficulty of using lines that are too long, try changing the text you just entered to a smaller size. Follow these steps:

1. Drag to select all of the body copy of the article (all of the text except the headline).

2. Pull down the Size menu, and select the 9-pt. size. The individual lines of the text will now contain so many words that your eye will have trouble reading them.

3 Why not save your document, to make sure all of that typing doesn't go to waste? Press ⌘-S (the shortcut for the Save… command on the File menu). You'll see the Save As dialog box. Name the document **Dog vs. Fox**, and click the Save button to complete the file-saving operation and close the dialog box.

Figure 5.5 shows the result of using 9-pt. text. We switched typefaces in this figure (and in Figure 5.6 as well), to show you how the text looks with different

---

FIGURE 5.5

Text is hard to read when there are too many words on a single line.

ANGRY DOG SUPPORTERS QUESTION Q. B. FOX CLAIM

Supporters of L. Dog today demanded a formal investigation of the claim by Quick Brown Fox that he "jumped over the lazy Dog." The Dog backers pointed out that there were no known witnesses to the jumping event and that Fox's veracity has been questioned on previous occasions, particularly regarding his account of the death of an acquaintance to whom he offered a ride across the river.

Furthermore, the Dog organization stated that Fox is "barking up the wrong tree" when he calls Dog lazy. Dog has stated repeatedly that his regular morning and afternoon naps are taken on doctor's orders and that he personally would prefer to chase cars all day.

Fox replied to the charges by saying, "If the case comes to trial, I will produce my witnesses at the proper time. I consider it a vile slur on my reputation when these animals allege that I'm lying about this jump and have no verification. In fact, I'm considering filing a suit for slander."

FIGURE 5.6

Text is hard to read when divided into columns that are too narrow for the font size selected (too few characters on a single line)

ANGRY DOG SUPPORTERS QUESTION Q. B. FOX CLAIM

Supporters of L. Dog today demanded a formal investigation of the claim by Quick Brown Fox that he "jumped over the lazy Dog." The Dog backers pointed out that there were no known witnesses to the jumping event and that Fox's veracity has been questioned on previous occasions, particularly regarding his account of the death of an ac-quaintance to whom he offered a ride across the river.

Furthermore, the Dog organization stated that Fox is "barking up the wrong tree" when he calls Dog lazy. Dog has insisted repeatedly that his regular morn-ing and afternoon naps are taken on doctor's orders and that he per-sonally would prefer to chase cars all day.

Fox replied to the charges by saying, "If the case comes to trial, I will produce my wit-nesses at the proper time. I consider it a vile slur on my reputation when these animals al-lege that I'm lying a-bout this jump and have no verification. In fact, I'm considering fil-ing a suit for slander."

fonts than those in the much-used Helvetica and Times Roman families. The heading in these figures is in Flare Bold, and the body copy is in Flare Regular, both from Digital Typeface Corporation.

Ⓢ EPARATING A HEADING FROM MULTIPLE-COLUMN TEXT

If you want to use a small font size to save space in a document, but you don't want the lines to be so long that they'll be hard to read, the solution is to separate those lines into multiple columns.

Before you can do this, to keep the headline in its present position—running across the full width of the page at the top of the document—you'll have to move the headline into a text frame. Otherwise, when you convert the text to multiple columns, MacWrite Pro will squeeze the entire headline into the first column.

Use the following steps now to convert your headline into a text frame (use this technique to convert any document heading into a text frame):

❶ Display the Tool palette, if it's not already available on your screen.

❷ Click to select the Text frame tool (remember, its icon contains a capital A), then drag to draw a frame around the two-line headline. As mentioned previously, the default settings for a frame drawn with a tool are that it will be opaque and not anchored to text, but with text wrap activated. Since text wrap applies to the bottom of a frame as well as the sides, all of the text you typed previously will move down to make room for the new text frame.

❸ Drag across the headline to select all of its characters, pull down the Edit menu, and select the Cut command. (Shortcut: press ⌘-X.) The headline will disappear from your screen, and the body copy will fill the gap by moving up next to the text frame.

4 Click inside the new text frame to select it, then pull down the Edit menu again and select the Paste command. (Shortcut: press ⌘-V.) The headline will reappear inside the text frame. Since you drew the frame around the headline while it was part of the main document text, the frame should be exactly the right size to display the headline. If, for some reason, it is not, you can drag a corner handle of the frame to resize it.

S WITCHING TO MULTIPLE COLUMNS

As you'll remember from Chapter 1, you can increase or decrease the number of columns for the main text of a document by clicking the column buttons in the ruler. The left button decreases the number of columns (unless the text is already in a single column). The right button increases the number of columns.

Try converting the Dog vs. Fox document into a three-column format. Follow these steps:

1 To convert the main text into a larger size than 9 pt., drag to select all of this text, then pull down the Size menu, and select 12- or 14-pt. (You can try both sizes; the size you'll prefer will depend upon the typeface you've chosen.)

2 Click the right column button twice to increase the number of columns to three. The text will automatically rearrange itself into three columns and the columns indicator will change to 3.

3 As soon as you're pleased with the font size for the columns, use the ⌘ and hyphen keys together to insert discretionary hyphens wherever necessary to avoid awkward gaps in individual lines.

Figure 5.6 shows the three columns displayed in 14-pt. Flare Regular. (Of course, the document has been reduced in size for reproduction in this book.) Although the lines have been hyphenated properly, you can see the opposite problem to the one shown in Figure 5.5: In this font size, the result is too few characters on a three-column line for easy reading. The solution would be either to reduce the font size or to make this a two-column document.

P REPARING TO USE VARIABLE-WIDTH COLUMNS

MacWrite Pro lets you use columns of different widths on the same page. By also dividing your pages into sections, you can change column widths as often as you like within a single document.

Next, try turning your Dog vs. Fox document into a page with variable column widths. What you'll do is display the entire "news story" you've already typed as the first column of a redesigned page. The remainder of the page will consist of a wider column that will display a feature interview with L. Dog's wife. Type the interview now, using the text displayed in Figure 5.7. This figure displays the Times Roman typeface family again, but you can use other typefaces if you prefer. Follow these steps:

1 Click the left column button twice to format the Dog vs. Fox news story as a single-column document again. If you entered the discretionary hyphens properly, these hyphens should all disappear, unless the words in which they were placed still happen to fall at the end of a line.

2 Type the headline for the interview and the interview itself below the end of the text you originally typed for the news

FIGURE 5.7

Type this headline and text for use on a page with columns of different widths

Valerie Dog Speaks Out

"Goodness, I'm just a house dog," Valerie Dog declared with a modest smile, "but I just can't sit on my haunches and say nothing when my husband is ridiculed in this manner." She was wearing a comfortable brown collar and reclining casually on the sofa in the large home she shares with L. Dog and their human staff.

She offered her interviewer a doggie biscuit, and when the offer was declined, proceeded to munch delicately on one herself. "I mean, after all, that Fox rascal never did jump over him, no matter what he says."

story. You'll soon rearrange all of the text to form your variable-width-column page.

The Section dialog box contains an option for activating variable-width columns. You can access this dialog box in any of the following ways:

- Pull down the Format menu, and select the Section... command.

- Press Option-⌘-S.

- Double-click the small box on the ruler that displays the current number of columns.

Regardless of the method you use to display the Section dialog box, you can convert any multiple-column document to variable-width columns by selecting the Variable Width button in the Columns section of this dialog box, as demonstrated in Figure 5.8.

You can then enter separate measurements for the width of each column, as well as the space between columns. But there's an easier method for changing to variable-width columns, which you'll use now.

FIGURE 5.8

Selecting
variable-width
columns

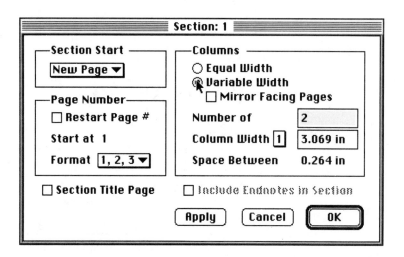

ⒸONVERTING SINGLE-COLUMN TEXT TO VARIABLE-WIDTH COLUMNS

Follow these steps to change the Dog vs. Fox document into a variable-width format:

1 Click the right column button to convert the document into a two-column format. The original news story will now appear in the first column, with the interview starting underneath it.

2 Click an insertion point below the last line of the news story (but above the headline for the Valerie Dog interview), and press the Enter key. (The Enter key is on the number keypad; it is *not* the Return key!) The interview will move to the second column.

TIP

Pressing the Enter key is the shortcut for pulling down the Format menu and selecting the Insert Break command, then selecting Column from the command's submenu.

3 Your goal is to make your document resemble the example in Figure 5.9. First, widen the second column (which now contains the interview) to approximate the width shown in the figure. To do this, you can bypass using the Section dialog box at all and drag the left column guide for the column to the left until the column has the width you want. To drag the column, simply position the pointer on the column guide, and hold down the Option key as you drag. (This action will also select the Variable Width button in the Section dialog box automatically, without displaying the dialog box.)

TIP

You can change either column width or the space between columns by holding down the Option key and dragging. As soon as you hold down the Option key, the pointer will assume one of the shapes shown in Figure 5.10. On the left is the shape of the pointer when used on a page guide with the Option key depressed, to drag and change column widths; on the right is the alternate pointer shape seen when dragging to change the spacing between columns

FIGURE 5.9

The Dog vs. Fox
document in a
variable-column-
width format

4 Next, as a substitute for inserting a picture of Valerie Dog (which you probably don't have), use the Picture Frame tool on the Tool palette to draw a frame to represent the picture. Place the frame in the approximate position occupied by the picture in the figure. If you have a drawing of a dog that you can place in the frame (or wish to create a dog portrait in a drawing program), feel free to do so.

5 Change the wording of the news-story headline, and/or the font size, to make it fit better into the space available for it.

6 If you have a casual script typeface available, this would be a good alternative to a standard headline typeface to use for the heading of the feature interview article. The typeface we used

FIGURE 5.10

Alternate pointer
shapes

in Figure 5.9 is Staccato 555, Bitstream's version of the Choc script typeface.

7 Adjust the hyphenation in the revised columns.

These actions will probably be all that you'll need to complete in order to display the Dog vs. Fox document in two variable-width columns.

Note, however, that we took one additional step: we created a separate transparent text box for the words Speaks Out in the heading for the interview so we could drag those words closer to the first two words in the heading than normal line spacing would permit.

Usually, you have to use a larger point size to make script typefaces noticeable than would be required for other typeface categories because these typefaces contain some characters with flourishes and/or long strokes that extend far above or below the area occupied by most of the characters. The large point size means that the program will use large default line spacing to accommodate those strokes, thereby spacing multiple lines of script text further apart than you may want. The use of a transparent text box for part of the text can easily correct this problem.

Since you've just created a rather complicated page (successfully, we hope!), you may want to save your revised Dog vs. Fox document and print it out. However, you won't need it again for exercises later in the book.

E XAMPLES OF SINGLE- AND MULTIPLE-COLUMN PAGES

Figure 5.11 shows the beginning of an article about the devastating 1906 San Francisco earthquake. The illustration is a photo of the damage done to the city hall by the earthquake. Because the font size used for the body copy is large and because the photo occupies so much of the page, each line contains only a few words, so the document is comparatively easy to read.

Note that a caption has been added under the photo; it was inserted in an opaque text frame with text wrap activated, so that the main text wraps around both this frame and the picture frame above it.

The typefaces used here are an interesting combination of the old and the new. The headline is in Abadi Extra Bold Condensed, designed by Ong Chong Wah for Monotype and introduced in 1988. The rest of the text is in fonts from the Plantin family, released by Monotype in 1913. Both typeface families are

FIGURE 5.11

A single-column
page on the 1906
San Francisco
earthquake

EARTHQUAKE RAVAGES 1906 SAN FRANCISCO

At 5:13 a.m. on April 18, 1906, the San Francisco city hall ceased to exist—at least, for all practical purposes. Seven million dollars' worth of ornate concrete and brickwork (at 1906 prices) separated from the steel framing and fell into heaps of rubble. Later the president of the chamber of commerce was to say that this catastrophe was "what comes of mixing bad politics and bad cement."

The city hall after the earthquake

However, the major reason for the building's collapse was the event that the world soon came to know as the San Francisco Earthquake.

When the earthquake struck, the city was prosperous and bustling. Enrico Caruso was in town, appearing in Bizet's *Carmen*. Young John Barrymore was visiting too, having recently finished his final performance on tour in *The Dictator*. The Bank of Italy—founded just two years before by 34-year-old A. P. Giannini—was becoming a respected entity in the city, with deposits totaling nearly a million dollars; this bank was one day to become Bank of America. The city boasted three major newspapers. Despite previous earthquakes in 1857, 1865, 1890, and 1898, the population of San Francisco had increased steadily. Some of the major buildings had been designed to be

available for the Macintosh directly from Monotype or through Adobe and are highly legible even when printed at low resolution.

Figure 5.12 shows the earthquake article converted to a two- column format, with the same main text but with the wording of the headline changed so it

FIGURE 5.12

A two-column version of the San Francisco earthquake article

San Francisco Splits Wide Open, and Its Great 1906 Monuments Become Rubble

At 5:13 a.m. on April 18, 1906, the San Francisco city hall ceased to exist—at least, for all practical purposes. Seven million dollars' worth of ornate concrete and brickwork (at 1906 prices) separated from the steel framing and fell into heaps of rubble. Later the president of the chamber of commerce was to say that this catastrophe was "what comes of mixing bad politics and bad cement."

However, the major reason for the building's collapse was the event that the world soon came to know as the San Francisco Earthquake.

When the earthquake struck, the city was prosperous and bustling. Enrico Caruso was in town, appearing in Bizet's *Carmen*. Young John Barrymore was visiting too, having recently finished his final performance on tour in *The Dictator*. The Bank of Italy—founded just two years before by 34-year-old A. P. Giannini—was becoming a respected entity in the city, with deposits totaling nearly a million dollars; this bank was one day to become Bank of America. The city boasted three major newspapers. Despite previous earthquakes in 1857, 1865, 1890, and 1898, the population of San Francisco had increased steadily. Some of the major

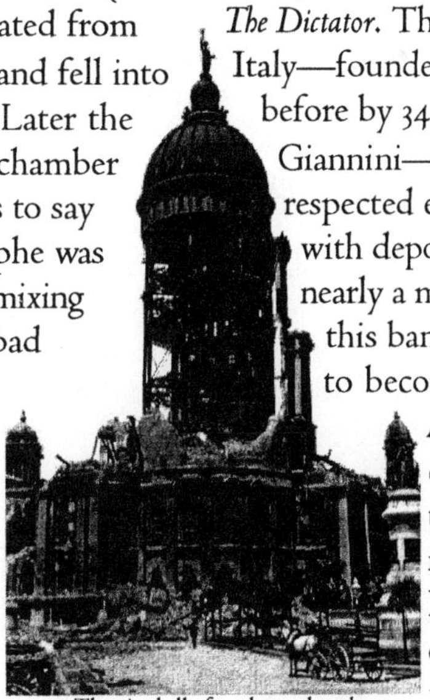

The city hall after the earthquake

will fit the new format. The picture is now centered on the page, with the text wrapped around the city hall itself rather than the frame containing it (because the picture frame was configured as transparent).

As discussed in Chapter 3, if you're using a PostScript-based printer, you may have to select Black & White in your Print dialog box in order to print text wrapped around an irregularly shaped graphic image; with other printers, you should have no problem printing the document correctly with Color/Grayscale selected.

This page looks very different from the single-column page dealing with the earthquake. Aside from the interesting placement of the photo, the main difference is the typeface family used. This is Centaur, rated by many as one of the most beautiful designs of this century. Centaur was created by Bruce Rogers for the Metropolitan Museum in 1914; the italic fonts are based on the 1925 designs of Frederic Warde and were originally released under the name *Arrighi*.

Centaur is available from Monotype or Adobe. Monotype has also released an Expert collection to accompany the basic typefaces. Centaur Expert contains some special characters seen in Figure 5.12, including the italic swash capital letters (swashes are those fancy swirls) used in the headline and lowercase numerals (numbers that extend above and below the height of most characters) seen in the references to time, dates, and the age of the founder of Bank of America. You can read more about expert collections and lowercase numerals in Chapter 6.

Our final example in this chapter uses typefaces that are far from classic and traditional; on the contrary, the typefaces are ultra-modern, in keeping with the subject matter. The page shown in Figure 5.13 has a heading in Glyphic (from Image Club). The body copy is in Cantoria, from Monotype—also sold by Adobe. The background illustration and the android are both from Image Club's DigitArt clip-art library.

This page is included to demonstrate that you can use multiple columns in different and creative ways; they needn't cover the entire page nor be separated only by white space or a printed vertical dividing line. In this figure, the heading and the two columns are each separate text frames. The heading was created by configuring the type color as white on a black background; the frame for the heading is transparent, to let the space scene show through behind the characters.

FIGURE 5.13

A modern theme illustrated through a multiple-column layout by using appropriate typefaces and artwork

S UMMARY

The success of a multiple-column document is dependent upon several factors discussed in this chapter—all of which should work together for the best effect.

- The text should be chosen with multiple columns in mind. Pick a typeface and font size that will look good in narrow columns.

- You should use the right number of columns so that the subject matter will be displayed to best advantage, and those columns should be the proper width to make a pleasing layout and ensure good readability.

- Hyphenation should be correct, and you should use discretionary hyphens whenever you enter hyphens manually.

- Any illustrations should be appropriate to the subject, and your typefaces should fit the subject too.

If some of these elements are poorly handled, the readers of your document may be irritated, dissatisfied, or unimpressed, and they may not even know why.

The next chapter provides you with more information about typefaces and how to use them.

Making the Most of Typefaces

CHAPTER 6

FEATURING

Using typefaces with discretion

How typefaces differ from one another

Learning useful definitions

How typefaces are named

How to kern your text

Using special characters

Installing and managing typefaces

Creating special effects

Does it really matter which typeface you use? Of course it does. As you've already seen in the earlier chapters, the right typeface can attract attention to your document, set the proper mood, increase readability, and establish a positive image for you or your organization. But the wrong typeface can make the document seem dull and uninteresting, mislead readers as to its nature and purpose, be difficult to read, or make you and your company appear amateurish and fly-by-night.

Although we've already provided you with some information about typefaces, we'll tell you much more in this chapter. You'll learn a few of the reasons why typefaces look different from one another, how to adjust the spacing between characters (*kerning*), where to find special characters, and how to use them. We'll also describe utilities that make it easier to work with typefaces. As we did in previous chapters, we'll identify the typefaces shown in examples so you can become more familiar with the many choices available.

T I P

Always remember that you can accomplish a lot with typefaces merely by changing the size, placement, and style of the fonts you use—even if you have only two or three typeface families available to you. For example, adding the Shadow or Outline attribute can often make an overused type design look fresh and different. To change the style of text, drag to highlight (select) the text, then select the style either through the Style menu or the Text palette.

Figure 6.1 shows the word *Sale!* presented in five different typefaces. Not all are appropriate for the subject, and some are more suitable than others.

The top example is Castle, a display typeface of the kind often called Old English. It is fitting for a church bulletin, but hardly for a retail sale.

The second typeface is called Aurea Inline. It's very elegant and reminiscent of ancient Rome; it would be a good choice for a luxury-car sale or an offering of fine jewelry.

The third example is good old Times Roman. It gets the message across in a straightforward, neutral manner, but certainly doesn't generate much excitement.

The fourth example is Stencil, which is intended to resemble the stenciling on the side of a packing crate. It would be suitable for a "warehouse sale."

FIGURE 6.1

The same message
presented in five
different typefaces

$\mathfrak{S}$ale!

SALE!

Sale!

SALE!

SALE!

Finally, we have a typeface with the intriguing name Too Much Opaque. This is an attention-getting, modern, informal typeface that you could use to sell many products, ranging from casual clothing to stereos.

The figure drives home the point that it helps to match the design to the project. But if you only had Times Roman available for announcing a sale, you might want to select italics or shadow styling, just to make the heading look a little different.

All of the above typefaces are available from Image Club. Stencil is also available from Adobe, Bitstream, and other vendors. Of course, you can find Times almost anywhere.

USING TYPEFACES WITH DISCRETION

The primary purpose of most documents is to communicate. The reader should understand the message and not be distracted by the medium. Therefore, if you're fortunate enough to have many typefaces available on your Mac, don't use them all in the same document. The result will look inept and confusing, rather than impressing those who see it with the quality and depth of your type collection. As a general rule, you shouldn't use more than two typeface families on the same page.

Figure 6.2 shows an example of what can happen when you break this rule. The document explains the origin of *uppercase* and *lowercase*, terms customarily used in the printing industry to differentiate between capital letters and all of the others.

The typeface in the first line of the heading is Blackoak from Adobe, a tribute to the wooden display fonts of the last century; couldn't you just see this one in a patent medicine ad?

The second line uses University Roman, an ornate and sophisticated design —sold by most vendors—that reminds us of the 1920s.

The main text starts with Pepita, a modern, casual script (imitating handwriting) that was created for Monotype in 1959 (also available from Adobe).

In the middle of the first sentence, we switch to Dorchester, a different Monotype script that is formal and could be used for wedding invitations.

The typeface for the last sentence is Poplar, a bold Adobe *condensed* typeface (condensed means with narrow characters) that would be suitable for announcing the result of a gunfight at the OK Corral.

Furthermore, this document breaks two other rules. First, it uses "straight up and down" quotation marks, such as you'd see in the output of a typewriter,

---

FIGURE 6.2

Mixing multiple typefaces of different kinds results in an unattractive and bewildering document

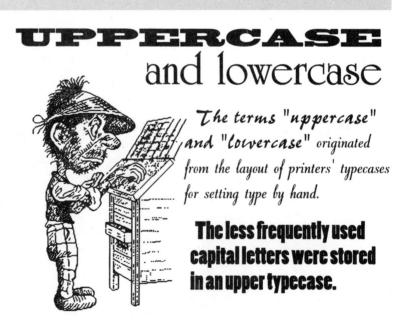

UPPERCASE
and lowercase

The terms "uppercase" and "lowercase" originated from the layout of printers' typecases for setting type by hand.

The less frequently used capital letters were stored in an upper typecase.

rather than the separate opening and closing marks that are customary in professional publications (more about this rule later in the chapter). Second, it uses two
script typefaces together. The effect of this combination is a little like a man wearing a plaid jacket with trousers in a different plaid.

Contrast this disaster with the version of the same document displayed in
Figure 6.3. Now we have only one typeface family—Cheltenham (from Bitstream), a
design introduced early in this century. Bold, regular, and italic variations within
this family combine to create a page that is easy to read and understand, as well
as pleasing to the eye.

EARNING HOW TYPEFACES DIFFER

As you've seen, typefaces can vary tremendously in their appearance and impact.
If you're aware of some of the causes of this diversity, you can do a better job of
selecting fonts in every document you create.

FIGURE 6.3

The same
document reset
entirely with
members of the
Cheltenham
typeface family

Uppercase and Lowercase

The terms *uppercase* and
lowercase originated from
the layout of printers'
typecases for setting type by
hand. The less frequently
used capital letters were
stored in an upper typecase.

TYPEFACE SIZES AND STYLES

Size is obviously one factor that separates one font from another. We mentioned earlier that font size is measured in *points* and that a point is approximately $\frac{1}{72}$ of an inch. But what is the practical effect of a change in font size?

If you don't know much about typefaces, it may help you to see a few actual font sizes. Figure 6.4 displays three representative Palatino Regular fonts in the actual point sizes listed. Palatino is one of the typeface families provided both with LaserWriter printers and with the System 7 operating system.

Style is another element that makes a font different. In Macintosh terms, the style consists of an attribute such as Bold or Shadow that you can add through the Style menu—or, within MacWrite Pro, through the Text palette as well. You can add any of these attributes and see the result instantly on your screen. If you're using a regular typeface that doesn't come with an italic counterpart, the operating system will slant the regular typeface to the right to provide the illusion of an italic version.

Unfortunately, there are two problems with this substitution. First, a typeface slanted to the right is properly called *oblique*, not italic. Many typeface families include only oblique variations rather than italic. If a typeface does include an italic, however, it may slant to the right, but its primary distinction is that the characters are designed differently than the regular or upright version. Slanting the regular version does not produce the same result.

Second, many typefaces are programmed so that a slanted (or pseudo-italic) version that you see on the screen will not print out. This restriction also applies to the boldface that the operating system can create by simply printing each character twice on the screen, the second time with a slight offset to make it wider. Real boldface in a typeface family is usually a different design from the regular typeface, not merely darker and wider.

FIGURE 6.4

Three Palatino
Regular fonts,
shown in their
actual point sizes

This is 12-pt. Palatino

This is 18-pt. Palatino

This is 24-pt. Palatino

Therefore, if the programmers have so decreed, you will see italic or bold on your screen, but on paper, you'll still see the original typeface. Typeface manufacturers create typefaces with these restrictions for two reasons: to encourage you to buy the separate italic and bold versions, of course, but also to preserve the purity of the design. The designer of the typeface deserves to see his work printed in the form in which it was created.

Figure 6.5 shows on the top line the ITC New Baskerville Roman (or regular) typeface (sold by Bitstream and several other vendors). The second line shows this typeface slanted by the operating system to imitate an italic. Directly under the imitation, you can see the real New Baskerville italic—quite a difference!

DEFINING TYPEFACES, FAMILIES, AND FONTS

Figure 6.6 provides you with visual definitions of a typeface family, a typeface, and individual fonts—already defined with words earlier in the book.

Remember, a *typeface* consists of all of the sizes in a typeface design having the same attribute or attributes, such as all of the sizes of Helvetica Regular. A *typeface family* is the term used for all of the typefaces belonging to the design, considered collectively. A *font* is one size of a typeface.

Pictured in Figure 6.6 is the Joanna family (from Monotype, also sold by Adobe), created by famed designer Eric Gill. An unusual characteristic is that the italic typefaces in this family are hardly slanted at all; they achieve their individuality by having narrower characters that are also drawn differently from the regular and bold versions.

FIGURE 6.5

A slanted regular
typeface compared
with a true italic

This is New Baskerville Roman
Slanted New Baskerville Roman
The real New Baskerville Italic

CH. 6

FIGURE 6.6

Illustrations of a typeface family, a typeface, and different fonts (reduced from actual sizes)

A typeface family

Joanna Regular
Joanna Italic
Joanna Semi Bold
Joanna Semi Bold Italic
Joanna Bold
Joanna Bold Italic
Joanna Extra Bold

A typeface

Joanna 10-pt. Regular
Joanna 12-pt. Regular
Joanna 14-pt. Regular
Joanna 18-pt. Regular
Joanna 24-pt. Regular

A font

Joanna 18-pt. Regular

A different font

Joanna 24-pt. Regular

TYPEFACE CATEGORIES

Typeface families are separated for convenience into specific categories, which we'll explain in this section. These categories are another factor in differentiating one typeface from another.

To begin with, typefaces are either *proportional* or *nonproportional* (discussed in Chapter 1). As shown in Figure 6.7, a nonproportional (or *fixed-pitch*) typeface resembles the traditional output of a typewriter, in that each character takes up the same amount of space on a line, regardless of its actual width. On the other hand, a *proportional* typeface allocates to each character only as much room as it needs.

Figure 6.7 is a dramatic demonstration of this difference. The Monaco nonproportional typeface (furnished with the Mac operating system) requires much more space for its characters than the proportional Neuzeit Grotesk (available from several typeface vendors), even though both share many of the same design properties.

Most typefaces used in computer printouts are now proportional, because these typefaces are easier to read and more professional in appearance. They eliminate awkward spaces between narrow characters in the same word.

The other big dividing line in identifying typefaces is between *serif* and *sans-serif typefaces* (*sans* is French for without). A sans-serif typeface has clean lines, without those small nubs or cross-strokes called serifs.

Usually, a serif typeface is easier to read for the main text of a long document because the serifs provide subtle clues that help a reader identify characters more quickly. On the other hand, a sans-serif typeface often looks more modern and clutter-free.

Incidentally, when typefaces without serifs were first introduced, critics in England thought these designs looked very strange indeed and termed them *grotesques*. The name stuck in many quarters, and some sans-serif typefaces carry the word Grotesque as part of their names today. (For example, Neuzeit Grotesk

FIGURE 6.7

Similar proportional and nonproportional typefaces

Monaco: nonproportional
Neuzeit Grotesk: proportional

is a German typeface; the name translates into English literally as "New Age Grotesque," which you could paraphrase as "Modern Grotesque" or "Modern Sans-Serif.")

Figure 6.8 gives examples of both the serif and sans-serif typeface categories, as well as two others: *decorative* and *script*. A decorative typeface is ornamental, intended primarily for display use in large sizes for headings and usually unsuited for use as body copy because of its intricate design. A script typeface imitates handwriting, and may be either casual or formal in appearance. Don't use a script typeface for your main text either, because script also makes for slow reading in large blocks of text.

Garth Graphic, the first typeface in this figure, and Shannon, the second, are designs released by Agfa and available either from Agfa or from the Adobe library; Adobe also sells the fourth typeface, Monotype's Script Bold. The third typeface, Moulin Rouge, can be obtained from Casady & Greene—a good source for unusual decorative designs.

Figure 6.9 displays three typefaces in another category: novelty. A novelty goes beyond decorative in offering a design that is often looked at for its own sake, may consist of characters resembling familiar objects or even people, and is frequently created with a sense of humor.

For example, in the figure you can see Bitstream's Old Dreadful, which was created by asking individual members of the Bitstream staff to submit the design for a single character. The result was a typeface including a capital I with two large eyes peering over its top and a capital D that looks like a c-clamp from a home workshop.

FIGURE 6.8

Examples of typeface categories: serif, sans-serif, decorative, and script

Garth is a serif typeface

Shannon is sans-serif

Moulin Rouge—decorative

Monotype Script Bold—script

FIGURE 6.9

Three novelty
typefaces

Bamboo is a novelty

I'm Old Dreadful

HERE'S BEEBOPP

The other novelty examples are Bamboo, which seems to be constructed from the hardy stems of that plant, and Beebopp, composed of geometric shapes combined in strange formations. These two typefaces were created by Image Club and are available only from that company. Image Club also sells novelty typefaces that resemble automobile bumpers and license plates, a neon sign, paper clips, children's blocks, twisted hairpins, and a brass plate on an office door (the last two licensed from Visual Graphics Corporation).

All Image Club typefaces were created with the help of Adobe Illustrator and Fontographer (a font editing program from Altsys Corporation). When you buy a typeface from Image Club, the company usually provides you with TrueType or Adobe Type 1 and Type 3 files (explained later in this chapter), *plus* the Illustrator and Fontographer files from which the typeface files were created. This means you can modify Image Club typefaces within Illustrator or Fontographer to create new designs for your own purposes. (Chapter 14 provides more information about modifying or creating typefaces.)

Needless to say, you wouldn't want to use a novelty typeface for long passages of text. However, employed carefully and with restraint, a novelty can draw attention to your message and often provide a chuckle as well.

THE MYSTERY OF TYPEFACE NAMES

Typeface designs are not protected by the copyright laws, but typeface names *can* be registered as trademarks. Consequently, if a digital type house wants to release a popular design to its customers and cannot lease the design from the original creators (or if the royalty payments asked would be too costly), the company often creates its own version of the design and releases it legally under a different name or a slightly different version of the original name. So when you buy and use typefaces, you may find it difficult to locate exactly what you're looking for.

For example, Optima was designed by Hermann Zapf and is a trademark of Linotype-Hell AG. The Bitstream version is called Zapf Humanist 601, and the Agfa version is CG Omega. Other names used by type foundries and manufacturers for similar products include Optimum, Optimist, OP, and even very different names such as Chelmsford, Musica, October, and Roma.

Some typeface companies include indexes in their catalogs that let you match up their own names for typefaces with the names used by others. Bitstream goes a step further; the firm provides a free utility to purchasers of its typefaces that can help you wade through the morass.

This utility is called Bitstream Analogue and functions as an INIT file you call up through your Apple menu. As shown in Figure 6.10, you can type a word like Helvetica and find out immediately that Bitstream sells versions of the Helvetica typefaces under the name Swiss. You will also see a list of other names applied to this design (in the *Industry family* section of the Analogue window), as well as other related information.

FIGURE 6.10

The Bitstream Analogue utility lists alternate names for typefaces

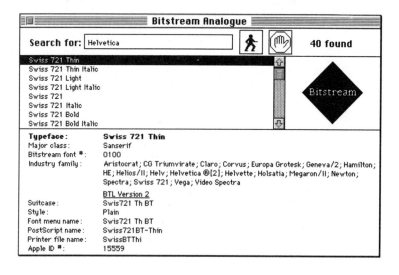

TERMS RELATED TO TYPEFACES

The appearance of a typeface is influenced by the shape and size of various parts of each character, as well as the manner in which the characters relate to each other and to the imaginary *baseline* on which they rest. Figure 6.11 shows the word *Verifiably* printed in Bitstream's Baskerville typeface, with key features labeled.

We've already discussed serifs (which are plentiful on the strokes of these characters), as well as the terms uppercase and lowercase.

The *x-height* of a typeface is the percentage of the total height represented by the distance between the baseline and the tops of the average lowercase characters; the term gets its name from the fact that the height of a lowercase letter x is usually a good criterion for determining this measurement. (Figure 6.12 illustrates the difference that x-height can make in the appearance of a typeface.)

An *ascender* is a stroke on a lowercase character that extends above the x-height. A *descender* is also a stroke on a lowercase character, but extends *below* the x-height.

A *ligature* is two or more letters of the alphabet combined into a single character. In Figure 6.11, if it were not for the use of the ligature, the dot over the lowercase i would conflict with the top of the lowercase f, causing a collision of sorts; the ligature eliminates the dot entirely. In most typefaces, several ligatures are included that don't appear on the keyboard but can be accessed by pressing special key combinations. Later in this chapter, we'll tell you how to locate these ligatures in the typeface files you're using.

FIGURE 6.11

Basic terms related to typefaces

As you learned in Chapter 2, *kerning* is the practice of moving characters closer together or further apart to improve their spacing within a word. We'll show you how to kern in a moment.

Now, take a look at Figure 6.12, which provides a graphic demonstration of the effect of a change in x-height.

FIGURE 6.12

Two versions of Kabel, with different x-heights

Geometric 231, Kabel version with a small x-height

ITC Kabel, Kabel version with a large x-height

The top line shows a few words in Bitstream's Geometric 231, a faithful rendering of Kabel—a typeface family designed by Rudolf Koch in Germany in 1927 and named in commemoration of the laying of the Atlantic Cable.

Directly under this sample, you can see ITC Kabel, created for International Typeface Corporation. Note that the shapes of the characters are the same as those of Geometric 231 but that the effect is entirely different because the x-height has been significantly increased. Geometric 231 has a refined, sophisticated look because of the long ascenders (made possible by the small x-height). ITC Kabel, on the other hand, looks bold, brassy, and somehow more modern. In Figure 6.12, both typefaces have been reproduced in the same point size.

International Typeface Corporation is noted for creating (and licensing to type manufacturers) many typefaces used in the advertising industry, where impact and legibility are imperative, regardless of the quality of the paper to be used. To produce suitable typefaces, ITC often takes an old or even classic design and produces a new version with a larger x-height. Some typeface users find such modifications very helpful; others prefer to have the original designs untouched. Bitstream caters to both groups by offering customers both their Geometric 231 *and* ITC Kabel. ITC Kabel is also available from Adobe, Image Club, and other vendors.

K ERNING YOUR TEXT

Most typeface manufacturers include kerning information for many character combinations within the computer files for each of their typefaces. Desktop-publishing programs can usually access this information and automatically kern character pairs that are listed. Unfortunately, most word-processing programs do not support automatic kerning; some programs won't even let you do manual kerning.

Fortunately, MacWrite Pro (like MacWrite II) does support automatic kerning. You can also do manual kerning, which is often desirable for headings and other text to be printed in large font sizes. (The lack of proper kerning can become painfully obvious when the characters are large.)

Figure 6.13 shows the words *Vote Today* presented without kerning and then properly kerned. In the top line, note the spaces between the *V* and the *o* in *Vote*, the *T* and *o* in *Today*, and, to a lesser extent, the *a* and *y* in *Today*. The bottom line shows all of the characters properly kerned.

Two of these particular kerning problems were caused by space being allocated for characters that actually did not need the entire area reserved for them. The capital *V* and *T*—in combination with a following lowercase character—look better when that unneeded space is tightened up through kerning. The capital letter can overhang the lowercase letter, making the word to which they belong seem much more of a unit.

The incorrect spacing between the lowercase *a* and *y* in *Today* was a more subtle problem. The *a* ends with a serif at the baseline; space was reserved for that serif. However, the design of the *y* that follows includes an indentation adjacent to the serif at the baseline of the *a*, so there was room to move the two characters closer together and narrow the gap.

FIGURE 6.13

Text without kerning (top) and with proper kerning

Vote Today
unkerned

Vote Today
kerned

You can carry kerning too far. You can move characters so close together that they seem to crowd one another, and readability suffers. Also, characters should seem to be evenly spaced. We say "seem" because sometimes optical illusions are at work. Don't measure the spacing; judge it with your eye. Spacing that looks even is the spacing that's desirable.

TURNING ON AUTOMATIC KERNING

You can turn on automatic kerning within MacWrite Pro that will automatically kern many character combinations. To do this, follow these steps:

1 Pull down the Edit menu and select the Preferences… command.

2 Select the Document section in the Preferences dialog box.

3 Select the Auto Kern box on the Document screen displayed in Figure 6.14, and click OK.

FIGURE 6.14

The screen of the Preferences dialog box where automatic kerning is selected

- For more precise character placement when printing to a laser printer, select Fractional Character Widths as well.

- This screen is also where you select or deselect Smart Quotes, a feature that changes the kind of quotation marks used in your document. The feature is explained in the next section.

KERNING MANUALLY

You can do manual kerning in two ways. In either case, you must begin by dragging to select the characters you want to kern. You can select more than two characters if you wish and then move them all closer together or further apart simultaneously.

One kerning method uses the keyboard. You hold down the Option and ⌘ keys, then tap the left arrow key to reduce the space between the selected characters or the right arrow key to increase the spacing. For finer adjustments, hold down the Shift key as well.

The other kerning method requires clicking the small arrows at the bottom of the Text palette. You click the left arrow to reduce the space between the selected characters (see Figure 6.15) or click the right arrow to increase the spacing. For finer adjustments, hold down the Option key as you click.

FIGURE 6.15

Kerning through
the Text palette

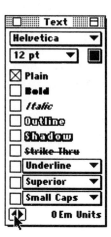

is that there will be slight differences between the spacing you see on the screen and the spacing that appears on paper. This disparity is most obvious if you're using a printer that supports the PostScript language, because your screen display is created with a different language—Apple's QuickDraw.

U SING SPECIAL CHARACTERS

Unlike a typewriter, typefaces on a Macintosh include many characters not shown on the keyboard. The extra characters available vary according to the typeface used and are determined by the designer and/or the manufacturer. Usually, you access these characters by pressing the Option key—or the Option key with the Shift key—in combination with a letter or numeral that appears on the keyboard. In this section, we'll explain some of these hidden characters.

USING PROFESSIONAL QUOTATION MARKS

Two helpful character substitutions can be made automatically from within Mac-Write Pro. The "straight-up-and-down" quotation marks usually seen in the output of a typewriter can be replaced by "curly quotes"—the separate opening and closing quotation-mark symbols seen surrounding quotations in professionally printed documents, magazines, and books.

If the Smart Quotes box is selected on the Document screen of the Preferences dialog box (refer back to Figure 6.14), the program will make these substitutions for you correctly every time you use the keyboard symbol to enter quotation marks.

Smart Quotes works by sensing whether you follow this symbol with a character (which would require an opening quotation-mark symbol) or follow the symbol with a space (requiring a closing quotation-mark symbol). The difference in appearance between these kinds of quotation marks is shown in Figure 6.16, illustrated with Monotype's Photina Bold typeface (also available through Adobe).

FIGURE 6.16

Typewriter and
professional
quotation marks

"typewriter quotation marks"

"professional quotation marks"

T I P

You can enter "curly quotes" manually in most typefaces by pressing the Option key in combination with the left bracket key (the key to the right of the letter p) to obtain the opening quotation-mark symbol and Shift-Option with the left bracket key to obtain the closing quotation-mark symbol.

USING THE RIGHT DASHES

On a typewriter, it's customary to enter two hyphens to indicate a dash between phrases in a sentence. Professional publications use a single symbol instead—either a long dash called an *em dash* or a shorter dash called an *en dash*. Fortunately, these symbols are among those hidden characters you can enter into your documents on a Macintosh. The em and en dashes are illustrated in Figure 6.17. The typefaces are Monotype's Amasis Bold and Bold Italic.

FIGURE 6.17

The differences
shown between
em and en dashes
and a hyphen

— *em dash*
– *en dash*
- *hyphen*

Don't use a typewriter dash merely composed of hyphens--like these. Use a real dash symbol—like this.

The key combination for an em dash is Shift-Option-hyphen. The key combination for an en dash is Option-hyphen.

USING ADDED CHARACTER SETS

You can obtain added character sets for some typefaces. These character sets provide alternate characters and symbols you can use to enhance the appearance of your documents. The result can often be a completely different look for the original typeface and sometimes an impressive increase in the readability of the text.

Take a look at Figure 6.18. What typeface is this? Actually, many of the characters are simply the familiar ITC Bookman Bold, available on most LaserWriter printers. However, the fancy, highly decorative characters were inserted from an additional typeface called ITC Bookman Bold Swash, available for personal computers (as far as this writer can determine) only from Image Club and the Font Company.

Image Club also offers ITC Bookman Bold Swash Italic, Outline, Outline Swash, and Contour, as well as the more common Bookman Light, Light Italic, Demi Bold, Demi Bold Italic, Bold, and Bold Italic variations. Incidentally, all of these Bookman typefaces are bundled by Image Club into one $90 package.

Adobe and Monotype both offer "expert" typefaces to expand some of their popular typeface families. For example, Adobe has created such additions to accompany Adobe families like Caslon, Garamond, Minion, and Utopia. The Adobe

---

FIGURE 6.18

A decorative effect is achieved by combining ITC's Bookman Bold typeface with another: Bookman Bold Swash

Caslon Expert Collection offers a good illustration of what these typefaces include. In the Caslon set you'll find lowercase figures (also called old style figures), small capitals, extra ligatures, fractions, superior and inferior figures (used in formulas and to number footnotes), superior letters (used in French and Spanish to abbreviate words), alternate characters (such as swash characters), and ornaments.

Figure 6.19 exhibits some of the Adobe Caslon old style figures, small capitals, and swash characters, plus an added ligature. The top paragraph in this figure includes only the characters in the standard regular and italic typefaces. As a result, note that the phrase *MORE ON MOZART IN VIENNA* acquires unwanted importance, as do the dates enclosed in parentheses.

The bottom paragraph shows the same text embellished by the addition of expert characters. First of all, the opening phrase in capital letters has been placed in its proper perspective through the use of small capitals instead. Swash italic characters have beautified the names of the Handel compositions listed, and the use of lowercase figures has de-emphasized the dates in parentheses.

An interesting and rarely seen ligature for the *st* letter combination has been added to the word *Feast*, combining the two characters into a single, graceful symbol.

FIGURE 6.19

A paragraph printed using standard Adobe Caslon typefaces (top), contrasted with the same text printed with typefaces from the Adobe Caslon Expert Collection

MORE ON MOZART IN VIENNA: He added wind-parts to Handel's *Acis and Galatea* (1788), *Messiah* (1789), *Ode to St. Cecilia's Day*, and *Alexander's Feast* (1790).

MORE ON MOZART IN VIENNA: He added wind-parts to Handel's *Acis and Galatea* (1788), *Messiah* (1789), *Ode to St. Cecilia's Day*, and *Alexander's Feast* (1790).

In addition to the Expert Collections, Adobe also sells smaller assortments containing only lowercase figures and small capitals to accompany many of the typefaces sold by the company.

Figure 6.20 displays a supplementary typeface created for a different purpose. Here the phrase *the quick brown fox* has been reproduced in a phonetic transcription—by the use of recognized phonetic symbols to show how the words actually sound. These symbols are part of Adobe's Stone Phonetic package, which provides phonetic symbols to match the standard characters in the ITC Stone Sans and Stone Serif families, sold by several vendors. The symbol sets include both the current symbols recommended by the International Phonetic Association, as well as alternate symbols customarily used in the United States and other countries. Stone Serif is shown in the figure.

FIGURE 6.20

The Adobe Stone
Phonetic typeface

ðə qwɪk bɹaᵘn fɒks

Other specialized symbol sets and typefaces offered by Adobe supply symbols in specialized categories such as astrology, audio, maps, chess, and music.

FINDING AND ACCESSING SPECIAL CHARACTERS

Some typefaces containing special characters are accompanied by charts showing the keys or key combinations you use to access these characters. If one of these typefaces works in conjunction with a standard typeface (as is the case with Stone Phonetic and Bookman Bold Swash), you must switch back and forth from one typeface to another through the MacWrite Pro Font menu—a tedious but necessary process.

If you don't have a chart showing the location of special characters in any typeface, you can use the Macintosh Key Caps utility (provided with the operating system) to find them. Figure 6.21 shows the Key Caps window in action.

While Key Caps is active, a special Key Caps menu appears that is really a Font menu from which you can pick a typeface to examine in the window. With the typeface chosen, you merely press a key or key combination such as Shift-Option to

FIGURE 6.21

The Key Caps
utility shows the
ITC Newtext
characters
available when the
Option key is
pressed

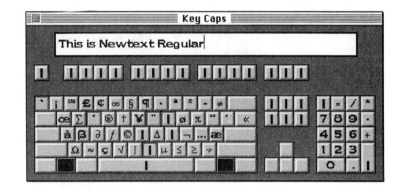

see which characters you can select by pressing those keys along with a regular key on the keyboard; the available characters are displayed in the window in the positions from which they can be accessed from your keyboard. You can type any character combination and see the result in the window. Figure 6.21 shows the characters available for ITC Newtext Regular when the Option key is pressed.

You open Key Caps by selecting it from the Apple menu.

Figure 6.22 shows another utility that is much more versatile than Key Caps. It's called BigCaps, and it's included free of charge when you buy any typeface from Dubl-Click Software. In the figure, the BigCaps window has been expanded to fill an entire 13-inch screen. You can even expand it to fill a two-page, 21-inch screen. This feature means that you have plenty of room to examine letter characteristics in a large size.

You can pick any font size you want from the BigCaps menu, which also lets you display the typeface with any style selected, see a chart of foreign accent marks you can apply, and even examine the characters in a typeface that isn't loaded into your system.

T YPEFACE FILE FORMATS

Typefaces for the Macintosh are available in three main file formats: bitmapped, Adobe PostScript, and TrueType.

In the early days of the Mac, many vendors sold bitmapped fonts, actually collections of fixed dots (like bitmapped graphic images) provided in specific font

FIGURE 6.22

Dubl-Click's
BigCaps font utility
has many features

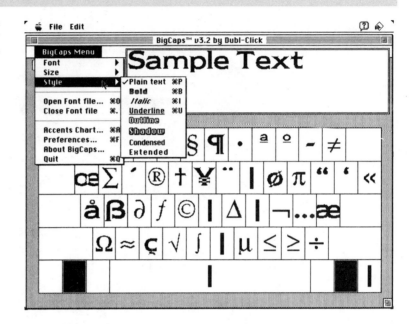

sizes. These fonts may look terrible if you try to print them in a size other than one you have stored on disk (because the odd size is approximated from the existing sizes) and are used primarily these days only to display the font image on your screen.

An Adobe PostScript typeface may be in a Type 1 or Type 3 format; Type 1 usually offers better quality, and most PostScript typefaces are now available in this format. These PostScript typefaces are created by many manufacturers other than Adobe, conforming to PostScript specifications provided by Adobe, and consist of small programming routines called outlines that will generate the typeface for printing "on the fly" in any size you want—thereby providing excellent printing quality. The printing outline works in conjunction with a bitmapped version of the typeface from which the screen image is created.

If you have the Adobe Type Manager utility, it will produce screen sizes not available on disk by using the PostScript printer outline file for information, thereby eliminating the jagged screen characters caused by the approximation of unavailable bitmapped sizes. Adobe Type Manager also makes it possible to print PostScript typefaces on non-PostScript printers such as ImageWriters and StyleWriters.

The third typeface category is TrueType, which automatically uses the same outline file to produce both the screen image and the printed version of a typeface; no bitmapped fonts are involved.

Although some major vendors sell only typefaces in the Adobe PostScript Type 1 format (which include both the printer outlines and corresponding bit-mapped screen fonts), other vendors offer their products in both Type 1 and True-Type formats.

ⓢ OURCES FOR TYPEFACES

We've provided names and sources for most of the typefaces displayed in the figures of this book; this information is usually located in text near each of the related figures. (You'll find addresses and phone numbers for these typeface vendors in Appendix B.) Of course, we used only typefaces we had available. You'll find other sources in magazines devoted to Macintosh software and hardware.

Several companies now offer their entire libraries—and even the libraries of competitors as well (with the payment of agreed-upon royalties)—in the form of CD-ROM disks. As is the case with some clip-art CD-ROMs, you can purchase type from most of these sources either by initiating a credit-card charge by phone to have the company provide a code that will "unlock" specific typefaces, or by paying a lump-sum fee to purchase the entire library in an unlocked form.

Figure 6.23 shows the contents of the Image Club LetterPress CD-ROM disk, with part of the "C" folder displayed in the superimposed window. As you can see in the figure, this CD-ROM disk contains over 260 megabytes of typefaces.

URW sells a CD-ROM disk for $895 that contains 3000 unlocked quality typefaces, meaning that each typeface costs only 30¢.

If your system includes a CD-ROM drive, buying typefaces on CD-ROM disks can be a convenient practice that will also save you many megabytes of hard-disk space.

ⓘ NSTALLING AND MANAGING TYPEFACES

If you use only a few typefaces, it's practical to install them in your System folder (although soon we'll recommend an alternative).

FIGURE 6.23

Part of the
contents of a
CD-ROM
type disk

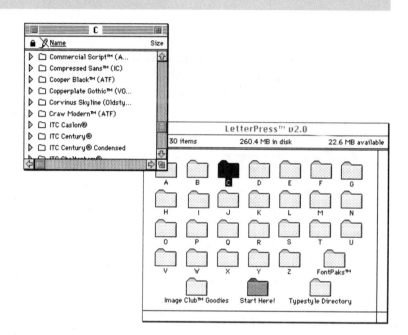

If your Mac is running under some version of System 6, you install typefaces through an Apple utility called the Font/DA Mover. In the right list box of the utility's window, you simply display and select the names of the typefaces or fonts to be installed. The left list box shows the typefaces and fonts currently installed. You click the Copy button to install the selected items.

The process is even simpler under System 7. All you have to do is drag the typefaces into your System folder; the system will do the rest.

However, under either System 6 or System 7, the more typefaces you have stored in the System folder, the slower your system will operate. A favorite font-management utility of those who use typefaces professionally is Suitcase, from Fifth Generation Systems, Inc. With Suitcase, you can store typefaces, sounds, and desk accessories anywhere you like on your hard disk and include them in your active Mac system only when you want to use them. This means that you could store, say, 200 typefaces on your hard disk and yet clutter up your system with only 15 that you need for the current day's work.

Suitcase has many other features. For example, it can compress typeface files so they take up less disk space, and it resolves conflicts between two typefaces with the same identification number. (The manufacturers assign each typeface a number by which the system keeps track of it when it's active.)

Suitcase also lets you establish groups of typefaces in named sets so that—with one command—you could activate 18 typefaces used only in a monthly report, or remove those typefaces from your active system again just as easily.

Figure 6.24 shows the Suitcase menu and main window, giving you some idea of the utility's capabilities.

FIGURE 6.24

The menu and main window for the Suitcase utility

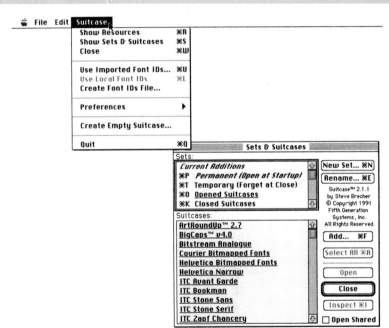

CREATING SPECIAL EFFECTS

You may want to buy any of several utilities that can create special type effects for inclusion in your documents. TypeStyler (from Broderbund) is an excellent example. Figure 6.25 shows a sign created in TypeStyler for a mythical magic shop.

The type was actually curved to match the illustration. The typeface is Raphael, one of a group provided with the utility and manufactured by Agfa. However, you can also use any Adobe Type 1 typeface in TypeStyler, which can twist and modify characters to produce thousands of interesting effects.

FIGURE 6.25

A sign for a magic shop with curved type produced by the TypeStyler utility

Ⓢ UMMARY

You've covered a lot of territory in this chapter. You've learned about some of the characteristics that make one typeface different from another, how to kern your text and use special characters, and the right way to insert dashes and quotation marks. In addition, you read discussions of type formats and special effects and received some tips on installing and managing your type collection.

Don't forget that Chapter 2 also explained how you can change the way your Font menu is displayed.

This book is full of examples using many different typefaces. By the time you've read it all, you should be familiar with many typeface families that you may find useful in your own work. However, if you can't afford to add to your system's basic fonts, don't worry. Changes you can make through the Size and Style menus will supply you with variety, and having few fonts to work with will keep you from making that fatal mistake of the beginning typeface collector—wanting to show off the entire collection on every page!

Chapter 13 provides tips on building a typeface library, and Chapter 14 tells you how to modify or even create typefaces.

Creating and Using Tables

CHAPTER 7

FEATURING

The advantages of a table frame

Using the Table menu

Creating a sample table

In many word-processing programs, you can create a table only by using your Tab key to divide information into columns. With MacWrite Pro's table frames, however, you have much greater flexibility. You can:

- create floating tables that you can drag anywhere you like on a page;

- set tables apart with special typefaces, graphics, borders, and backgrounds;

- wrap your main text around tables;

- place tables partially or entirely in front of or behind other elements on the page;

- change the size and formatting of individual cells in a table;

- merge the contents of one or more cells;

- sort the contents of cells; and

- move text into or out of a table in order to exchange information with other documents or programs.

This chapter covers all of these subjects.

A single table can consist of as many as 100 cells; however, the table must be entirely contained within a single page. You can paste a graphic image into a cell, and you can choose from 81 colors and 64 patterns for table shading and coloring. You can either print or hide the grid (the borders, divisions, or boundaries between cells) and include or eliminate a border around the entire table frame.

Figure 7.1 shows a typical example of one kind of table you can create. In this figure, the drawing of the angel (from Dubl-Click's WetPaint library) and the headline (in Adobe's Mesquite typeface) are not part of the table, though they could have been placed in large cells within it. Note that the entire table (the frame) is surrounded by a border and that the cell borders are composed of thinner lines than the table border. Other possibilities would have been to add a background for the table and select colors and/or patterns for both the border and the background.

FIGURE 7.1

A table created
by placing data
within a formatted
table frame

AUTHORS WHO LIVED 90 YEARS OR MORE

Author	Age at Death
Howe, Julia Ward	91
Shaw, George Bernard	94
Sophocles	90
Walton, Izaac	90
Wodehouse, P. G.	94

I NSERTING A TABLE FRAME

The first step in creating a table is to insert a table frame into your document. You can accomplish this either by using the Insert Table… command from the Frame menu or by drawing the table after selecting the Table Frame tool from the Tools palette.

In either case, as soon as you issue the command or drag to define an area for the table, you'll see the Insert Table dialog box. If the dialog box has appeared as a result of issuing the Insert Table… command, you'll be expected to enter the number of rows and columns you want and also the column width.

The default entries are shown in Figure 7.2: a table with two rows and two columns, each column 3.229 inches wide. The dialog box will look exactly the same if you use the Table Frame tool to draw the table, except that you won't see a Column Width box, because you will have automatically established the column width by drawing a frame of a particular size.

FIGURE 7.2

The Insert Table
dialog box as
displayed if a table
has been created
through the Frame
menu rather than
through the Tool
palette

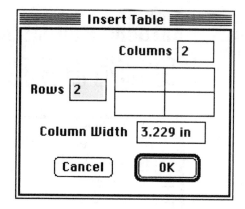

Follow these simple steps to draw a table frame:

1 If necessary, display the Tool palette (by pulling down the Frame menu and selecting the Show Tool Palette command).

2 If the palette is blocking the area where you want to draw the frame, drag the palette by its title bar to a more convenient location.

3 Click the Table Frame icon on the palette to select the Table Frame tool (it's in the middle of the second row). The pointer will change into the shape of crosshairs.

4 Drag to draw a table frame the size you want, as demonstrated in Figure 7.3. The dimensions of the table will be displayed in the lower-left corner of your screen. As soon as you release the mouse button, the Insert Table dialog box will appear.

5 Enter the number of rows and columns you want in the table, and click OK. The dialog box will close.

As soon as the dialog box closes, two other changes will occur on your screen: an empty table frame will appear, containing cells for the number of rows and columns you specified, and a new Table menu will appear on the menu bar. This menu is displayed only while a table is selected.

Drawing a table
frame with the
Table Frame tool

ⓤ SING THE TABLE MENU

The first three commands on the Table menu (see Figure 7.4) let you perform operations on the contents of the current table.

The Table To Text command converts the contents of the table into ordinary text. You can use this option either to eliminate the table and make the information it contains a part of the main text of the document or to export the data for use in another program.

The Table menu,
displayed only
when a table is
selected

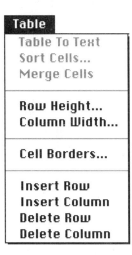

The Sort Cells… command brings up the dialog box shown in Figure 7.5, from which you can choose to sort selected cells in ascending or descending order, to use ASCII values in performing either kind of sort (which may change the sorting position of some items, since capital letters have different ASCII values than lowercase letters), and to sort the entire row rather than merely the selected cells.

The Merge Cells command combines the contents of selected cells into one cell.

ADJUSTING ROW HEIGHT AND COLUMN WIDTH

Below the Sort Cells… and Merge Cells commands, you'll find Row Height… and Column Width… commands, which are used only to change the dimensions of currently selected rows or columns.

As indicated by the ellipsis (the three dots) after each of these command names, invoking either command will bring up a dialog box. Here you can enter precise measurement specifications; you can select more than one row or column either by dragging across those you want to change, or by clicking a cell to select the first item, then holding down the Shift key and clicking to select additional rows or columns. If you want to select rows or columns that are not next to each other, hold down the ⌘ key as you click.

When the Automatic button in the Row Height dialog box is selected, as it is by default, the program will automatically adjust the height of each row to accommodate its contents. Alternatively, you can enter a minimum row height measured in points (see Figure 7.6). You might use this option to make the rows

---

FIGURE 7.5

The Sort Cells
dialog box

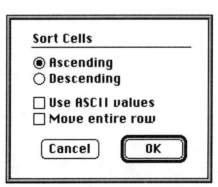

FIGURE 7.6

The Row Height
dialog box

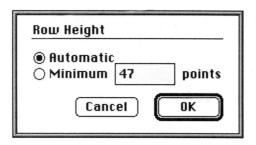

in a table all the same size even if some cells contain smaller fonts.

The Column Width dialog box contains only a data box in which you can enter a specific column width in points (see Figure 7.7).

TIP

You can also adjust column widths more easily but less precisely by placing the pointer on the boundary line between two columns and dragging to the left or right. Any time you place the pointer on one of these boundaries, its shape will change to show two vertical lines flanked by left- and right-facing arrows, indicating that the pointer is in position to make a change in the width of the adjacent table cells.

When you widen one column by dragging a boundary, MacWrite Pro automatically narrows the other adjacent column, thereby maintaining the outer dimensions of the entire table. If you want the table itself to change in size to accommodate a changed column width, hold down the ⌘ key as you drag.

FIGURE 7.7

The Column Width
dialog box

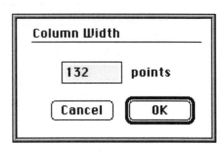

MOVING CELL BORDERS

The Cell Borders... command displays the Cell Borders dialog box, in which you can use pop-up palettes to change the appearance of the borders of cells you've selected. You can specify various combinations of single or double lines and use a color instead of the default black. You can also apply any one of a variety of patterns to the borders and (as demonstrated in Figure 7.8) change the line width.

To check the effect of your selections before "making them official," click the Apply box. Click the OK box when you're satisfied with the results, or, of course, click Cancel to abort any changes.

FIGURE 7.8

Selecting border
line width
in the Cell Borders
dialog box

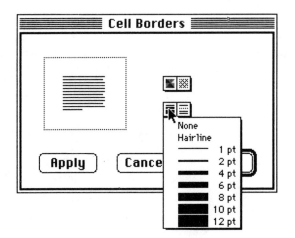

TIP

Remember that, although you change the type of line, width, pattern, and color for the borders of selected cells in the Cell Borders dialog box, you add a background or a special border to the entire table by using options on the Tool palette instead. The entire table constitutes a frame, and you use the Tool palette to select background and border options for any frame.

INSERTING AND DELETING ROWS AND COLUMNS

The remaining four commands on the Table menu simply let you insert or delete rows or columns. The Insert Column command will insert a new column to the left of the currently selected column. The Insert Row command will insert a new row above the currently selected row.

If you've selected more than one row or column before issuing either command, MacWrite Pro will add the same number of rows or columns as you've selected.

The Delete Row and Delete Column commands will delete all selected rows or columns.

CREATING A SAMPLE TABLE

Now try creating a table yourself. Figure 7.9 shows a printout of the table you'll be producing—a summary of the championships that tennis pro John McEnroe has won in the U. S. Open tournament.

Although you could create this table by merely setting appropriate tab stops, placing the table in a table frame means that you can experiment with changing cell sizes, adding a border and/or background, and dragging the table to a new

FIGURE 7.9

A printout showing the table feature used to present tennis statistics

John McEnroe's U. S. Open Wins

Year	Opponent	Score
1979	Vitas Gerulaitis	7-5, 6-3, 6-3
1980	Bjorn Borg	7-6, 6-1, 6-7, 5-7, 6-4
1981	Bjorn Borg	4-6, 6-2, 6-4, 6-3
1984	Ivan Lendl	6-3, 6-4, 6-1

location. You can also print the grid of cell borders —although this option was turned off when Figure 7.9 was printed.

Figure 7.10 is a reproduction of a MacWrite Pro screen, showing the structure and positioning of the text, picture, and table frames making up this page on John McEnroe.

You may not have a suitable tennis illustration to use (this one is from Dubl-Click), so you can substitute an empty picture frame if you like. For future reference, however, note the positioning of the clip-art drawing we used. The racket protrudes slightly into the area occupied by the heading (made possible by configuring the picture frame containing the drawing as transparent), and the feet of the tennis player touch the top of the table. This positioning helps tie the entire page together: the heading, the illustration, and the table appear to be a single unit, part of one message, rather than seeming to be three separate entities that just happen to be located on the same page. Such integration can greatly improve the effectiveness of this kind of layout.

The typeface family we used is ITC Bauhaus, available from Bitstream and other vendors. You can use any fonts installed on your Mac. Just be sure that you pick typefaces that can be easily read, since statistics are involved.

FIGURE 7.10

The page is composed of separate text, picture, and table frames.

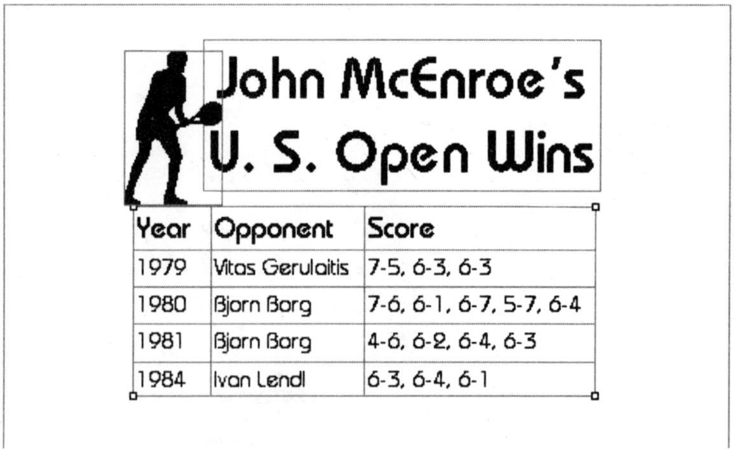

John McEnroe's
U. S. Open Wins

Year	Opponent	Score
1979	Vitas Gerulaitis	7-5, 6-3, 6-3
1980	Bjorn Borg	7-6, 6-1, 6-7, 5-7, 6-4
1981	Bjorn Borg	4-6, 6-2, 6-4, 6-3
1984	Ivan Lendl	6-3, 6-4, 6-1

CREATING THE TABLE HEADING AND ILLUSTRATION

Now follow these steps to create the heading and illustration that will appear above the table:

1 Start a new document (shortcut: press ⌘-N), and make sure the Tool palette is displayed (by selecting Show Tool Palette from the Frame menu).

2 Click the Text Frame tool to select it, and drag to create a text frame of the approximate size indicated in Figure 7.10. (Although this figure doesn't reproduce the screen elements in their actual sizes, you can judge the size you need by drawing the frame in relation to the top and side page guides that are visible in the figure.)

3 Pull down the Font menu, and select the typeface you want to use for the heading.

4 Pull down the Size menu, and select the font size you want. (We used 36 pt.)

5 Select a font style (such as Bold or Shadow) from the Style menu, if this choice is necessary for the proper display of the typeface you've chosen.

6 Click the Center alignment button on the ruler, to center the words you're about to type.

7 Type the first line of the heading: **John McEnroe's**, and press Return to move to the second line.

8 Type the second line of the heading: **U. S. Open Wins**.

9 Click the Picture Frame tool in the Tool palette, and draw a picture frame the correct size to contain the illustration of a tennis player.

10 If you have a drawing available that you want to place in the picture frame, use the Insert... command on the File menu to insert the file into the frame.

CREATING THE TABLE

Last, create the table itself. Follow these steps:

1 Click to select the Table Frame tool on the Tool palette, and draw a table of the approximate size you'll need. As soon as you release the mouse button, the Insert Table dialog box will appear.

2 In the dialog box, specify a table 5 rows deep and 3 columns wide, and click OK. The table frame will appear, divided into the number of rows and columns you've requested. At this point, all of the cells in the table will be the same size.

3 Drag cell boundaries to make the cells the relative sizes shown in Figure 7.10.

4 Drag to select all of the cells in the top row of the table, then select the typeface, point size (we used 18-pt. here), and style (if necessary) that you want to use for the column headings.

5 Click to select the upper-left cell of the table, and type **Year**. Press Tab to move one cell to the right.

6 Type **Opponent**, and press Tab to move one more cell to the right.

7 Type **Score**.

8 Drag to select all of the blank cells still remaining in the table (the bottom four rows), then select the typeface, point size (we used 14-pt.), and style (if necessary) that you want to use for the information in the table.

9 Click the first cell in the second row, and type **1979**. Press Tab to move right one cell.

10 Continue to enter the remainder of the data in the cell as shown in Figures 7.9 and 7.10.

11 Rearrange the three completed frames slightly if necessary, to obtain the best composition possible. (If you resize any cell so that it's too small to display the text it contains, you'll see a warning message; respond simply by making the cell slightly larger until the problem disappears.)

12 So that the document will print without cell boundaries or borders showing, click anywhere within the table to select it, then select the Cell Borders command from the Table menu, choose as the line-width the None option in the small line-width palette in the dialog box, and click OK.

13 Save the document under an appropriate name and print it.

T I P

You'll notice that we had you select all of the cells that would use a particular font before doing any typing. Then you selected the first cell in the series and started typing. If you use this procedure, you can enter all of the data in any such series of cells without selecting the typeface, size, style, and alignment all over again for each cell you enter.

REFINING YOUR TABLE

Now, if you want to experiment with adding a border around one or more cells, feel free to do so (through the Cell Borders... command). You can also add a background and/or border to the entire table through the options on the Tool palette. If you have a color monitor and/or printer, you can also experiment with the effects you can achieve by changing colors on cell borders or on a table border or background.

S UMMARY

You've learned how easy table frames can make the job of creating tables and integrating them into your documents. Remember, you can wrap your main text around a table frame just as you can around words in a text frame or a graphic image in a picture frame. Furthermore, the options for special formatting assure you of being able to make a table stand out from the rest of a document.

Using Shared Data and Files

CHAPTER 8

FEATURING

Learning System 7's Publish and Subscribe features

Sharing the files on your Macintosh

Setting up the networking control panels

Specifying user privileges and restrictions

Accessing other Macs from your computer

M acWrite Pro fully supports the Publish and Subscribe options of System 7, as well as the built-in networking capabilities of this version of the Mac operating system.

These capabilities mean that you can embed all or part of a document in another document—even within another application—and have all copies of the original document updated automatically whenever the original is changed. You can also exchange files with the operators of other Macintoshes that are connected to yours only through the same LocalTalk cables that let the Macs share a printer.

First we'll cover the Publish and Subscribe options.

SING SYSTEM 7 PUBLISH AND SUBSCRIBE FEATURES

If your Macintosh is running under System 7, you'll see a Publishing command on the MacWrite Pro Edit menu. Highlighting this command will display the submenu shown in Figure 8.1.

The terms Publisher, Subscriber, and Edition on this submenu have these specific meanings:

> A *publisher* is any part of a document that has been set up for sharing through the Publish and Subscribe feature of the operating system.

> An *edition* is a copy of the publisher saved as a separate file; it's through an edition that other documents and applications can access the shared material.

> A *subscriber* is a copy of the edition that has been included in a document; you can set up a subscriber so that it's updated automatically every time the publisher is changed, thereby changing the edition.

Now let's see how a publisher is created and used. As we proceed, we'll explain each item on the submenu at the appropriate time.

FIGURE 8.1

The System 7
Publishing options
available through
the Edit menu

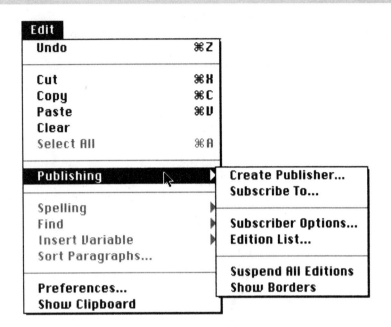

CREATING A PUBLISHER

To create a publisher, follow these steps:

1 Select the material to be published. You can do this by dragging to highlight the area that you wish to publish. As an alternative, if you want to publish the entire contents of a MacWrite Pro frame, you can merely click the frame to select it; selection handles will appear at each corner of the frame.

2 Pull down the Edit menu, highlight the Publishing command, and select Create Publisher... from the Publishing submenu. The Publisher dialog box will appear.

3 In the dialog box, specify a name for the edition to be created and the name of the folder to contain the edition file.

TIP

You can reduce the likelihood of confusion and errors by ending the name of any edition file with the word edition. *Another recommended procedure is to store all of your editions in a special folder called Editions.*

4 Click the Publish button to create the edition and close the dialog box. This action publishes the material and makes it available for subscription by anyone authorized to access the edition and therefore to include it in a document. (See the networking portion of this chapter for information on how file access can be restricted.)

Figure 8.2 illustrates this sequence, showing the Publishing dialog box superimposed over the Women's Fashion document introduced in Chapter 4.

FIGURE 8.2

Publishing a graph
displayed
in a picture frame

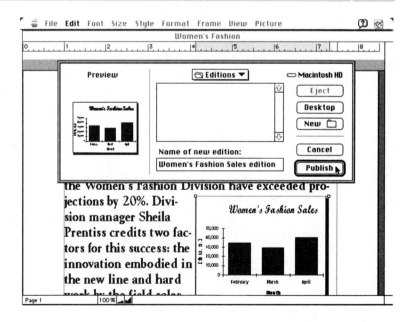

Within the document, the picture frame has been selected that contains the sales chart previously pasted in from Excel 4. The small preview window in the dialog box displays a small reproduction of the selected area, so the user can be sure the selection is what is wanted. The title *Women's Fashion Sales edition* has already been entered as the name of the edition file to be created for this publisher. All that remains to be done in publishing this material is to click the Publish button.

SUBSCRIBING TO AN EDITION

To subscribe to an edition, you don't have to prepare a picture or text frame in advance, as you would if you wanted to paste the contents of the Clipboard into a frame. As soon as you issue the Subscribe To... command and make your selection in the resulting dialog box, a frame of the appropriate type and size will be created automatically, configured as in-line and anchored to the main text of the document at the position where the pointer was resting before the command was issued. In other words, the subscriber will function as if it were just another character or series of characters in the text.

Of course, you can change the mode of the new subscriber frame through the Modify Frame dialog box (accessed by pulling down the Frame menu and issuing the Modify Frame... command). In many instances, you would want to reconfigure the frame to be unanchored, opaque, and with text wrap activated. In this way, you could drag the subscriber frame to any desired location in the main body of the text and have the text automatically realign itself around the frame.

If you prefer, however, you can prepare a text or picture frame in advance and then create the subscriber within that frame. The advantage to this alternative is that you can make the subscriber fit into a predetermined area within the document.

Follow these steps to create a subscriber by this second method:

1. Open the document that is to contain the subscriber, and—using either the Text or Picture Frame tool on the Tool palette—draw a frame of the size you want at the position you've selected for it within the document.

2. With the new frame selected, pull down the Edit menu, highlight the Publishing command, and select Subscribe To... from the submenu. The Subscribe dialog box will appear.

3. If necessary, change folders within the dialog box until you see the file name for the edition you want.

4 Highlight the name of the edition. A miniature preview of the edition will appear at the left side of the dialog box.

5 Click the Subscribe button. The contents of the edition will appear within the frame you've just prepared.

6 If the frame is a picture frame and the edition doesn't fit within it correctly, select the frame if necessary, then pull down the Picture menu, and select the Fit Contents to Frame command. The edition will be resized to fit the frame.

7 If the frame is a text frame and the edition doesn't fit within it correctly, select the frame if necessary, pull down the Edit menu, and choose the Select All command. All of the text in the frame will be highlighted—even text that isn't displayed if the frame is too small to show it all. Then pull down the Size menu and pick new point sizes for the text until you find a size that makes all of the text fit.

Figure 8.3 illustrates this sequence. Here a picture frame within a corporate report document has been prepared to receive the Women's Fashion Sales edition. The name of this file has been highlighted in the Subscribe dialog box, which displays a small preview version of the edition. All that remains to be done to create the subscriber is to click the Subscribe button.

Figure 8.4 is a printout of a page from the corporate report, showing the subscriber inserted as part of the report, with text wrapped around the contents of the edition. If the graph is updated within the original Women's Fashion document, the copy of the graph within the report will be updated automatically as well.

Incidentally, the typeface used in Figure 8.4 is Letraset Rialto, available through Digital Typeface Corporation. This particular typeface is unusual in that it's decorative and rather ornate, yet easy to read even when used as body copy.

USING SUBSCRIBER OPTIONS

Once you've created a subscriber in a document, you can change the default procedure for updating the subscriber. To make changes, start by selecting the Subscriber Options... command from the Edit menu's Publishing submenu. This action will display the Subscriber Options dialog box shown in Figure 8.5.

FIGURE 8.3

Subscribing to an
edition, using
a predefined
picture frame

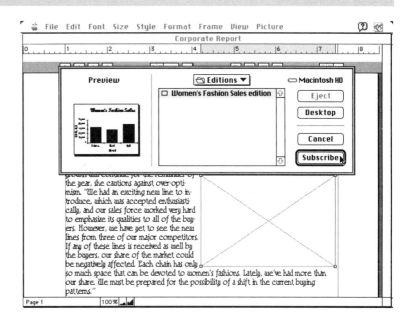

FIGURE 8.4

The contents of the
edition displayed
as part of a report

Corporate Report: Women's Fashion Division

The Women's Fashion Division reports sales of $30,000 to $40,000 a month for the quarter just concluded. These results are 20% above projections for the period. Although manager Shiela Prentiss is pleased by these figures and anticipates that this growth will continue for the remainder of the year, she cautions against over-optimism. "We had an exciting new line to introduce, which was accepted enthusiastically, and our sales force worked very hard to emphasize its qualities to all of the buyers. However, we have yet to see the new lines from three of our major competitors. If any of these lines is received as well by the buyers, our share of the market could be negatively affected. Each chain has only so much space that can be devoted to women's fashions. Lately, we've had more than our share. We must be prepared for the possibility of a shift in the current buying patterns."

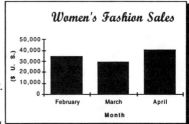

FIGURE 8.5

The Subscriber
Options dialog box

Here, as you can see, you can click a button to switch from automatic to manual updating from the latest edition. You can also click the Get Edition Now button to get the latest edition immediately, the Cancel Subscriber button to cancel the subscriber entirely, or the Open Publisher button to open the original document containing the publisher so you can edit the material in the edition.

In addition, you can select a box to retain any formatting changes you've made in the subscriber; if the box is not selected, formatting changes will be wiped out the next time the edition is updated. (For a subscriber picture frame, this option is labeled Keep Picture Changes; for a subscriber text frame, the option is labeled Keep Subscriber Style Changes.)

The following section provides more information about options relating to editions.

DECIDING WHEN TO GET EDITIONS

You might think that anyone using a subscriber would want the document containing it updated every time the publisher issued a new edition. Occasionally, however, there are good reasons for delaying an update or—indeed—canceling the subscriber entirely.

For example, when you click the Cancel Subscriber button, you'll be asked, "Are you sure you want to remove this subscriber?" The question implies that the contents of the related edition will disappear forever if you respond by clicking the Yes button. However, in actuality all this action does is break the link between the publisher and the current document. The contents of the latest edition received will remain in the document, but future updates to the edition will not be received. Therefore, if your goal was to discuss sales figures for February, March, and April in the current document, you might want to break the link; you would not be interested in replacing a chart covering those three months with an updated edition reporting on May, June, and July sales.

You might want to delay an update instead of canceling it because you don't want a subscriber changing while you're modifying its appearance. (Style changes you can make to a subscriber include changing the typeface used if the subscriber is a text frame.) Therefore, in this case it would make sense to specify in the Subscriber Options dialog box that you want to receive new editions only when you request them manually.

The timing of the issuance of editions is further controlled by options in the Preferences dialog box. As Figure 8.6 illustrates, you access this dialog box by selecting the Preferences... command from the Edit menu.

You then scroll the dialog box and click the Publishing icon in order to display the screen within the dialog box that's devoted to publishers and subscribers. Here you can choose to Update New Subscribers Automatically or On Request

FIGURE 8.6

The Publishing screen within the Preferences dialog box

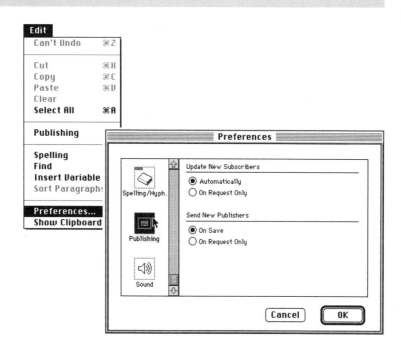

Only. You can also elect to Send New Publishers automatically when the originating document is saved (by selecting the On Save option), or On Request Only.

Changes you make within the Preferences dialog box apply only to the current document, unless you save the document in a special format described in Chapter 9.

USING THE EDITION LIST

The Edition List... command on the Publishing submenu displays the Edition List dialog box shown in Figure 8.7.

Here, by clicking the appropriate button, you can see a list of all of the publishers or all of the subscribers included in the current document.

If the All Publishers button is selected, you can click a button to Send All Editions Now, or another button to Cancel All Publishers.

If the All Subscribers button is selected, you can click a button to Get All Editions Now, or another button to Cancel All Subscribers.

The Options... button is active only if the list shows subscribers; clicking this button simply displays the Subscriber Options dialog box we discussed previously.

FIGURE 8.7

The Edition List
dialog box

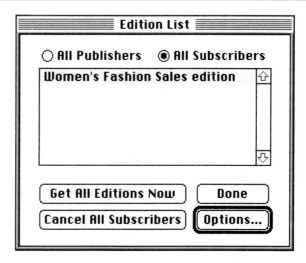

SUSPENDING ALL EDITIONS

The Suspend All Editions command is self-explanatory. When selected, this command is preceded on the menu by a check mark and temporarily prevents any changes to editions relating to the current document.

SHOWING BORDERS

When selected, the Show Borders command displays a light gray border around the portions of the document included in publishers and a dark gray border around portions of the document that are subscribers. These borders are displayed in addition to any borders associated with frames.

Displaying publisher and subscriber borders can be particularly helpful if the publishers and subscribers consist of text embedded within the main text of the document itself. If this command is not selected, you'll have no way to see the boundaries of these publishers and subscribers—unless they're displayed in a different typeface.

Once the Show Borders command has been selected, it changes on the menu to the Hide Borders command and can be used to conceal the publisher and subscriber borders again.

These borders appear only on the screen and do not print.

Ⓢ HARING THE FILES ON YOUR MACINTOSH

As you've learned, you can use the Publish and Subscribe feature of System 7 for the automatic updating of one document you've created from another that you've also created. It's not necessary that both documents be MacWrite Pro files. Obviously, if more than one person uses your Macintosh, you can subscribe to an edition that someone else has created in an application such as MacDraw Pro or Microsoft Word or Excel; and the person using those applications can subscribe to editions you have published.

Be aware, however, that some applications run under System 7 but do not support Publish and Subscribe.

You can also share editions (or any folder or hard drive) with the operators of other Macintoshes connected to your network, provided the other computers are also running under System 7 and using applications that support Publish and

Subscribe. This section will explain how to accomplish this goal using only System 7 and Apple's standard LocalTalk cables that can connect multiple Macs to the same printer.

USING THE NETWORKING CONTROL PANELS

If you work in an organization that has delegated networking responsibilities to one or more technical experts, you may not need to be involved personally in setting up and using the control panels related to exchanging files between Macintoshes under System 7. However, you should understand the basics of how these handy control panels work.

Under System 7, you can access a variety of control panels by selecting Control Panels from the Apple menu at the upper-left corner of your current menu bar. When you highlight the Control Panels option, you'll switch to the Finder from MacWrite Pro or any other application that might be active, and the Control Panels window will open. This window contains control-panel icons for regulating the operation of Mac features ranging from setting the current date and time to adjusting mouse speed. Four of these control panels relate to file sharing and networking: Sharing Setup, Users & Groups, Network, and File Sharing Monitor. The icons for these control panels are shown in Figure 8.8.

The Sharing Setup Control Panel

The first step in setting up a Mac so that its files can be shared by other computers is to open the Sharing Setup control panel and enter required information. The top section of the control panel is called Network Identity. Although this name would seem to indicate an area for establishing the identity of the network, in actuality the section

FIGURE 8.8

The control panels used in sharing files

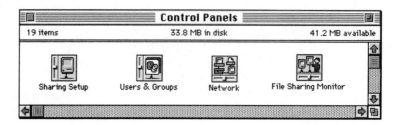

is provided so that the user of the computer can identify this particular computer *to* the network.

The section provides text boxes for entering Owner Name, Owner Password, and Macintosh Name.

> **Owner Name** refers to the individual or department responsible for the security and allocation of access privileges for this Macintosh; in a small organization, the owner might be you yourself as the principal user of the Mac.
>
> **Owner Password** is optional but strongly recommended, since using a password prevents other users of the computer from changing items that are the responsibility of the owner or accessing any files not approved for access by the owner. The password can consist of up to eight capital and/or lowercase letters. Passwords are case-sensitive, meaning that you must match the use of capital and lowercase letters when you're asked to provide the password.
>
> **Macintosh Name** is the name the operators of other computers must select to gain access to this Macintosh. In a small organization, this name might be the type of Mac, such as a Quadra 950 (if there was only one such computer on the network; a unique name is required). On the other hand, the name could be the name of an employee assigned to that Mac or the name of the department in which the computer is located. Figure 8.9 shows the Sharing Setup dialog box with Corporate shown as the Owner Name and Accounting Dept. as the Macintosh Name.

The two lower sections of this dialog box let you activate file sharing and program linking.

File sharing must be activated in order for any other computer to access the files on your Mac; in addition, one or more folders or hard disks in your system must be specifically approved for sharing, and only those volumes will be accessible. (We'll explain shortly how to set up folders and disks for sharing.)

FIGURE 8.9

The Sharing Setup
dialog box

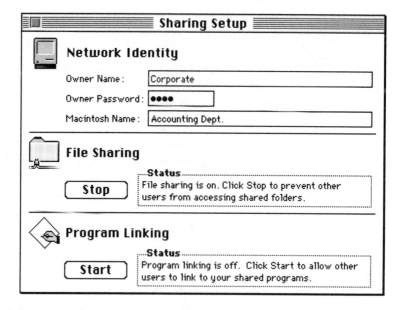

Program linking lets the operators of other computers access and use programs on your Mac as if these applications were resident on their own computers. Of course, you must be sure a particular program is licensed for this kind of access before sharing the program.

The Users & Groups Control Panel

The Users & Groups control panel is where the owner specifies access privileges for individual users and groups. Using groups can be a time-saver because you can set up specific privileges for a group and then automatically grant various individuals the same privileges by making them members of the group.

Figure 8.10 shows the Finder File menu headed by two commands that are added to the menu when the Users & Groups control panel is open. (You can open any control panel by double-clicking on its icon.)

In this figure, the New User command has been selected, which adds a new individual user to the Users & Groups control panel shown at the right side of the figure. You replace the placeholder New User as a user name with the name of an

FIGURE 8.10

Adding a new
user to the
Users & Groups
control panel

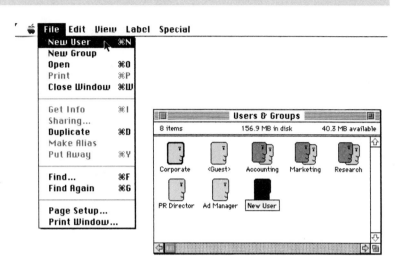

individual who will receive certain privileges you will select. You add a new group
in the same way, through the New Group command.

A user icon labeled Guest appears by default in this control panel. If you
wish, you can let network members access files by logging onto your computer as
Guest, without being registered as users with individual passwords. All guests will
be subject to whatever privileges or restrictions you've assigned to the Guest user
icon. Double-click on a user icon to display its contents.

Figure 8.11 shows the contents of a user icon for Linda Perez. As you can
see, she has been assigned a password to use in accessing your files. (For security
reasons, a password is represented on the screen as a series of bullets.) You've allowed her to access folders or hard disks set up for sharing and to change her own
password if she wishes. However, she is not authorized to use programs installed
on your Mac.

Linda Perez is a member of three groups: Accounting, Marketing, and Research. You make a user a member of a group by simply dragging the user's icon
on top of the group; the user icon will still be displayed independently in its
original position, but a special icon will have been added to the group to represent
that individual.

FIGURE 8.11

The contents
of a user icon,
showing the user's
privileges,
restrictions,
and group
memberships

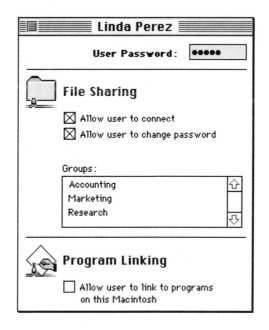

When you've finished establishing access privileges for a person such as
Linda Perez, you click the close box. At this point, you see the message shown in
Figure 8.12, asking if you want to "Save changes to user information" for Linda
Perez. Click the Save button if you do want to put these access privileges into effect.

Figure 8.13 shows the Marketing group. As you can see, members of the
group are represented by individual "portrait" icons that resemble pictures hanging on a wall.

FIGURE 8.12

An Alert message
asking if user
access changes
should be saved

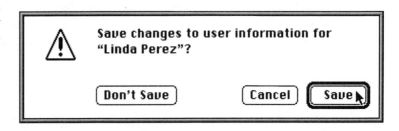

FIGURE 8.13

The members
of a Marketing
group—each
symbolized
by a "hanging
picture" icon

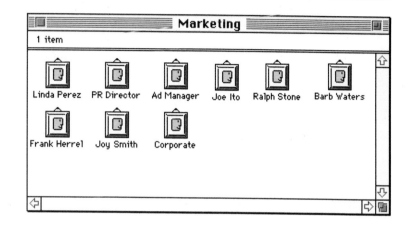

The Network Control Panel

Your Mac system may include a Network control panel. Here, if you have access
to more than one AppleTalk network from your computer, you can select the network with which you want to connect.

Figure 8.14 shows a Network control panel with two options: connecting to
the built-in LocalTalk network we're describing, or to an EtherTalk network.

FIGURE 8.14

The Network
Control Panel,
showing LocalTalk
and EtherTalk
options

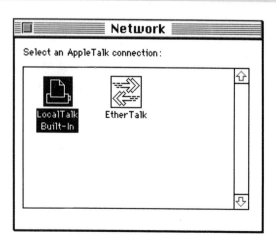

When you attempt to change your network connection by clicking one of these icons, you'll see the Alert message shown in Figure 8.15, cautioning that changing your AppleTalk connection "will interrupt current network services." Of course, you click OK if you want to proceed with the change anyway, or click Cancel if you want to wait for a time when important services will not be interrupted.

FIGURE 8.15

The Alert message seen when trying to change the AppleTalk network connection

The File Sharing Monitor Control Panel

The fourth System 7 control panel related to sharing files and networking is called the File Sharing Monitor. It shows you at a glance which items you've designated for sharing and who is using your files at the moment you display this control panel.

As a security precaution, you can instantly highlight any name in the Connected Users list and click the Disconnect button to terminate that user's current access to your files. (Then, if you didn't want this user to share your files at any future time either, you could also drag the user icon for the individual into the trash.)

Another feature in the File Sharing Monitor is a horizontal bar graph that depicts the current File Sharing Activity on a scale ranging from Idle to Busy. This control panel is shown in Figure 8.16.

SETTING UP ITEMS FOR SHARING

No one operating another Mac can access any of your folders or hard disks unless you've set them up for sharing. (You cannot share floppies.) In most cases, it's not a good idea to set up an entire hard disk for sharing because you'll be letting other

FIGURE 8.16

The File Sharing
Monitor
control panel

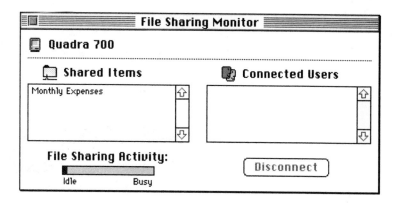

users of your network access folders and files unrelated to their actual needs. However, the procedure for sharing either a folder or a hard disk is the same. In the same way, you can also share access to a CD-ROM drive attached to your Mac, which can be a very practical move in situations where other Macs on your network don't have CD-ROM drives or have different CD-ROM disks loaded.

As is the case when you use the control panels related to sharing and networking, you set up folders, disks, or CD-ROM drives for sharing from the Finder, not within MacWrite Pro or any other application—even if a folder to be shared contains only MacWrite Pro files.

First, highlight the icon for the item to be shared. Then, as demonstrated in Figure 8.17, pull down the File menu, and select the Sharing... command. (This command appears on the menu only when you're using the Finder.). A Sharing window will appear, headed with the name of the folder or other item you've selected for sharing, as shown in Figure 8.18.

By examining Figure 8.18, you can see that, although an item is shared, you can still restrict the kind of access you will permit for it. For example, you could grant a particular user or group the right to see all folders and files contained within the shared folder and to make changes. Using the Everyone selection boxes, however, you could restrict all others accessing the folder so that they could look at folders and files but not make changes.

You'll note that there is an Owner line in the dialog box too. Here you can restrict your own access privileges to this shared item if you wish, or even assign ownership of the item to some other individual or group.

FIGURE 8.17

Selecting a folder
to share

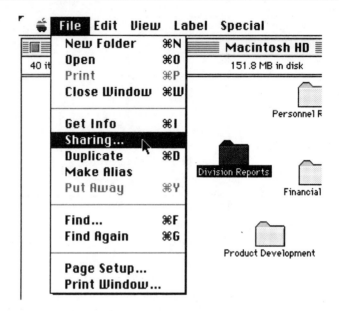

FIGURE 8.18

The Sharing
window for the
selected folder

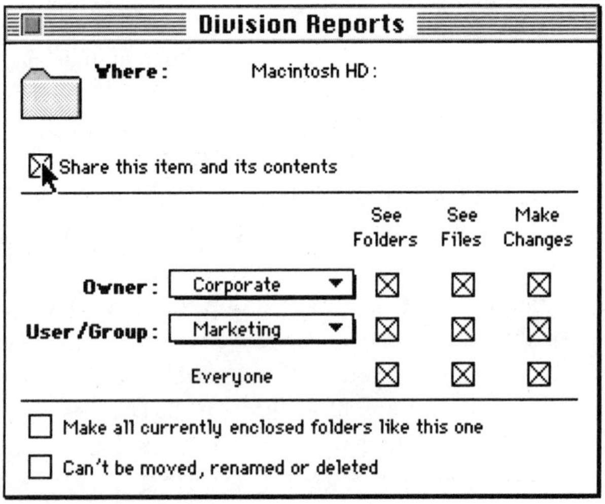

DANGER

Be careful about giving away your ownership of folders or drives in your Mac system—even when an item is to be used primarily by someone else. A new owner could change your access privileges and keep you from using the item again. In particular, if you insist on assigning your ownership to someone else, be sure you copy or remove your personal files before relinquishing ownership.

Make all currently enclosed folders like this one The *Make all currently enclosed folders like this one* selection box at the bottom of the dialog box lets you automatically pass on the same privileges and restrictions to all folders contained within this folder or drive. Clicking this box could be a time-saver, but remember that the availability of this feature means that you can also assign different privileges and restrictions to the enclosed folders.

If you do select this box, you'll immediately see the Alert message shown in Figure 8.19, asking if you're sure you want to "change all folders inside this one to show these privileges?" Of course, you click OK if that is your intention.

Can't be moved, renamed or deleted If you activate the *Can't be moved, renamed or deleted* selection box, you keep users from moving, renaming, or deleting a shared folder—a security measure.

FIGURE 8.19

The Alert message seen if you activate the selection box assigning the privileges and restrictions of the current folder to other folders within it

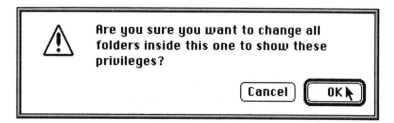

Saving Your Sharing Settings

When you've finished making selections in a Sharing window, you click the close box. You'll then see another Alert message asking if you want to save these changes to access privileges (see Figure 8.20). As soon as you click Save, the changes will go into effect, and the folder or drive is available for access by other users of your network.

FIGURE 8.20

The Alert message seen when you've just closed a Sharing window after making changes

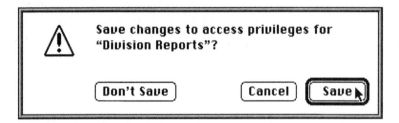

A shared folder looks different than other folders. Figure 8.21 shows the shape of an unshared folder on the left, contrasted with a shared folder on the right (which appears to have cables connected to its lower edge). If you're the owner of a shared folder, you'll see a black tab on the folder, also shown in Figure 8.21.

ACCESSING OTHER MACS FROM YOUR COMPUTER

The previous section explained how to set up folders or drives on your own Macintosh for sharing. This section will tell you how to access files on other Macintoshes from your Mac.

FIGURE 8.21

An unshared folder (left) and a shared folder

Personnel Records

Division Reports

SELECTING THE MAC TO ACCESS

First, pick the Mac you want to access. Pull down the Apple menu and select the Chooser option (as if you were going to select a printer), then double-click the Apple-Share icon. This action displays a list of available Macs or file servers with which you can connect. A *file server* is simply another computer used as a storage area for files to be used by members of a network.

The Chooser list box showing your connection choices is headed by the prompt "Select a file server" even if the rest of the network consists only of another Macintosh sitting next to yours and sharing the same LaserWriter-compatible printer. If a Mac connected to your network is turned off, its name will not appear on the list.

Figure 8.22 shows the Chooser window displaying the names of three file servers or computers that are available. The names are picked up by System 7 from the information entered as Macintosh Name in the Sharing Setup control panel of the computers involved. Therefore, a name such as *Sales Dept.* may actually represent a computer such as a Mac Classic, a IIci, or a Quadra.

FIGURE 8.22

The Chooser window, showing network connection options

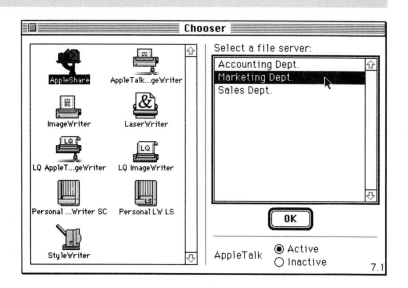

LOGGING ON TO THE CHOSEN MAC

Once you've selected a "file server," you'll see the dialog box shown in Figure 8.23, where you click the appropriate button to log onto the other computer either as a guest or registered user.

If you log on as a registered user, you must provide your name and any password that has been assigned to you. If you've been given permission by the operator of the other computer to change your password, you can also do that from this dialog box, clicking the Set Password button after typing the new password to save it for future use.

CHOOSING ITEMS TO SHARE

When you've made all of the necessary entries in this dialog box, click OK to proceed to the next dialog box, which presents a list of items available for sharing on the other computer, as shown in Figure 8.24.

If you want to use an item regularly, you can activate the check box after its name to have the item loaded onto your Mac every time you start it. However, although an item appears in this dialog box as available for sharing, the owner of

---

FIGURE 8.23

Connecting to
another computer
on your network

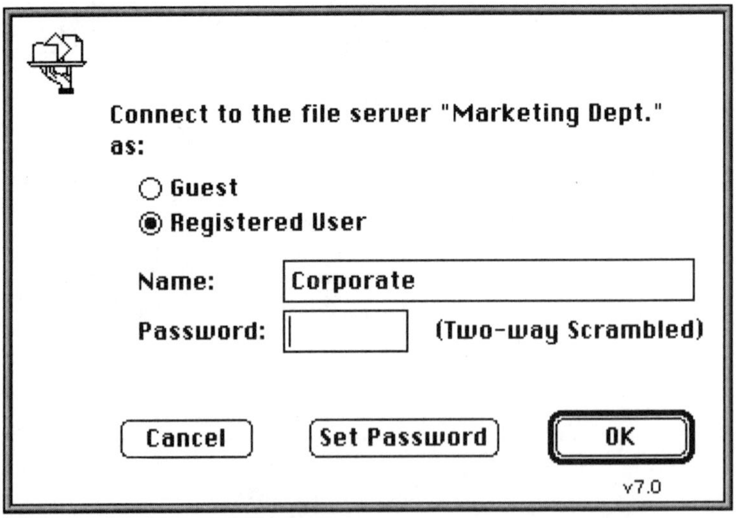

Connect to the file server "Marketing Dept."
as:

○ Guest
◉ Registered User

Name: | Corporate |

Password: | | (Two-way Scrambled)

(Cancel)   (Set Password)   [OK]

v7.0

The list of items
on a Mac that
are available
for sharing

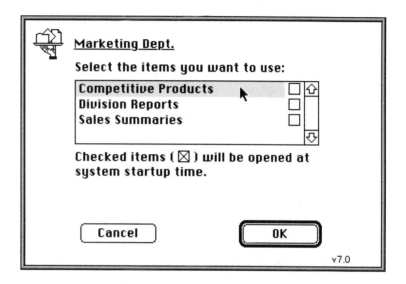

the computer may not have given you access to all of the folders or drives listed. For example, you might select an item you'd like to have appear on your desktop "at system startup time" only to see the warning message shown in Figure 8.25, indicating that the item is not available to you.

The warning
message seen if a
network user
selects a file for
startup access
when access has
not been granted

After you select one or more items in this second dialog box and click OK, those items will appear as icons displayed under the icon for your hard disk on your desktop, as demonstrated in Figure 8.26—provided, of course, that you have the proper access privileges for those items.

You can double-click one of these shared-item icons to open it, just as you would a regular disk, folder, or file icon, and you can also drag the icon onto your hard disk to copy the contents of the shared item onto your Macintosh.

If program linking has been approved in the host's Sharing Setup control panel and in your user icon, the items available for sharing can include programs stored on that computer, which you can then run as if they were installed on your own Mac.

DANGER

Remember, to share programs, you must be sure that you or your organization has been authorized by the software publishers to run their applications on more than one computer.

SHARING PRINTERS

An AppleTalk network lets you share several LaserWriter or LaserWriter-compatible printers, as well as folders and drives. Setting one of these printers up for sharing requires only that the printer be turned on and plugged into the network through the standard LocalTalk cables. Figure 8.27 shows a choice of LaserWriter-compatible printers displayed in the Chooser.

In addition to LaserWriter-compatible printers connected through the LocalTalk cables, you can also connect a printer such as an ImageWriter or StyleWriter to your own Mac for your personal use only, through your modem port—if that port is not already in use for another device such as a modem or a MacRecorder microphone.

FIGURE 8.26

The icon for a shared item from another computer appears under the standard hard-disk icon

Macintosh HD

Competitive Products

FIGURE 8.27

A choice of
LaserWriter-
compatible printers
displayed in the
Chooser

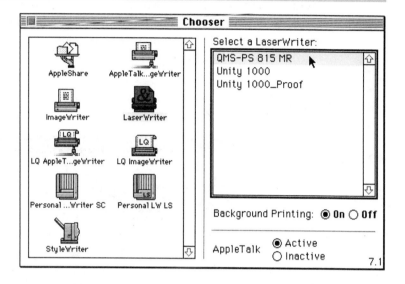

If your modem port is already in use but you want to connect a personal printer anyway, you can do so by purchasing an accessory such as MultiPort (manufactured by the Silicon Valley Bus Company). MultiPort combines a hardware device containing numerous port and ADB connections with software that controls those connections, so you can add printers, microphones, and ADB devices such as a trackball or a graphics tablet and switch between them at will.

Figure 8.28 shows the MultiPort control panel where port switching is accomplished. You can rename the port connections at any time to match your own configuration.

Ⓢ UMMARY

You have powerful connectivity tools at your disposal because of the new features added in System 7 and supported by MacWrite Pro. If your Mac is running under System 7, you can easily share files or portions of files with other applications or other computers, complete with automatic updating when the original files change. In addition, with the proper approvals, you can even run programs installed on another computer as if they were resident on your own Mac.

You can print your MacWrite Pro documents (and other files as well, of course) on any of several printers that may be linked by LocalTalk cables to your Mac and to other Macs with which you're sharing folders or programs. Moreover, you can connect a personal printer to your modem port that cannot be accessed by others on your network.

FIGURE 8.28

The port control panel for the MultiPort accessory

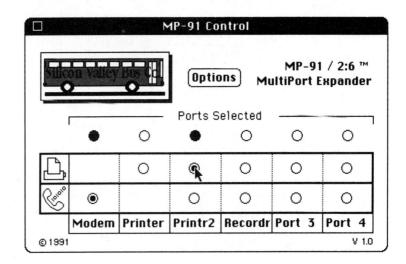

Using Shared Data and Files

CHAPTER 9

F EATURING

Changing style defaults

Picking a new default typeface

Selecting display, measurement, and operational preferences

Customizing your system

Y ou can change many aspects of the way MacWrite Pro works, in order to suit your own preferences and needs. To apply your changes to all future documents, start a new document containing your preferences, then issue the File Menu's Save As ... command. In the Save As dialog box, press the box below the words Save As to pop up a list of the format in which you can save a file. Save the new document in the special MacWrite Pro Options format. A file bearing this name and implementing your choices will be created in the Claris folder within your System folder. To restore the original defaults, simply drag this MacWrite Pro Options file into the Trash.

You can change numerous defaults through the Preferences dialog box. In addition, you can change other defaults by creating or revising character and paragraph styles, which were introduced in Chapter 2.

Let's discuss these style options first because the right choices can save you a lot of time.

D EFINING AND CHANGING STYLES

If you know that you'll be using certain style features most of the time that are different from the defaults, don't hesitate to replace those defaults with new selections of your own.

CHANGING THE DEFAULT TYPEFACE

For example, one of the basic decisions in word processing is picking the typeface you want for a particular document. The default font in MacWrite Pro is 12 pt. Helvetica Regular.

If you'd rather use 10 pt. Times Roman for 80 percent of your documents, does it make sense to change the typeface and size nearly every time you begin a document, in order to use your choice? Not if you can possibly avoid this drudgery. Come to think of it, what if you don't like Helvetica and would rather not use it at all? Now you're faced with selecting a typeface (and perhaps a different size) *every* time you start a new document—unless you can find an alternative method of operation.

Fortunately, there is an easy alternative. You can pick a new default font that will be ready for use every time you begin a document. Then, on those occasions when you do want to use a different typeface or size, you can still access those Font and Size menus and make other choices.

The first step is to open the Define Styles dialog box. You do this by selecting the Define Styles... command from the Style menu. Initially, the dialog box will come up in a mode that displays all existing *paragraph* styles (as distinguished from *character* styles) and with New 1 already entered in the text box as the name for a new style the program assumes you're about to create. However, if changing the default font is the only style change you want to make, you may as well do that by merely modifying the default paragraph style. To do this, click the Default style in the list box to highlight it; the name Default will now also appear in the text box, as shown in Figure 9.1.

You could now click the Copy button to make a copy of this style for modification, click the Remove button to delete the style (but don't ever do this with your one and only style!), or click the Cancel button to close the dialog box without saving any changes. Click OK only when you've made new changes you want to put into effect.

Other options in this dialog box let you switch to the Character, Paragraph, or Tab dialog boxes, base a new style on No Style or on an existing style if you like, and specify that the style you're creating will be followed in a document by another named style. (For example, in a book, you might want a chapter-introduction paragraph in a certain style to be always followed by the style you're using for the main text of the book.)

In Figure 9.1, note that when you highlight a style in the list box, the box at the right shows the present components of that particular style. This summary of the style is displayed only for your information. To modify the style, you must use one of the other dialog boxes represented by buttons.

The Define Styles dialog box contains a Use Character Info box that is selected by default. With this box selected for a paragraph style, that style will pick up the current Character dialog box settings as part of the paragraph style. Therefore, in this instance, the information box at the right does pick up 12 pt. Helvetica as the default font, even though no specific character styles have been created. Although it can be handy to have character style information added automatically to a paragraph style, you'll have tighter control if you deselect the Use Character Info box and define both styles separately.

FIGURE 9.1

The Style menu,
shown with the
Define Styles...
command selected,
and the Define
Styles dialog box,
which is opened by
the command, with
the contents of the
Default paragraph
style displayed

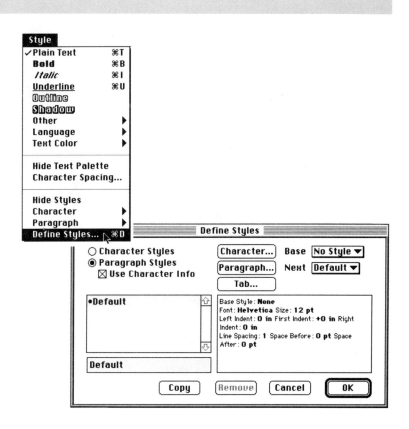

to a paragraph style, you'll have tighter control if you deselect the Use Character Info box and define both styles separately.

To change the default font from the Define Styles dialog box, click the Character... button; this action will bring up the Character dialog box. Here, as demonstrated in Figure 9.2, you can place the pointer on the current default typeface (Helvetica, in this case) and press to reveal the choice of typefaces available in your system.

Figure 9.3 shows that the list of available typefaces will expand both above and below the dialog box on your screen if you have a large quantity of typefaces installed.

(Figure 9.3 was captured from a SuperMac 21-inch monitor, which can display two complete pages simultaneously; the list of typefaces extends upward and downward for the entire length of a page, even though Adobe Type Reunion was

FIGURE 9.2

Selecting a new
default font in
the Character
dialog box

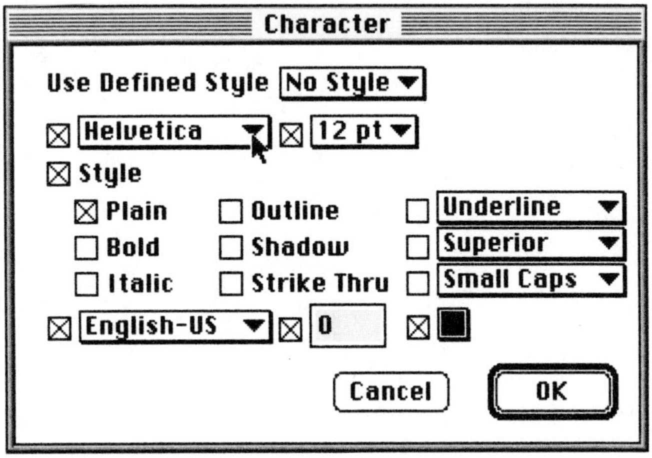

used to consolidate each typeface family as a single entry in the list. Any one of these typefaces could be selected as the new default. The default typeface can be changed as frequently as the user wishes.)

After you've changed the default typeface (and the default point size as well, if you like), click OK to close this dialog box; you'll be returned to the Define Styles dialog box, where you started.

Although nearly all other options in the Character dialog box are self-explanatory, note that the options on the bottom line change the dictionary in use, the character spacing (replace the zero with a number to move all characters further apart), and the color of the text (black is the default).

CHANGING OTHER STYLE DEFAULTS

If you want to change the default indentations and line spacing as well, click the Paragraph... button, make your changes, and click OK to return again to the Define Styles dialog box. (Figure 2.30 in Chapter 2 illustrates the Paragraph dialog box.) You can click the Tab... button to access the Tab dialog box in the same manner if you want to change the default tab alignment or spacing. (The Tab dialog box was discussed in Chapter 1; see Figure 1.4.)

FIGURE 9.3

The list of typefaces in the Character dialog box will expand upward and downward if many typefaces are installed

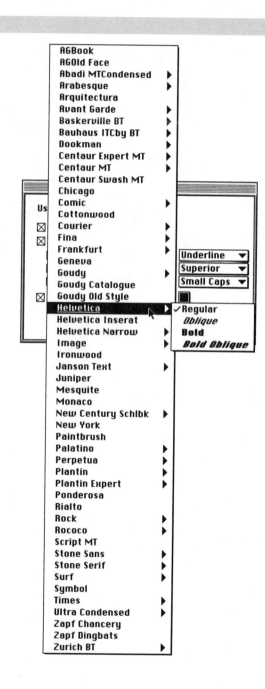

After you've completed all of the changes you want in the subsidiary dialog boxes, click OK again to close the Define Styles dialog box and put your changes into effect.

U SING THE PREFERENCES DIALOG BOX

As mentioned in Chapter 8, you access the Preferences dialog box by selecting the Preferences... command from the Edit menu. This dialog box is divided into several separate screens, each of which contains items for controlling some aspect of MacWrite Pro's operation. You display the screen you want by clicking the appropriate icon in the scroll box at the left side of the dialog box.

SELECTING DOCUMENT PREFERENCES

Figure 9.4 shows the contents of the Document screen, the first on the list.

FIGURE 9.4

The Document
screen in
the Preferences
dialog box

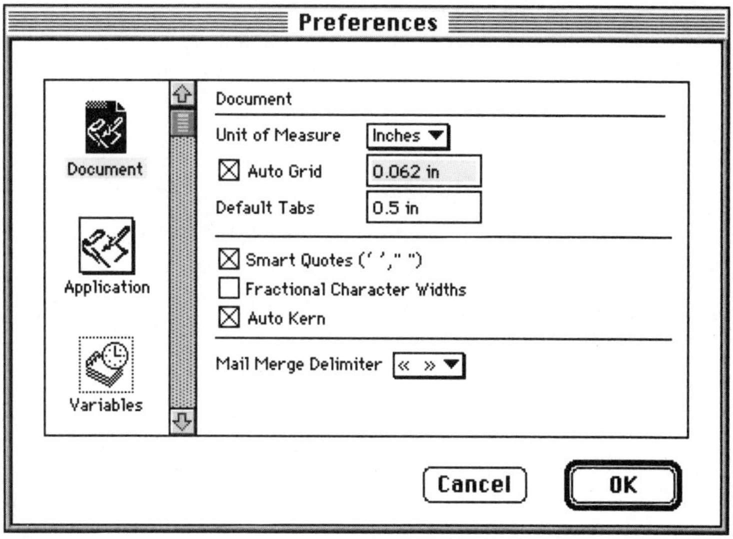

Changing the Unit of Measure

Here you can change the unit of measure for the program from the default of inches to inches decimal, picas, points, millimeters, or centimeters. Press the downward-pointing arrow to display these options.

Auto Grid

The second item on this screen is Auto Grid. When this option is activated, the elements of a document align themselves to an invisible grid, which means you can place multiple items in a straight line more easily. You determine the size of the grid cells by the number you place in the entry box to the right of the selection box for the Auto Grid.

TIP

For some documents, you may want to deactivate the Auto Grid so that you can make more precise adjustments in the placement of objects.

Choosing Default Tabs

The default tab setting is 0.5 inches, meaning that a document will automatically contain a tab stop every one-half inch—unless you've added a different tab arrangement to the ruler. If you want some other uniform tab spacing, you can enter a different number in this entry box.

Smart Quotes

When Smart Quotes is selected, the program will automatically enter separate opening and closing quotation-mark symbols as you use the quotation-mark symbol on your keyboard—the rule being that the closing quotation-mark symbol will be used when the symbol is followed by a space; otherwise, the opening quotation-mark symbol will be used.

This rule works very well, and we suggest that you use Smart Quotes unless you want some special effect. For example, you might want to disable Smart Quotes just before typing sample program code containing quotation marks—since these symbols in computer programming must be generic, "straight-up-and-down" quotation marks, rather than the separate "curly quotes" opening and closing symbols that you usually see in professional documents. (Figure 6.16 in Chapter 6 illustrates the difference between these different kinds of quotation marks.)

TIP

Deactivating (or activating) Smart Quotes while creating a document doesn't change the formatting of any quotation marks already entered. To do so, you must retype the text involved after changing the Smart Quotes setting.

Fractional Character Widths

If you select Fractional Character Widths, the spacing between individual characters will be more precise when the document is printed, although the document may print more slowly.

Auto Kern

With Auto Kern selected, pairs of characters that are usually kerned (see Chapter 6) will be automatically kerned as you type.

Mail Merge Delimiter

The final option on this screen, Mail Merge Delimiter, relates to mail merge operations that are explained in Chapter 10.

SELECTING APPLICATION PREFERENCES

You can see the contents of the Application screen in Figure 9.5.

Changing the User Name

The first item in the Application screen lets you change the user name that Mac-Write Pro will apply to documents you create. Initially, if you're running under System 7, this name is picked up by the program from the owner name that has been entered in the Sharing Setup control panel of your computer. (Chapter 8 contains an explanation of this control panel.) However, you can enter your own name in this text box as the creator of your documents (unless you have a supervisor who wants some other name shown).

FIGURE 9.5

The Application
screen

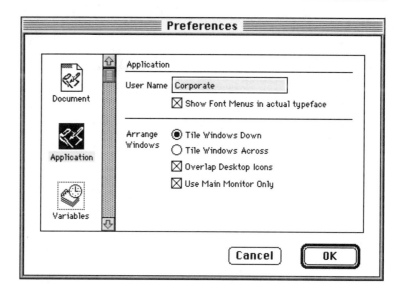

The user name will be saved with the document; you can see the name and other statistics by selecting Document Info... from the View menu. If you've revised a document that someone else originated, and if the user name has been changed before you create the revision, both the name of the original author and your name will appear in the Document Info window, as shown in Figure 9.6.

Using the Text Count Utility

In this window you can also click a Count button to obtain a count of any of these items that are selected:

- characters
- words
- lines
- paragraphs

Once you click the Count button, the name of this button will change to Pause; click Pause to interrupt the count temporarily on a long document so you

FIGURE 9.6

The Document Info
window

Document Info

Text Count

☐ Selection ☒ **Main Body**

☒ **Characters** -- 1,640
☒ **Words** -- 277
☒ **Lines** -- 24
☒ **Paragraphs** -- 3

Document: Relocation Bids
Original Author: Nancy Steinberg 9/15/93
Last Revision: Rosa Vidal 9/19/93
Revision #: 1
No. Pages: 1 **Total Time:** 6:22
No. Sections: 1 **Size on Disk:** 3K

(Copy) (**Done**) (Pause)

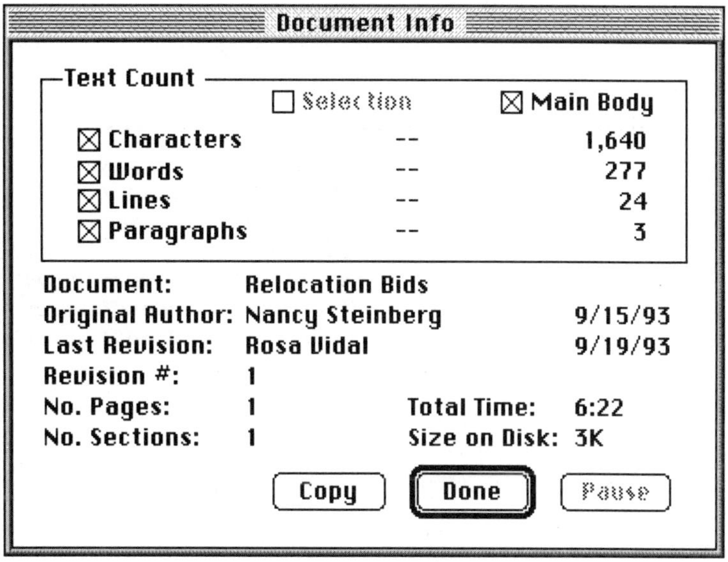

can look at the statistics calculated to that point. Click Copy to copy the contents of the Document Info window to the Clipboard for pasting into a document. By clicking appropriate boxes you can run the text count either on a selected portion of the document (the Selection box) or on the entire main text entered (the Main Body box).

Show Font Menus in Actual Typeface

Beneath the User Name text box, the Application screen contains a selection box you can activate to display the actual typefaces when you open your Font menu.

Your reaction might be: "Seeing the actual typefaces? What a convenience when you're making a choice! Why wouldn't I want to see the actual typefaces all of the time?"

There are three reasons why you might not want to show the actual typefaces. First, when you display the list of typefaces in this way, you can't group the typefaces into families with a utility such as Adobe Type Reunion; you'll see separate listings for bold, italic, and bold italic variations, thereby making your menu very long if you have many typefaces installed. Second, displaying the actual typefaces will slow down your access to the Font menu. And, finally, if you use typefaces that consist of decorations, symbols, or expert characters, you'll see a few of these rather than a typeface name, because the characters to create the name are not present in the typeface.

T I P

If you're using the Suitcase utility to manage your typefaces, you can have it both ways. You can configure Suitcase to show actual typefaces when you hold down a modifier key such as the Shift key as you open the Font menu. When you don't hold down the modifier key, you see the standard Mac Font menu; all of the typeface names are shown in the operating system's Chicago typeface customarily used on menus, and, if Adobe Type Reunion is installed, the names will be gathered into families.

Arranging Windows

The remaining options on the Application screen regulate how MacWrite Pro will overlap multiple file windows when you issue the Arrange Windows command from the View window.

You can choose to have windows tiled down or across your display, to overlap icons on the Desktop or not, and whether or not to have the open windows arranged across the screens of two monitors, if you have two attached to your system and turned on.

Of course, if you have a large-screen display or rarely have more than one file open at a time, these options will be of little importance to you. Otherwise, making the right decisions here can make the juggling of multiple files a lot more convenient.

SELECTING VARIABLES PREFERENCES

Variables are those items you can insert into your documents that are either derived from the system clock (the date and time) or calculated by MacWrite Pro for you (page numbering). As you can see by looking at the Variables screen reproduced in Figure 9.7, you can adjust the formatting of all of these elements to suit your preferences.

FIGURE 9.7

The Variables
screen

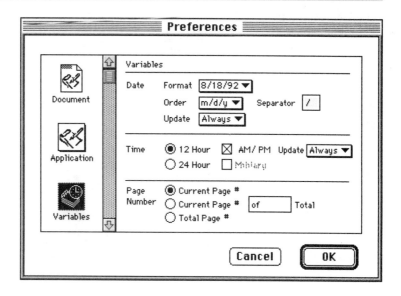

You can also choose to have the date and time updated Never, Always, When Modified (when changes have been made), or Next Open (which means the next time the document is opened); the default is to update these items Always, meaning whenever possible.

You actually insert a variable into a document through the Edit menu's Insert Variable command, shown in Figure 9.8. Note that—in addition to the date, time, and page number—you can also insert the section and revision number and the name of the document.

SELECTING XTND PREFERENCES

The XTND Prefs screen lets you view the list of translators installed with your copy of MacWrite Pro; translators are files that help you exchange documents with other applications. Click the Update button to see changes that have been made to the list.

From this screen you can also click the Set... button to specify your operational preferences for any translators that provide such options.

The XTND Prefs screen is shown in Figure 9.9.

FIGURE 9.8

The Insert Variable
command on the
Edit menu

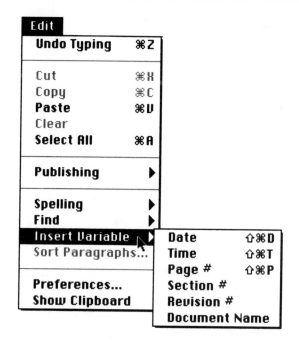

SELECTING COLOR PREFERENCES

From the Color screen (if you have a color monitor), you can assign colors of your
choosing to many of the elements of your MacWrite Pro environment:

- indents and tabs
- page guide lines
- column rules
- frame rules
- invisible characters
- tick marks
- ruler icons
- ruler background

FIGURE 9.9

The XTND
Prefs screen

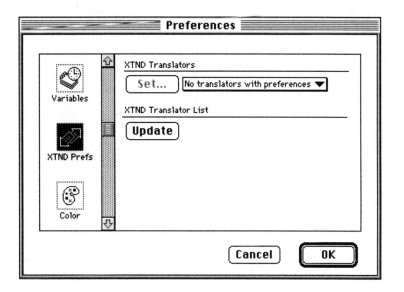

- page background
- frame anchors

To assign colors, you merely press the sample box to the left of a name on this screen; a palette of available colors will drop down, from which you highlight the one you want.

If you don't like the colors you've chosen—or find that they're hard to read—you can always click the Default Colors button to return all of the colors to their original values.

The Color screen is shown in Figure 9.10.

SELECTING SPELLING/HYPHENATION PREFERENCES

The options on the first line of the Spelling/Hyphenation screen relate to the program's Spell As You Type feature. If you activate this option by clicking the selection box that begins the line, MacWrite Pro will either beep when you type a word not in its dictionaries or flash the menu bar, according to which button you've selected. Some find

FIGURE 9.10

The Color screen

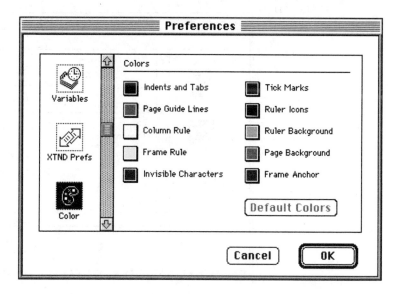

this interaction very helpful; others find it very irritating. Fortunately, the decision as to whether or not Spell As You Type is active lies in your hands.

The remaining options on this screen control how end-of-line hyphenation is handled. For example, as shown in Figure 9.11, you can decree how many hyphens in a row will be accepted; the options are Unlimited (the default) or a fixed number ranging from one through seven.

You can also specify the following:

- that the smallest word to be hyphenated will consist of a certain number of characters (the default is five)

- the minimum number of characters before and after a hyphen (the defaults are zero and 2)

- whether or not capitalized words will be hyphenated (by default, they will be)

For most users, these defaults work satisfactorily.

FIGURE 9.11

The Spelling/
Hyphenation
screen

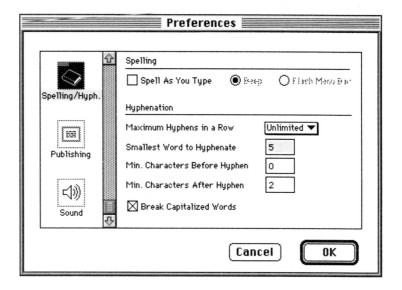

The next screen in the Preferences dialog box is called Publishing and was shown and explained in Chapter 8. The final screen is Sound, explained in the following section.

SELECTING SOUND PREFERENCES

The Sound screen controls the sound quality and volume used for the recording of sound notes. The quality selections are labeled Good, Better, and Best, as shown in Figure 9.12.

Recordings of higher quality require more disk storage space. The default maximum note size is 44K, although you can change this to any other size you wish, limited by the storage space available on your hard disk. With a maximum size of 44K, a Good recording can run for a maximum of 12 seconds, a Better recording for 6 seconds, and a Best recording for only 2 seconds.

If you increase the maximum note size to 100K, for example, you can then make a Good recording up to 27 seconds in length.

The final option on this screen is Speaker, which you use for volume adjustment. Drag the slider to the left to decrease the volume or drag it to the right to increase it.

FIGURE 9.12

The Sound screen

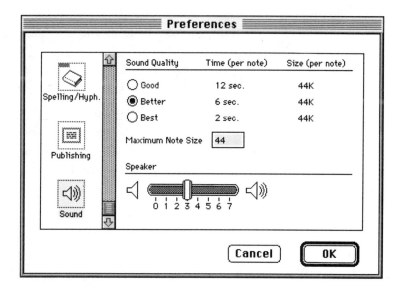

CUSTOMIZING YOUR SYSTEM FOR MACWRITE PRO

In addition to establishing your preferences within the program, you can make modifications to your system that will make your work within MacWrite Pro more productive and of a higher quality.

We've already suggested that you obtain inexpensive utilities such as Suitcase and Adobe Type Reunion. If you plan to produce publications with MacWrite Pro, a large monitor would be helpful too, since you could then see one or two entire pages at a time and modify them in that configuration. A large monochrome monitor will suffice for many jobs—available at prices ranging from a few hundred dollars for a full-page monitor to less than a thousand dollars for some two-page models.

If you're doing a lot of layout work—dragging objects back and forth with your mouse, rather than primarily straight typing—you may want to check out alternate input devices.

For example, the Kensington Turbo Mouse is actually a large trackball; because of its method of construction and programmable buttons, you can perform such tricks as holding down a key to move the pointer very slowly and precisely, clicking a button to lock the trackball into a drag configuration so you can move objects without accidentally dropping them into an unknown folder halfway to your destination, and making the pointer jump automatically to places on your screen you need to access frequently, such as the File menu and the Trash. The street price of the Turbo Mouse is a little over $100.

HIGH-RESOLUTION PRINTERS

For really professional-looking results from your desktop, you may want to consider a high-resolution laser printer. Several relatively inexpensive printers are available now that offer 600 dots-per-inch resolution instead of the traditional laser standard of 300 dpi. Among these are models from Apple, Dataproducts, Hewlett-Packard, and QMS that can be used to print the output simultaneously from both Macintosh and PC computers. The street price of some of these printers is less than $2,000.

For even higher resolution, you can consider LaserMaster printers offering 1000 and 1200 dpi, with built-in hard disks for typeface storage. These units match the resolution of some service-bureau imagesetters that prepare documents for the publishing industry.

TIP

If all of these high-resolution printer choices are out of the question for you because of budget considerations, you can still save important documents as PostScript files (a Print menu option) and have them printed through a service bureau at resolutions up to 2400 dpi.

When do you need high-resolution output? Of course, it's desirable in any document that is to be printed in large quantities for the general public—not just for distribution within your own organization. However, give high-resolution strong consideration if your document uses intricate artwork or delicate typefaces in small sizes, whose fine strokes may be lost when reproduced at 300 dpi.

UMMARY

After you've become familiar with the factory MacWrite Pro defaults, feel free to change those that don't match the way you want to work. In fact, since you can create and name a variety of different character and paragraph styles, you can change to a different set of style defaults in seconds to handle a particular project, then immediately switch to other styles for the next job. You probably won't want to change settings quite as often in the screens of the Preferences dialog box, but these specifications are easy to modify too.

Using the Mail Merge

CHAPTER 10

F EATURING

Selecting symbols (delimiters) to mark changeable text

Creating a data file of information to be merged

Producing a form letter for use with merged data

Merging based on conditional statements

Printing a document with merged data

With the mail-merge feature of MacWrite Pro, you can easily create professional form letters for your business or organization. The word *"merge"* is used because the procedure involves inserting personalized information from a database into each copy printed of a standard letter, thereby making the copy appear to be a personal letter written to the person who receives it.

The database can consist of nothing more elaborate than a list of names and addresses created in MacWrite Pro or created in some other application and imported as an ASCII text file. The only stipulation is that the names and addresses in the database must be divided by tab stops or commas into data categories or *fields* such as First Name and Last Name. The field names are used in the form letter to indicate where the database information is to be inserted.

With practically no effort, you can also do a little programming to personalize letters even further. For example, you could insert commands into a form letter for club membership renewal to congratulate any member who has belonged to the club for five years or more—provided, of course, that this information is included in one of the fields of the database.

This chapter will guide you through the steps necessary to create both databases and their accompanying form letters.

Ⓢ ELECTING DELIMITERS

Changeable fields in a mail-merge letter are separated from the main, fixed body of the text through the use of *delimiters*, symbols used to mark the beginning and end of any text containing field names or mail-merge commands.

The default delimiters are double opening and closing angle brackets (<< and >>)—the same symbols used in French-language publications to represent quotation marks. However, you can use the document screen of the Preferences dialog box (as shown in Figure 10.1) to change the default delimiters to either of two other sets of brackets: [and] or { and }. (Remember, you access the Preferences dialog box by selecting the Preferences… command from the Edit menu.)

We'll use the default delimiters in this chapter. Obviously, if you'll be creating form letters in French, you may want to change the default to avoid a conflict with quotations you might include in the main text of these letters.

FIGURE 10.1

The choices
available for
mail-merge
delimiters

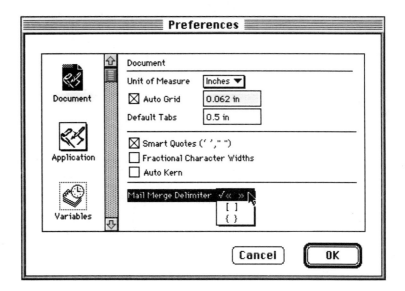

ⒸREATING A MAIL-MERGE DATA FILE

The easiest way to learn how mail merge works is to try it. So, if you have a Mac handy as you read this book, try the examples explained in this chapter to create a small database and a form letter that utilizes the database. If you also have a printer available, you can see for yourself how MacWrite Pro will follow the instructions you embed in a document to create a variety of personalized versions of the letter. You can use all of the procedures we'll explain in order to create mail-merge documents for your own projects.

First, you'll need the database to be used. Let's say that you work for an imaginary company called Tours For Singles, headquartered in Canyon City, New Mexico. (As far as we know, there's no such city. In addition, if you're familiar with the places listed in our database, you'll be aware that the street addresses and ZIP codes we supply are not correct either. After all, we don't want any real person at a real address being inundated with unwanted mail from readers who are trying out mail merge!)

Tours for Singles wants to send a letter to its customers that will announce a forthcoming tour of Europe. This particular letter will be in the form of a personal note from the president of Tours for Singles and will be personalized not only by the use of the customer's first name in the salutation but also by a reference to the fact that the customer took part in last year's tour or a previous tour, as the case may be.

Therefore, the database will contain a field named Tour in addition to fields for the customer's first name, last name, street address, city, state, and ZIP code.

Figure 10.2 shows the data file that you'll be creating.

Follow these steps to create the file:

1. Open a new MacWrite Pro document, and drag a tab marker from the align-left tab marker box at the left side of the ruler to create a new tab stop at the 2 ¼-inch position on the ruler.

2. Drag an additional tab marker to each of the remaining tab-stop positions shown in the ruler in Figure 10.2. When you're finished, you'll have all of the tab stops in place that you'll need for the data to be entered.

FIGURE 10.2

The data file for a
mail-merge project

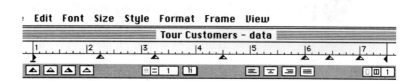

Last Name	First Name	Street or P.O.	City	State	ZIP	Tour
Hammersmith	Frederick	25866 Hillcrest	Grosse Pointe Farms	MI	48123	90
Nehru	Anup	6000 55th St.	New York	NY	11234	91
Pemberton	Nancy	P.O. Box 14682	Running Springs	CA	91234	91
Rizzo	Barbara	81 Bench View	Boise	ID	81234	92

3 Select an easy-to-read typeface in which to display the data on your screen.

- You don't have to use this typeface in your printed letter, but a very readable typeface is a help when you're setting up a data file or the mail merge codes within a letter itself.

- After this work is done, you can change the typeface to a more decorative replacement before printing.

- We used Times Roman in these setup examples, rather than the default Helvetica.

4 Each column produced by the tab stops will contain one field of the database you're creating, and the first line of the document must contain the names you're assigning to each field. To establish these field names, begin by typing **Last Name** on the first line as the name of the first field.

5 Press Tab, and type the name of the second field: **First Name**.

6 Enter all of the remaining field names in the same manner, as shown in Figure 10.2. (If you run out of space on the first line before you've typed all of the field names, don't worry. The text will wrap automatically to accept the reminder of your entries. However, you must enter all field names before pressing Return to end the line officially.)

7 On the following lines, enter all of the customer records shown in Figure 10.2. Each line below the first line constitutes a single *record* in the database: the line contains all of the information about one customer.

8 Save the file in the standard MacWrite Pro format, using the name **Tour Customers - data**.

9 Close the file.

T I P

You can use a data file created in another program. Simply create the file using these guidelines and save it in a plain text (ASCII) format.

TARTING THE FORM LETTER

Now that the data file is ready, you need to create the form letter itself. Obviously, such a letter would normally be printed on a letterhead, although in these days of high-resolution printers, you might be able to print the letterhead itself as part of the document. For this exercise, you'll have to take this second approach, since we haven't provided you with any stationery for the Tours for Singles company.

Figure 10.3 shows how such a letterhead might be designed; we've used two Casady & Greene typefaces in this figure—Harlequin Extra Bold for the name of the company and Highland Gothic for the city and state. We saved the file under the name Tour Letter for merging.

Create your own Tours for Singles letterhead with any typefaces installed on your Mac that you believe would be appropriate. Shortly you'll be issuing the Mail Merge... command, as also shown in Figure 10.3, to start preparing the actual form letter to appear in the file under the two-line letterhead.

FIGURE 10.3

Issuing the Mail Merge... command in a document that already contains a company letterhead

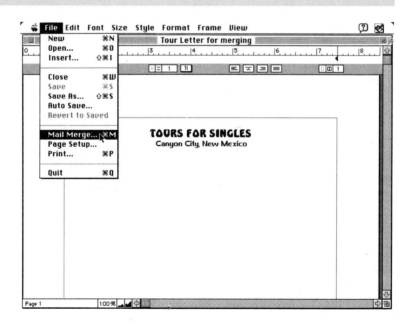

Since the purpose of this exercise is to show you how to enter mail-merge codes and commands, we haven't cluttered the example by starting the letter with a date. However, don't forget that in your own work you can further automate a form letter by making MacWrite Pro insert the current date from your Mac's system clock every time you print a new merged copy of the letter.

You enter the date through the Insert Variable command explained in Chapter 9, after choosing the date format you want through the Preferences dialog box, also explained in Chapter 9.

Follow the steps below to create the form letter beneath the Tours for Singles letterhead. First, you'll load the merge data file into your Mac's memory in order to select fields from the file for insertion into the letter.

1 Pull down the File menu, and select the Mail Merge... command. (Shortcut: press ⌘-M.) A window will open prompting you to "Open Merge Data File." You can either select a merge data file from the folder contents displayed in the list box, or switch to another folder before making your selection. Since you just completed creating the file called *Tour Customers - Data*, that file should be contained in your current folder (although you may need to scroll the list box to display the name).

2 Highlight this file name, and click the Open button to open the file. Once the file is open, you'll see the Mail Merge dialog box rather than the file itself. This is the result you want; the data file is loaded but not shown during either the building of a form letter or the actual merge-printing process.

Incidentally, you can't use a merge data file for either of these purposes unless it is opened through the File menu's Mail Merge... command rather than the Open... command.

3 As shown in Figure 10.4, select the necessary field names one at a time to enter the first name and last name as the first line of the customer address (with a single space in between the field names so that the two names don't run together when printed). Position the insertion point where you want each field name, highlight the name, then click the Insert Field Name button to place the name on the page. Delimiters will automatically be added around each name entered into the document.

4 Select only the *Street or P.O.* field name to serve as the second line of the address.

5 Enter the *City*, *State*, and *ZIP* field names as the third line of the address. Scroll the Field Name box to display the ZIP field name. After the *City* field, be sure to enter a comma followed by a space. Also, separate the *State* and *ZIP* fields with a space.

6 Skip a line by pressing Return twice, and type the word **Dear** followed by a space, to begin the salutation of the letter.

FIGURE 10.4

Inserting field
names into the
form letter

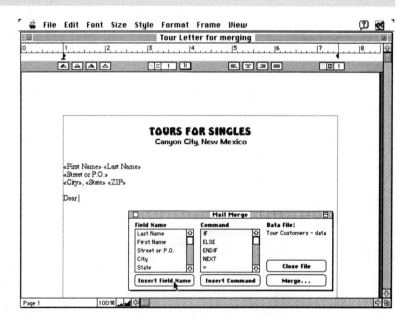

7 Then, as specifically illustrated in Figure 10.4, insert the *First Name* field name again, so that this line when printed will contain the word "Dear" followed in each version of the letter by the first name of a customer. Add a comma after the field name. (If the format of this letter was to be formal, you'd use a colon at this point rather than a comma.)

8 Close the Mail Merge dialog box, either by selecting Hide Mail Merge from the File menu or by simply clicking its close box.

TIP

You can format text inserted by mail merge so that it appears in a different typeface, size, or style than the main body of a document. For example, if you were working in the credit department of a retail store, you might want to do this in sending out letters to customers to call attention to an increase in their credit limit.

To format inserted information differently, simply drag across the field name inside the delimiters, and make the changes you want through the Font, Size, and Style menus. If you have a color printer, you can also change the color of inserted text, either through the Style menu or the Text palette. The appearance of the field name will change to reflect your changes.

ENTERING THE FIRST THREE SENTENCES

The main body of the letter starts with three sentences that don't require the insertion of any mail-merge coding. Type these sentences now:

> **We're planning a one-month tour of Europe, leaving June 16th from New York City. The tour is just for singles and will include top attractions that everyone will find exciting. Each year we visit different places, so you can have fun with us year after year without getting bored!**

Now that you've entered this text, you'll be adding two more sentences to the paragraph that require some simple mail-merge programming.

INCLUDING AN IF STATEMENT IN YOUR FORM LETTER

MacWrite Pro lets you go beyond merely inserting text from a series of database records into a specific area of a form letter. (Remember, the information on each customer constitutes a *record*.) You can tell the program to add one item of information if a certain condition exists (determined by a *logical test*), or to add a different item of information if the condition does not exist. Such instructions are called a *conditional statement*.

Conditional statements are used every day by computer programmers and frequently by those who enter formulas in spreadsheet programs. In MacWrite Pro, these statements consist of:

commands (terms used in defining, limiting, or ending the statement)

operators (symbols or words that represent the relationship between two values)

values themselves (usually, a field name followed by specific text or a number that may be contained in that field within some of the records in the data file)

operands (text from the merge data file that will be operated upon by the conditional statement—in other words, text that will be inserted or not, according to whether or not a condition is met)

If a conditional statement specifies a search for certain text in a field of the database records, that text must be enclosed in double quotation marks.

You can use the following commands: IF, ELSE, ENDIF, NEXT, AND, OR, and NOT.

IF precedes the listing of the first condition to be met within a conditional statement.

ELSE precedes an instruction stating what the program is to do if that first condition is not met.

ENDIF ends the entire conditional-statement sequence.

NEXT skips the current record and moves on to the next if specified conditions are not met; for example, a department store might decide not to send a merchandise offer to customers who are listed in its mail-merge database as behind in their payments.

AND, OR, and NOT modify a condition; for example, you might want to include a certain offer in a sales form letter if the recipient—according to the database—is married AND has a high income.

You can use the following operators (included with the commands in the Command list box of the Mail Merge dialog box):

=	equals or matches exactly
<>	does not equal
<	is less than
<=	is less than or equal to
>	is greater than
>=	is greater than or equal to
CONTAINS	contains the following text

Figure 10.4 shows the Mail Merge dialog box with the first few field names displayed that have been defined in the merge data file of tour customers. Under the heading Command, the dialog box also displays the first few commands and operators you can use to stipulate special conditions under which the text of the form letter will be changed.

Figure 10.5 presents another view of this dialog box in which the remaining field names are displayed, along with some of the other commands and operators that are available.

In our Tours for Singles example, we want to personalize the form letter not only by referring to customers by First Name but also by adding a certain sentence if a customer took the tour last year and a different sentence if the customer did not take the tour last year but did so in some previous year. To accomplish this, you'll need to enter a conditional statement incorporating the IF and ELSE commands as well as the text to be inserted.

FIGURE 10.5

The Mail Merge
dialog box,
showing some
commands and
operators and five
field names from
the merge date file
of tour customers

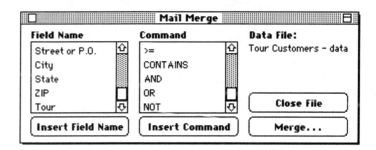

As you've already learned, you can enter field names and commands through the Mail Merge dialog box by highlighting the item you want in one of the list boxes and then clicking the button below the list box to insert the item into your document. However, you can also enter mail-merge field names, commands, and conditional statements by typing them—provided you're careful not to misspell any of the names. Try this alternate approach now to enter the conditional statement required in the tour form letter:

1 If necessary, click just after the exclamation point ending the last sentence you typed, to make this position the insertion point for the statement you'll type.

2 Type the following material, being careful to duplicate all characters and capitalization used and to insert the same number of spaces (if any) between words or commands: **<<IF Tour = "92">> We enjoyed having you with us last year and hope that you'll join us again. <<ELSE>> We missed you last year, but hope you can join us this time. <<ENDIF>>**

This is what the conditional statement really says: "If 92 is stored in the Tour field of a record (meaning that the customer participated in the 1992 tour), tell the customer that his or her presence was appreciated last year and that the company hopes the customer will also sign up for the upcoming tour. However, if this condition is not met (if the Tour field doesn't contain 92), tell the customer instead that his or her presence was missed on the last tour and that the company hopes the customer will sign up again for this tour."

The command IF must precede the listing of the condition and the entry of the text to be inserted if the condition is true, the word ELSE must precede the listing of the alternative text to be used, and the command ENDIF must end the entire statement.

All three of these command names must be entered in capital letters and must be enclosed within the mail merge delimiters currently in use (<< and >>). The spaces entered will provide the proper spacing when one of the conditional sentences is inserted into the form letter.

C OMPLETING THE FORM LETTER

The remainder of the form letter will appear in each version printed. Enter these elements now:

1 Press Return after completing the conditional statement, to enter a blank line before the next paragraph.

2 Type the following text: **The itinerary isn't complete as yet. What we need from you now is simply an indication of your interest in receiving full details. If we hear that you're thinking about signing on for this exciting cruise, we'll rush complete information to you as soon as it's available.**

3 Press Return, then press Tab as many times as necessary to place the insertion point at about the 4-inch position on the ruler.

4 Type **Sincerely,** and press Return.

5 Tab to the 4-inch position again, and type **Tina Prentiss** as the name of the person signing the letter. (We changed typefaces here and used Casady & Greene's Phoenix Script typeface to simulate a personal signature. If you have a script typeface installed in your system, you could pull down your Font menu and select this typeface before typing the name. Script typefaces usually look better and are easier to read in larger sizes, so if you've been typing in a 12-pt. font, you may want to use the Size menu to increase the font size for the signature to 14 pt.

6 If necessary, change the font back to the same one used for the main part of the letter, press Return, tab over to the 4-inch position, and type Tina's title: **President**.

7 Save the file again (or for the first time if you haven't done so previously), using the name **Tour Letter for merging**.

Your form letter is now complete and should resemble Figure 10.6.

MERGING THE DATA FILE WITH THE FORM LETTER

In order to print an individualized version of the form letter for each customer, the data file must be merged with the form letter. Follow these steps if you have a printer available and ready for use:

FIGURE 10.6

The completed form letter

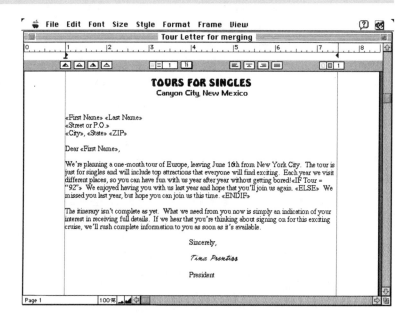

1 If necessary, use the File menu to display the Mail Merge dialog box again. (Shortcut: press ⌘-M.)

2 Click the Merge… button. You'll see the Merge dialog box shown in Figure 10.7. By default, this dialog box should be set to merge all data file records.

3 If the All option button is not selected to merge all records, click it now. (If you wanted to merge and print letters for only a portion of the records in the data file, you could enter the record numbers in the From and To entry boxes. You can determine record numbers either by counting the appropriate lines in the data file or by assigning each line its own record number in a separate field added to the file.

4 Click the Merge button to begin the merging and printing. Since you created only four records for the data file, you should see the results of your programming in a few minutes.

FIGURE 10.7

The Merge dialog box with its default settings

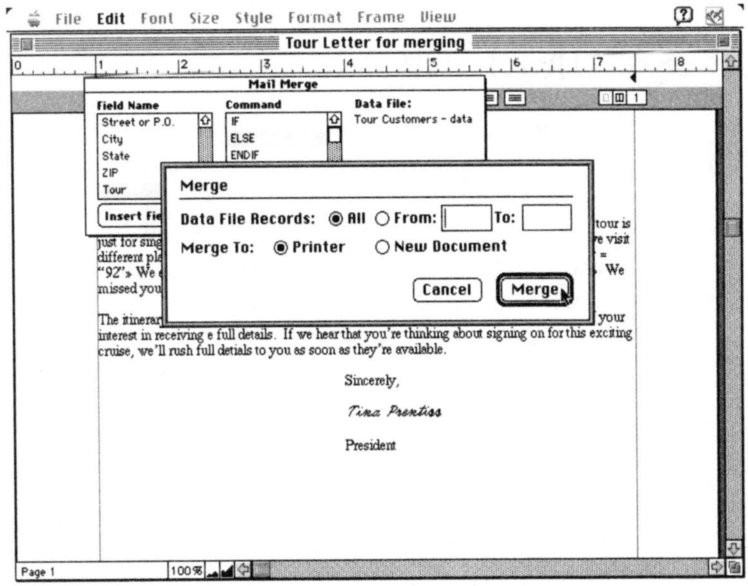

The Merge dialog box offers an additional option—to merge to a new document instead of to the printer. You could use this option if you wanted to create personalized form letters for printing at some later time.

T I P

In creating both merge data files and form letters, be sure to name the files so that one or more words in the title identify the file as either a data file or form letter. This practice can help you avoid confusion and potential embarrassment.

Remember, neither kind of file will print properly without being merged with the other. A data file will be simply a list of information in columns (or separated by commas, if you use that method of separating fields). A form letter will be a meaningless jumble of understandable sentences combined with merge codes and commands. It really does help to identify the files with names that indicate their purpose.

Figure 10.8 is a printout of the merge document produced for one of the data-file records—with all of the text of the letter (except the letterhead) changed to the Phoenix Script typeface. This change produces a letter that resembles a personal note from the president of the company offering the tour.

S UMMARY

Preparing and printing form letters can be a painless process. However, the key to success is attention to detail. Commands and field names must be entered absolutely correctly.

Be careful to use the correct number of spaces between merge commands and information and the main text of the document; if you want the letter to contain two spaces between sentences, make sure that you don't enter two spaces before the first delimiter for material to be inserted and then enter two more before the actual text to be inserted—that would make a total of four!

Also, be sure that you plan the "personalization" of the letter so that it works properly. For example, if the Tours for Singles company also operated tours of a more general nature, it might be a mistake to include the customers of all of the tours in the same merge-file database. Doing so might someday result in Tina Prentiss accidentally thanking a long- and happily-married man for joining all of her previous tours for swinging singles!

FIGURE 10.8

A printout of the form letter with all of the text reproduced in a script typeface

TOURS FOR SINGLES
Canyon City, New Mexico

Frederick Hammersmith
25866 Hillcrest
Grosse Pointe Farms, MI 48123

Dear Frederick,

We're planning a one-month tour of Europe, leaving June 16th from New York City. The tour is just for singles and will include top attractions that everyone will find exciting. Each year we visit different places, so you can have fun with us year after year without getting bored! We missed you last year, but hope you can join us this time.

The itinerary isn't complete as yet. What we need from you now is simply an indication of your interest in receiving full details. If we hear that you're thinking about signing on for this exciting cruise, we'll rush complete information to you as soon as it's available.

Sincerely,

Tina Prentiss

President

Choosing the Right Layout

CHAPTER 11

FEATURING

Managing design elements

Using basic layout types

Making the design enhance the message

The effectiveness of your MacWrite Pro documents will be strongly in-fluenced by the way in which you design them. Before people read the first word, they'll be impressed favorably or unfavorably by what they see—your choice of typefaces and artwork and the *layout*—the way elements are used and arranged on the page. This chapter gives you some pointers on how to utilize the design alternatives at your disposal.

SELECTING THE RIGHT PREFERENCES SETTINGS

If you want to create pages that are precisely designed and printed, begin by making certain that you've selected operational preferences appropriate to what you're trying to do.

For example, as mentioned in Chapter 9, if you want to position objects with great accuracy, pull down the Edit menu, select the Preferences... command, and—in the Preferences dialog box—click to remove the X from the Auto Grid selection box (unless this option has already been deactivated).

Also in this dialog box, Smart Quotes should be selected for the automatic insertion of the correct opening and closing quotation-mark symbols. Select Fractional Character Widths and Auto Kern in order to print laser documents with precisely-aligned characters. Figure 11.1 shows the dialog box with the correct choices made to accomplish these goals.

The Auto Kern option provides capabilities not available in most word-processing software. With the option selected, MacWrite Pro takes advantage of the *kerning pair* information included in most typeface files and will move certain character combinations closer together automatically so they appear next to each other in the exact relationship specified by the designer of the typeface.

Having Auto Kern means that you can include unusual, decorative typefaces in a page layout that would otherwise require tedious manual kerning that might never achieve the proper results. (See Chapter 6 for an explanation of manual kerning.)

Most manufacturers include kerning data in each typeface file for approximately 150 to 300 kerning pairs. However, one manufacturer—URW—offers 1,000 kerning pairs. The benefits of automatic kerning are dramatically illustrated by the example shown in Figure 11.2.

FIGURE 11.1

Choices in the
Preferences dialog
box that provide
greater precision

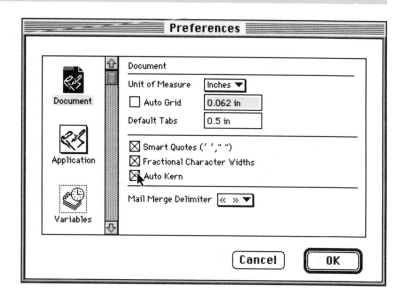

FIGURE 11.2

Automatic kerning
moves the **Q** and **U**
in **Quota** closer
together.

Here the word *Quota* is displayed in URW's version of the Plaza Swash typeface. Note that—because of automatic kerning—the tail of the capital Q intrudes far into the space belonging to the lowercase *u*, with very pleasing results. (You'll see this innovative typeface again later in the chapter.)

S ELECTING AND MANAGING DESIGN ELEMENTS

In creating a design, professionals consider not only the typefaces to be used but the exact size, color, and positioning of all text included in the design. In addition, they take into account many other factors that affect design. For example, the noted designer Takenobu Igarashi defines ten design elements that influence his work: the dot, line, grid, plane, surface, circle/triangle/square (geometric shapes), letters (the typefaces), structure, color, and *aimai*—a Japanese term representing the enigmatic quality or essence of a design.

Regardless of the kinds of elements that make up your own document designs, make sure that these elements complement each other and contribute to a coordinated whole.

Don't combine an Old English typeface with a border reminiscent of the Roaring Twenties and a drawing executed in the latest modern style.

Try to use only one or two typeface families on a page; if you use members of two families, the families should be very different from each another.

If you can't find a clip-art border that looks right with the typefaces you've entered in a frame, use a plain border that you can create within MacWrite Pro through the Tool palette (see Chapter 2).

Position drawings and photos carefully so they're in balance with other elements. You don't have to be a design wizard; just drag frames to new locations until the result satisfies you, bearing in mind that an object should be displayed prominently if you want the reader to pay special attention to it.

Ⓤ SING STANDARD LAYOUTS

Most page layouts fall into a few standard categories. If you create layouts that fit one of these categories and adhere to a few basic rules, you will probably avoid serious design problems.

SYMMETRICAL LAYOUTS

Amateurs tend to center everything. The result is a *symmetrical* layout in which the elements usually balance one another. However, the result may appear dull and uninteresting.

One way to make a symmetrical layout more effective is to group as many objects as possible so that there are few separate design elements on the page. The opposite of this technique would be to place exactly the same spacing between all of the elements displayed—a procedure that can make a layout monotonous and keep the reader from determining easily what is important.

The brochure cover shown in Figure 11.3 is an exception to this rule. The layout is completely symmetrical, yet the piece accomplishes its goals in a professional manner.

There are three design elements (not counting the border): the title of the brochure, a cute illustration that reinforces the message in the title, and a short sentence that tells those who receive the brochure what it's all about.

FIGURE 11.3

A symmetrical
layout

Getting Our Products to Market

**The chairman explains our company
sales policies and how you can help.**

Since these three elements are closely related in purpose, it's appropriate to give them all prominence on the page. The title is at the top and is in a large font size, so it will be noticed and read first. The drawing of the pigs going to market is also large and will be noticed next; since the title will have already been read, the drawing will be understood immediately in its proper context. The sentence of explanation is displayed in a much smaller font size, but the white space around it makes it important too.

What would other positioning options have accomplished? If the drawing had been moved higher to group it with the title—to reduce the number of design elements on the page—the page would have appeared top-heavy because of the font size of the title and the bulk of the drawing. In addition, the explanatory sentence would have become an orphan.

On the other hand, if the drawing had been moved down to group it with the sentence, the title would have seemed to bear little relationship to the drawing.

The drawing is clip art from the Dynamic Graphics library. The title typeface is Bitstream's Oz Handicraft. The explanatory sentence was printed in Monotype's Perpetua Bold, also available through Adobe. The border is clip art from Image Club and was inserted into the document by placing it into a picture frame of its own; we used the Move to Back command on the Frame menu (discussed in Chapter 2) to display the frame containing the border behind the other elements of the page.

TIP

In a word-processing document that consists primarily of many paragraphs of text, it's often hard to avoid a symmetrical layout; even if the text is divided into multiple columns, the columns will usually be the same width if they all contain text for the same article.

Sometimes you can vary such a layout by running a decorative border down one side of the page only, inserting a drawing or photo so that some of the text will wrap around it, or using a grayed-out illustration as a background or "watermark" for the page (a technique demonstrated in Chapter 3; see Figure 3.13).

HYBRID LAYOUTS

Of course, you can create a layout that has characteristics of two or more layout types—for example, symmetrical and *asymmetrical* (simply meaning "not symmetrical"). In an asymmetrical layout, elements are not centered. You balance them by such techniques as opposing a large, dark element with a small, light element made more substantial by surrounding it with white space.

Consider the poster reproduced in Figure 11.4. The three lines at the bottom of this page are definitely symmetrical, as is the border. However, the illustration

THE
mind
EXPANDS

Dr. Blair explores the future of thought
UNIVERSITY AUDITORIUM
8 p.m. Thursday   Tickets $10

and the title of the lecture are asymmetrical elements that balance one another because of their relative positions on the page and the white space surrounding the title of the lecture.

The futuristic typeface in the title is Lynz, from Image Club. The remainder of the text was printed in Antique Olive Bold Condensed, available from Adobe and other vendors. The illustration is from the Dynamic Graphics library. The border is from the Image Club library.

ASYMMETRICAL LAYOUTS

Asymmetrical layouts are often more interesting than their symmetrical cousins, for two reasons: you have more leeway in how you can position elements and you can surprise the reader with arrangements of objects that are unexpected—or, at least, not completely predictable.

In the ad for an art exhibit shown in Figure 11.5, the name of the imaginary gallery and the dates of the exhibit have been positioned so close to the illustration that all of these components become a single design element on the page.

Actually, the only other element worthy of consideration is the name of the exhibit, since the narrow border is so neutral as to be hardly noticeable. The two design elements balance because of their positioning on the page.

In this instance, after the name of the exhibit is read, the eye is drawn irresistibly to the group at the bottom of the page. The reasons are the dramatic diagonal positioning and the fact that eyes trained to read from left to right and top to bottom will usually follow that pattern in looking at such a design.

Note that the paintbrush in the hand of the elf helps draw the reader to the name of the gallery and the dates of the exhibit, since the brush seems to point at these items.

This drawing is also from the Dynamic Graphics library. The name of the exhibit is in Plaza Swash; for the rest of the text, we used another typeface in the same family: Plaza Ultra. The typefaces are available from URW.

GEOMETRIC LAYOUTS

Some layouts don't belong to the categories we've already discussed. For example, if a page is composed of elements in the shapes of rectangles, triangles, and/or circles—whether these elements be text blocks, decorations, or illustrations—the layout is considered to be *geometric*, regardless of its symmetrical or asymmetrical characteristics.

Geometric forms were given a big boost in the art world of the 1920s when the famous Bauhaus design school of Germany promoted their use. Among the designs that were inspired by these teachings were two typeface families that are

FIGURE 11.5

An asymmetrical
layout

popular today—Bauhaus and Gill Sans; the characters in both families are based on geometric components.

In laying out a page, never forget that communication is your primary goal. If the reader can't easily read the page or becomes confused, you haven't accomplished your purpose. You can find this rule broken every day in magazines devoted to design or the graphic arts. Invariably, the editors will include one or more articles that invite you to turn the page rather than reading them—because the magazine has subordinated communication to design.

FREEFORM LAYOUTS

When you look at an attractive layout that doesn't seem to be symmetrical, asymmetrical, or geometric, it may be *freeform*. This is a style of layout in which there is a definite plan, but the eye is led to its significant elements by a subtle arrangement of elements that can sometimes be compared to the fitting of pieces in a small jigsaw puzzle.

Figure 11.6 is a design for the cover of an imaginary mystery novel.

Note that—because of the careful arrangement of the elements—the eye follows a roundabout path down the page. First, you're drawn to the words "A SALLY HALL MYSTERY" because this text is black, surrounded by a generous quantity of white space, and located at the top of the page.

Then you notice that the large characters to the left and below this text constitute a title for the book: "The Smoking Gun." From the title, your eye moves right and down to take in the illustration. Finally, you read the name of the author. This is a freeform layout.

The title typeface is Adobe's Ironwood, with shadow styling added. The rest of the text is printed in Helvetica Inserat, an interesting variant of Helvetica that is also available from Adobe. The illustration is from the Dynamic Graphics library.

DESIGN TIPS

When the design of a document is an important consideration, it's often helpful to enter most or all of your text elements in frames. You will then have complete freedom to drag both text and illustrations to new positions and place them in

FIGURE 11.6

A freeform layout

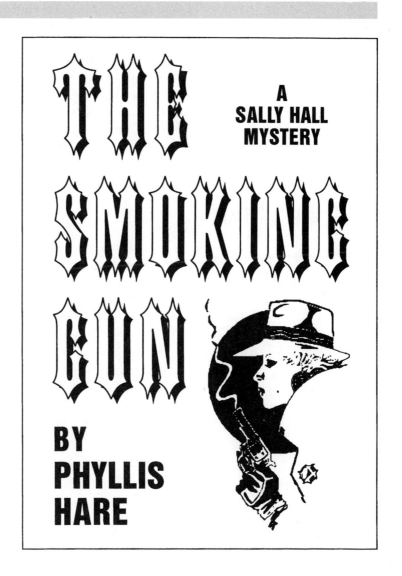

front of or behind each other to accomplish your goals. You have very few options available to you for rearranging text that is not in frames.

To enclose an entire page within a border, place the border in a frame by itself and move it behind the other components of the page using the Frame menu's Move to Back command, as demonstrated in the examples in this chapter.

Use a frame also to display a vertical line for separating columns. If you don't have a drawing or paint program in which to create the vertical line—or a satisfactory clip-art line you can insert—use MacWrite Pro to give an empty frame a border and move that frame behind the other elements of the page. Then place each column of text and the heading in their own frames and position all of the frames so that only one vertical line is visible from the frame containing the border. You can also drag a completely empty, opaque frame in front of a border to hide any part of it.

S UMMARY

If you're using decorative typefaces that require special kerning, display the Preferences dialog box and turn on both Auto Kern and Select Fractional Character Widths. Turn off the Auto Grid feature if you want to reposition objects in small increments.

Always plan the layout of your documents before you start creating them. You'll avoid many awkward combinations of elements and unnecessary revisions. Suit the kind of layout to the subject matter, rather than attempting to force the subject to fit the layout. And never lose sight of the message you're trying to convey. Make sure that your layouts give prominence to important elements and de-emphasize those that are inconsequential.

Creating Publications with Flair

CHAPTER 12

F EATURING

Using, creating, and editing stationery files

Using the files on the free disk

You can create standard files for special purposes and save them as stationery, a file format that lets you reuse copies of a file again and again without running the risk of accidentally deleting or changing the original. This chapter will tell you how to create and use stationery files—sometimes called templates.

In addition, we'll explain the completed stationery files contained on the free disk you can obtain from Image Club by mailing the coupon in the back of this book; these particular files use special typefaces and clip-art drawings, which are also included on the disk. These stationery files let you perform tasks ranging from producing eye-catching invitations to printing envelopes with both the return address and the address of the recipient positioned perfectly.

USING A STATIONERY FILE

To use a stationery file, all you have to do is open it, make the changes or additions you want, and print it.

When you open any stationery file, the title bar will show the name *Document1* (or the word *Document* followed by some other number, if you've opened other new files previously in your current MacWrite Pro session). The reason is that—since this is a stationery file—you're actually opening a copy of the original. If you want to save the file after you make changes, you can use any name you like. However, don't use the original name of the stationery file itself or you will overwrite that file stored on disk and lose it.

There is an exception to this statement. If a stationery file is *locked*, you can't overwrite it even if you do try to save another file under the same name. A locked file cannot be replaced or deleted, whether or not it's a stationery file. If you try to save a different file under the name of a locked file, you'll see a warning message similar to the one shown in Figure 12.1.

Next, you'll learn how to create and edit stationery files, including how to lock and unlock them.

CREATING A STATIONERY FILE

The first step in creating your own stationery file is merely to create, in the usual way, a MacWrite Pro document that is in the exact form you want. If other people

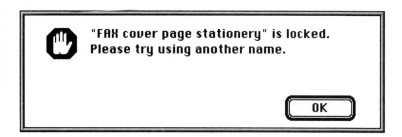

FIGURE 12.1

A warning
message seen
when trying to
save a file with the
same name as an
existing locked file

> "FAX cover page stationery" is locked.
> Please try using another name.
>
> OK

are to work with the stationery file, this means that you may want to leave certain lines blank or occupied only by a question mark or the name of an item.

In instances where the user may not be able to figure out from this kind of information what sort of answer or data entry is expected, you may want to use the alternate technique of inserting "placeholder" text that is to be replaced by the user with the actual text desired. For example, in a budget report, a placeholder paragraph might state: "Replace this text with a brief explanation of why the cost overrun occurred."

Your document should include any artwork, borders, or typefaces that you want to make part of the stationery file. The graphic images will be stored with the file. However, typefaces used will be picked up from those installed on the Mac in use. Therefore, if you want to create a stationery file that is to be used on other Macintoshes, you must make certain that each of these other Macintoshes has available the typefaces specified in your document.

Once your document is in the condition you want it, it's a good idea to print it as a final check against any errors. Then you turn it into a stationery file by the simple act of saving it in that format. Follow these steps:

1. Press ⌘-S to display the Save As dialog box (or pull down the File menu and select Save… or Save As…). The Save As dialog box will appear.

2. In the Save As section of the dialog box, press the name *Mac-Write Pro* to display the list of alternate formats in which you can save a file.

3. Highlight *MacWrite Pro Stationery* on this list and release the mouse button.

4 Give the file a name descriptive of its purpose. We recommend that you end this name with the word *stationery* to identify its file type.

5 Click the Save button to confirm your choices and save the file.

OCKING A FILE TO PREVENT CHANGES OR REPLACEMENT

As soon as any file has been created and saved to disk, you can lock the file. A locked file cannot be changed, replaced by being overwritten by another file saved with the same name, or deleted by emptying the Trash with the file in it.

N O T E

You can drag any file into the Trash, but if you then try to empty the Trash with a locked file in it, you'll see a message stating that this item cannot be deleted because it's locked. You can delete locked items in the Trash if you hold down the Option key before selecting the Empty Trash... command from the Finder's Special menu.

Use this procedure to lock a file:

1 Switch to the Finder either by clicking some visible part of it, or (under System 7) by selecting Finder from the Application menu in the upper-right corner of your screen. (If you're using a previous version of the operating system operating under MultiFinder, you can click the icon in the upper-right corner until you're returned to the Finder.)

2 Click once on the icon for the file to be locked (to select the file), pull down the Finder's File menu, and select Get Info. The Info window will appear, which tells you what kind of document is selected, its size, where it's stored, and when it was created and last modified. (You can also add comments to this window if you wish.)

3 As demonstrated in Figure 12.2, click the Locked selection box to select it.

FIGURE 12.2

Locking a file through the Info window

④ Click the close box to close the window. The file will now be locked. (You can unlock the file again by repeating the same routine, except that you *deselect* the Locked box.)

The *Stationery pad* option is provided with the operating system to let you create stationery files in programs that don't themselves have an option for saving a file as stationery. Therefore, when using MacWrite Pro, ignore this item.

TIP

Locking a file is only a method of preventing accidental changes or deletion. It's not a security system. Anyone using a Mac with a locked file can use the Get Info command to display the Info window—just as you can—and click the Locked box to unlock the file. However, you can use programs such as Apple's At Ease to provide greater protection.

At Ease supplies a simple environment with large icons suitable for children or other inexperienced computer users; through this program you can restrict access to any files you wish and even force the user to save files to a floppy rather than your hard disk. A computer user can't change or bypass At Ease without providing a password if you've activated the password option. At Ease is included with version 7.1 of the operating system.

E DITING A STATIONERY FILE

As mentioned previously, when you open a stationery file, you won't see the file; you'll see a copy. So how would you edit a stationery file?

The secret is to hold down the Option key before you select the Open... command from the File menu. Then, when you select the stationery file, you'll open the original.

However, if you make revisions to the file and try to save it again as a stationery file with the same name, you'll see the warning message shown in Figure 12.3, letting you know that you can't save the file in that way.

You'll see this message even if the file is unlocked. You have two ways around this problem. You could save the file in the regular MacWrite Pro format rather than as stationery; of course, you wouldn't want to do that because then the file wouldn't be stationery anymore. The practical alternative is to save the file as stationery, but under a new name. For example, if the original file was named "Sales Report stationery," you might want to name the revision something like "Sales Report stationery 2" or "Sales Report rev stationery." (The *rev* is short for *revised.*) Actually, the second name is better because list views of file names (any view not showing icons) often don't display the end of a long name, due to lack of space.

FIGURE 12.3

The warning message seen when trying to save the revision to a stationery file under exactly the same name

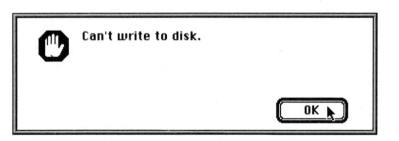

U SING THE FILES ON THE FREE DISK

The files on the free disk offered with this book are of two kinds. First, the disk includes a group of files in the MacWrite Pro stationery format that you can use to create popular types of documents with very little effort because the hard work has already been done for you. These files contain professional clip-art drawings that have already been integrated into the documents. You can use the drawings as part of these stationery files and also copy them through the Clipboard into other documents for your own purposes.

These free drawings have been supplied through the courtesy of Image Club, with the understanding that you can use them as professional clip art is normally used. This means simply that, although you're welcome to use the drawings in your own work, you can't copy them for use by others, and you can't sell them as part of a clip-art library.

Second, the stationery files also use typefaces provided by Image Club. Because of the way the Mac operating system works, the typefaces are not stored within the stationery files. You must install the typefaces into your system before you start MacWrite Pro for the purpose of using the stationery files. Chapter 6 explains how to install typefaces.

Like the clip art, you can use the Image Club typefaces in your own documents as well as in the stationery files. Some of these typefaces are part of a typeface family. If you're especially impressed by one or more of these designs, you may want to buy the entire family from Image Club.

The remainder of this chapter will explain the features of each of the stationery files on the free disk and how to use each file.

T I P

Remember that you can modify any of these stationery files to suit your own needs. You can use different typefaces or artwork and rearrange or resize the components of any layout. However, it's a good idea to work with copies and leave the files on the floppy disk in their original form. In that way, you can always revert to the original if you don't like the result of your revisions or want to use the files for a different purpose at a later date.

USING ENVELOPE STATIONERY

You can print envelopes with most printers that work with Macintoshes, by making special hardware adjustments. For example, on most LaserWriter models or compatibles, all you have to do is adjust the manual feed guides on the paper cassette to the width of the envelope and open the face-up tray at the back of the printer. (With this tray open, the paper path goes straight through the printer from front to back instead of curving, thus reducing the possibility of paper jams.) Then you can feed each envelope in by hand. (Apple and some other printer manufacturers offer envelope cassettes for automatic feeding.)

The real trick in printing an envelope is to position both the return address and the recipient's address so they will appear in the proper areas and not miss the envelope entirely. The file on your free disk called Envelope Stationery solves this problem for LaserWriter and compatible printers. (If you have some other kind of printer, use this stationery file as a guide and produce your own stationery file by experimenting with margin settings and text positioning until you get the combination to suit your needs.)

When you issue the Open... command from the File menu and select Envelope Stationery, your screen will resemble Figure 12.4 (except that you may have to scroll the Document1 window to see all of the print area if you have a small-screen monitor).

Note that this form contains placeholder text to show you where your return address should go, as well as the address of the person who is to receive the envelope. If you used the file regularly, you would probably want to revise the file to include your own name and address in the return-address area; otherwise, you would have to replace this placeholder text every time you addressed an envelope.

For the convenience of most users, we selected Helvetica 12-point Regular as the font for the addresses—since this is the default font in MacWrite Pro. However, you may want to change this—perhaps copying the typefaces and artwork used in your organization's letterhead.

We left a generous bottom margin to accommodate large envelopes, but be aware that text entered in most of the empty space below the placeholder addressee name and address will not fit onto a standard #10 envelope.

Since you insert the left end of an envelope first to print it on a LaserWriter or compatible, the horizontal option must be selected under Orientation in the Page Setup dialog box, to rotate the printing of text 90 degrees. Otherwise, the addresses would print across the end of an envelope instead of across the wide dimension. We've already made this selection for you as part of this stationery file.

FIGURE 12.4

The Envelope
Stationery file
displayed on a
large-screen
monitor

If you want to change the margin settings we used—in order to use the file on a different kind of printer—make your changes in the Document dialog box (accessed by selecting the Document… command from the Format menu). Figure 12.5 shows this dialog box with the settings used in our stationery file.

USING REPORT STATIONERY

The stationery file called Report Stationery provides an attractive, convenient format you can use for a one-page report of any kind. The word REPORT appears at the top of the page in Image Club, the modern typeface with a drop-shadow effect to which Image Club has given its company name; this type is displayed in a text

FIGURE 12.5

The Document
dialog box, with
the settings used in
the Envelope
stationery file

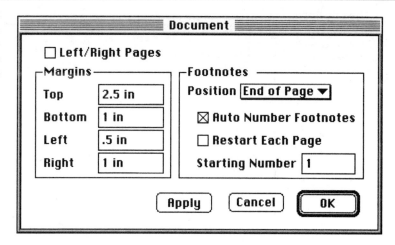

frame. As shown in Figure 12.6, the remainder of the page below this heading is offset slightly to the right and enclosed in another text frame with a border. Although we used Times Roman as the typeface in the placeholder for the body text, of course, you could use any typeface installed on your Mac.

TIP

If you open any of these stationery files that include typefaces—without having previously installed those particular typefaces in your system—you'll see a warning message saying "This document uses fonts not installed in your System file." The message will then list one of these missing typefaces by name, preceded by the word "possibly." As soon as you click OK to acknowledge the message, the file will load with the Chicago typeface automatically substituted for missing typefaces. The substitution will usually make the document look terrible; the spacing will be wrong, and some words within text frames may not even be displayed.

To correct this problem, all you have to do is close the file, clicking the No button when asked if you want to save these changes to the file. Then quit MacWrite Pro, install the missing typefaces either directly into your System folder or through a utility such as Suitcase (see Chapter 6 for instructions on installing typefaces), restart MacWrite Pro, and reopen the stationery file. The file should now be displayed correctly, without a warning message.

FIGURE 12.6

A printout of
the Report
stationery file

USING CELEBRATION STATIONERY

You can use the file called Celebration Stationery to announce almost any kind of event—from an anniversary sale in a retail store to the successful conclusion of a fund-raising campaign. The balloons, confetti, and streamers in the Image Club illustration help establish a festive mood (see Figure 12.7), as does the casual Image Club Paintbrush display typeface used. (The placeholder for your own text regarding the event uses Helvetica Bold.)

FIGURE 12.7

A printout of the
Celebration
Stationery file

USING INVITATION STATIONERY

The Invitation Stationery file is more elaborate. Here the design recalls the Art Deco period. (*Art Deco* is a distinctive design style introduced in the 1920s that continued in popularity through the 1930s.) The typeface in the heading is Image Club's Arquitectura, and the free disk provides you with a special typeface for the body copy: Image Club's Fina (seen in the "Place Your Message Here" placeholder shown in Figure 12.8).

You could use this stationery file for inviting friends, associates, customers, or employees to any party, exhibit, or show where the message can be short and you want to add an element of elegance. Each of the components of this page has been displayed in its own frame, so you can easily rearrange or delete any of them you wish.

USING NEWSLETTER STATIONERY

If your organization needs an informal newsletter, you can start with the two-column model shown in Figure 12.9—the Newsletter Stationery file.

Again, each part of the page appears in its own frame, including the placeholder for the headline (which uses Chicago as its temporary typeface). The typeface in the upper-right corner is Image Club's Comic Book Two. The word "Input" is actually part of a clip-art drawing that includes the arrow. The happy "family" within the picture frame (this "family" includes a Mac Classic computer!) is another Image Club clip-art graphic.

T I P

You may want to do some manual kerning (see Chapter 6) in stationery files in order to move some characters in the headings closer together or further apart so they will print properly on your particular printer. However, never adjust character spacing in this way until after you've printed a sample of the file. Kerning may look terrible on the screen and print perfectly because of the differences between the QuickDraw computer language used to draw the screen image and the language used by the printer.

In rare instances, your printer may not have enough memory to print a file with complicated graphic images. If you ever experience this problem with a printer using the LaserWriter print driver, you can sometimes complete the printing by selecting Unlimited Downloadable Fonts in a Document *from the Options screen of the Page*

FIGURE 12.8

A printout of the
Invitation
Stationery file

A printout of the
Newsletter
Stationery file

Setup dialog box. This option reduces memory requirements by load-ing fonts only as they're needed. Your other alternative would be to edit the file to simplify it. Remember though that a printer with limited memory may print an intricate file perfectly—but take half an hour to do it. Patience is still a virtue!

USING NOTICE STATIONERY

The Notice Stationery file reproduced in Figure 12.10 is suitable for any notice you wish to "post." The page has a burlap background such as might be used on

FIGURE 12.10

A printout of
the Notice
Stationery file

a bulletin board. Four giant, stylized pushpins hold the "Notice" in place. The unusual typeface used for the heading is Image Club's Rock-A-Billy. Of course, the message placeholder uses our old friend Helvetica.

Each of the pushpins is in its own frame, so if you want to change their size or use them individually, it's easy to do so. See Chapter 3 for instructions on moving and sizing frames.

Ⓢ UMMARY

In this chapter, you've learned how to create your own stationery files and also how to use the files included on the free disk. Stationery files can save you a great deal of time if you automate them as much as possible. So don't use a stationery file and change the typeface from Helvetica to Bookman Italic every time you open the file; in this kind of situation, create a copy of the stationery file with Bookman Italic as the default typeface, and use the copy!

Also, don't forget that you can lock a file to prevent accidental deletion.

Building a Typeface Library

CHAPTER 13

FEATURING

How to make one typeface look like many

Learning typeface classifications

Help from free typeface utilities

Using free fonts you didn't know you have

Using the standard LaserWriter typefaces

Locating new typefaces for your library

Th) here was a time when very few typefaces were available for the Macintosh. Now you can easily build an impressive library. You can choose from a bewildering array of designs, so you have the opportunity of selecting a typeface with exactly the right characteristics for presenting any message.

Of course, there are a couple of catches to this seemingly ideal situation. One drawback is that having a multitude of choices means that the inexperienced type user has the freedom to choose typefaces that are completely wrong for the job at hand. The other drawback is budget. If you have little money to spend on extra typefaces, you must take care to buy only designs versatile enough that you can reuse them again and again for many different kinds of projects.

This chapter explains how typefaces are categorized, displays samples in the various categories, and tells you how and when to use typefaces and where to buy them. You'll also learn about some helpful free utilities provided by typeface vendors.

C REATING VARIETY FROM A SINGLE TYPEFACE

If you have no money at all to spend on extra typefaces, remember that by using a little ingenuity you can make a single Macintosh typeface appear in numerous different guises.

Figure 13.1 illustrates this point. Here is the familiar Times Roman displayed in more than a dozen different ways. We generated the variations by mixing boldface, italics, capitals, small capitals, outline, and shadow effects in assorted combinations. We also combined different point sizes within the same word and compressed and stretched the spacing between characters; you can make such spacing changes either through manual kerning or by placing each character in its own transparent text frame and then dragging the characters into the relative positions you want.

FIGURE 13.1

Displaying one
typeface in
different ways

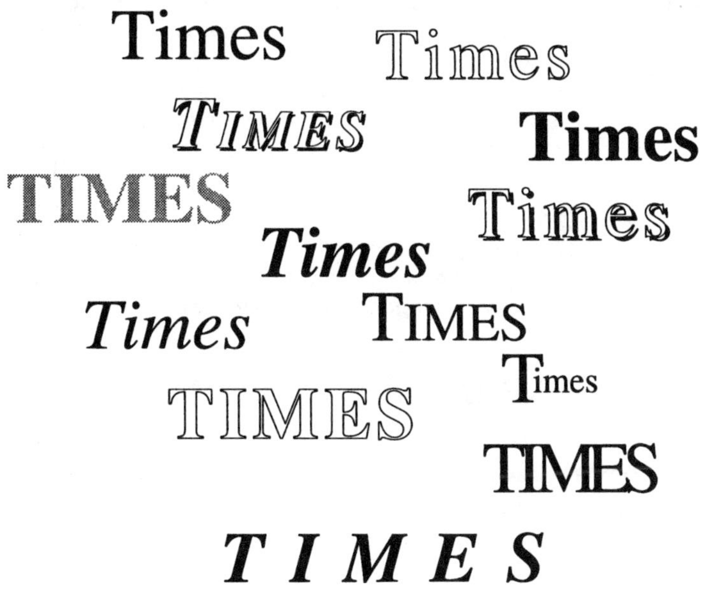

Times Times

TIMES **Times**

TIMES Times

Times

Times TIMES

TIMES Times

TIMES

TIMES

L EARNING TYPEFACE CLASSIFICATIONS

In Chapter 6 we explained some basic typeface categories, including serif, sans-serif, decorative (a term applied to certain display typefaces), script, and novelty (basically, another display subcategory). We also defined a few terms for characteristics that distinguish one font from another, including proportional and nonproportional, point size, italic, oblique, and x-height. However, if you're going to build a type library, it's helpful to be familiar with more precise terms that professionals apply to different designs. Some of these terms may be included as part of a typeface name. For example, a professional will instantly visualize specific characteristics as applying to any typeface that has the words Old Style as part of its name.

There is no complete agreement in the printing and publishing industries as to the typeface classifications to be used. Therefore, we'll give alternate names for some classifications and define subcategories used by many professionals.

T I P

Helpful clues in evaluating a typeface for your needs are knowing the name of the designer and when the face was released. Just as a writer of mystery novels is likely to infuse each story with certain characteristics and place the story in a particular period of history, every typeface designer has certain preferences, strengths, and weaknesses and produces designs that reflect the trends of the period.

This chapter provides the designer's name and the date released for many of the typefaces discussed. When you're looking for typefaces on your own, bear in mind that the name of a typeface often includes the name of its designer—examples include Gill Sans, Goudy Old Style, Benguiat Gothic, and Zapf Chancery.

DEFINING SERIF TYPEFACE CATEGORIES

In order to understand the characteristics applied to various serif typeface groups, you need to know the meaning of two additional terms used to define them: *stress* and *bracketed*.

Stress refers to the degree of incline (or the axis) formed by the relationship between the thick and thin portions of rounded letterforms such as the *bowl* (the enclosed round or oval area) of a letter like O or Q. As illustrated in Figure 13.2, there are two kinds of stress: *inclined* (wherein the axis is at a slant) and *vertical* (with little or no slant to the axis).

Bracketed refers to a curved or rounded intersection between the main vertical stroke (stem) of a character and a serif. In a character with *unbracketed* serifs, there is no rounding of this intersection. The difference is demonstrated in Figure 13.3.

The following definitions explain major serif typeface classifications, including some alternate names and subgroups:

> *Old Style.* Typefaces in this category may have been designed during the last few years, but their major design characteristics were established during the 15th to 17th centuries. They have little contrast between thick and thin strokes and feature inclined stress and bracketed serifs.

FIGURE 13.2

The difference between inclined and vertical stress

FIGURE 13.3

The difference between bracketed and unbracketed serifs

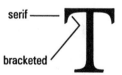

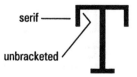

- A subgroup called *Venetian* or *Humanist* has a diagonal bar on the lowercase e (see ITC Weidemann in Figure 13.4 below).

Major categories of
serif typefaces

Old Style (Venetian, Humanist, Garald)

Goudy Old Style
ITC Weidemann

Transitional

Adobe Caslon
Baskerville

Modern (Didone)

Bauer Bodoni
ITC Fenice

Egyptian (Slab Serif, Mechanistic)

ITC Lubalin Graph
Rockwell

- Another sub-group called *Garald* or *Aldine* has a horizontal crossbar on the lowercase e and a slightly greater contrast between thick and thin strokes than the Venetian group. The name Garald is sometimes spelled Garalde and was formed by combining the names Garamond and Aldus.

Transitional. These typefaces contain characteristics of both the Old Style and Modern classifications. (Modern is defined in the next paragraph.) Since contemporary designers have incorporated whatever elements they wanted from both of these major groups, many typefaces created in the 20th century fall into the Transitional category. Transitional typefaces have a noticeable variation between thick and thin strokes, a horizontal bar on the lowercase e, an almost vertical stress, and, usually, flat-topped serifs. The characters are usually wider than their Old Style counterparts.

Modern. This style was originated in the late 18th century by designers such as Firmin Didot and Giambattista Bodoni. The last names of these two men have been combined to form the word *Didone*, an alternate term used for Modern typefaces. The Modern classification is distinguished by an extreme variation between thick and thin strokes (the thin strokes are often hairline in width), vertical stress, and, frequently, unbracketed serifs.

Egyptian. This category was introduced in England in the early 19th century and was named Egyptian because artifacts from Egypt were very popular at that time, due to the British defeat of Napoleon's expedition to that country. Egyptian typefaces are also known as *Mechanistic* or *Slab Serif* and can be readily identified by their square-cut, unbracketed serifs that are typically the same weight as the main stroke or stem. The stress is vertical.

- A subcategory of Egyptian is *Clarendon*; these typefaces have bracketed serifs.

Figure 13.4 illustrates these major serif typeface classifications.

The typefaces shown in Figure 13.4 are all well-known, suitable for many kinds of documents, and available from several vendors. The following paragraphs provide brief notes on each.

Goudy Old Style was designed in 1915 by Frederic Goudy, one of America's most respected typeface designers, and is distinguished by ascenders that are slightly higher than the capital letters; for example, compare the top of the lowercase l in *Old* with the capital O that precedes it. Goudy is an excellent choice when you want an elegant text face.

ITC Weidemann was designed by Kurt Weidemann. Kurt Strecker completed the master drawings. Released in 1983, this family has become popular as a contemporary alternative to traditional condensed typefaces.

Adobe Caslon—released in 1990—is the work of Adobe's Carol Twombly and is based on an early 18th century design by William Caslon. The United States Declaration of Independence was set in Caslon, a favorite of Benjamin Franklin, who used Caslon fonts regularly in his printing business. Over a hundred years later, author/playwright George Bernard Shaw specified that Caslon be used for all of his books.

Adobe Caslon has a smaller x-height than other recent Caslon revivals, in keeping with the original design, and is accompanied by an expert collection that adds old-style figures, small capitals, special ligatures, and other extra characters.

Baskerville was designed by John Baskerville in 1762, and its reincarnations are widely used for text throughout the world. The ITC version is called ITC New Baskerville and features a larger x-height than the version shown here.

Bauer Bodoni is considered by many the most authentic of the variations of Bodoni's original 18th-century design. Heinrich Jost created it in 1926. Its hairline thin strokes make it appropriate only for use in large point sizes if your printer has poor resolution.

ITC Fenice is the brainchild of Italian designer Aldo Novarese and was released in 1980. Its contemporary style features a combination of classic characteristics, condensed characters, a large x-height, and subtle serifs. A good choice for both text and display use, since its thin strokes are more substantial than those found in Bodoni.

ITC Lubalin Graph was created in 1974 as a seriffed companion to the sans-serif Avant Garde, designed by Herb Lubalin—one of ITC's founders—and discussed later in the chapter. Lubalin Graph features a very large x-height, prominent square serifs of the same weight as the main strokes, and simple character shapes. It prints legibly under difficult conditions and is appropriate for both text and display use.

Rockwell was created in 1933–34 by Monotype designers. One of the most famous of Egyptian or Slab Serif designs, its sturdy proportions lend authority to both paragraphs of text and headings.

N O T E

The regular (upright, non-italic) typeface in a seriffed family is often called Roman—as in Times Roman. The reason is that the design of the capital letters in early Old Style typefaces was based on the shapes of letters carved in stone on the monuments of ancient Rome.

OTHER TYPEFACE CATEGORIES

We explained in Chapter 6 that sans-serif typefaces are simply those without serifs. Script typefaces are those that imitate handwriting or hand lettering. There are more designs in both of these categories than you might realize, some of which are displayed later in this chapter.

Almost any typeface can be used in a large size for display purposes, as a title or heading. However, display typefaces are usually characterized as those intended primarily for use in large sizes. Often these styles are so ornate or detailed that they don't reproduce well in small point sizes and become difficult to read. Of course, a typeface used for display could fall into some other category too, such as Old Style or Script, because of its design characteristics.

The type style often called Old English—used in the headings of some church bulletins and Christmas cards—falls into a category called *Blackletter*. You'll see a variety of samples from this group later in the chapter.

F REE TYPEFACE UTILITIES

We mentioned Bitstream's free Analogue typeface name–finding utility in Chapter 6. Several other vendors offer useful free typeface utilities with the purchase of their typefaces.

Monotype includes a free typeface-identification utility called the Browser on the company's FoneFonts CD-ROM disk. As shown in Figure 13.5, with this utility you can select a classification such as Old Style and see a list of all typefaces on the disk included in that category.

When you select a typeface name, a large sample of the typeface is displayed, which you can print if you wish. You can also click an icon to display a brief history of the typeface, including the year it was created and the name of the designer. Another option will display the visual representation of typeface categories shown in Figure 13.6.

Type Specimen is a Varityper utility that can print a series of handy specimen pages for any typeface that is currently resident either on a printer hard disk or in the memory of a laser printer. Figure 13.7 shows the Text Sizes sample page printed for Digital Typeface Corporation's version of Goudy Old Style Regular; the point sizes range from 7-point to 18-point.

Figure 13.8 shows the Display Sizes sample page printed for the Clarendon Bold typeface also sold by Digital Typeface Corporation; the point sizes range from 24-point to 96-point.

FIGURE 13.5

Monotype's free Browser utility provides information about any typeface selected in a category, as well as a sample of the typeface.

FIGURE 13.6

The Browser includes a visual representation of major typeface categories.

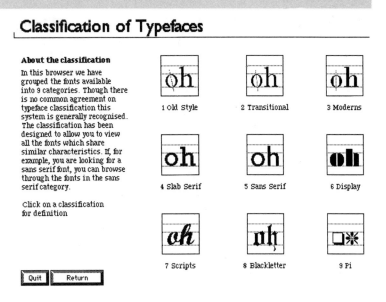

Classification of Typefaces

About the classification

In this browser we have grouped the fonts available into 9 categories. Though there is no common agreement on typeface classification this system is generally recognised. The classification has been designed to allow you to view all the fonts which share similar characteristics. If, for example, you are looking for a sans serif font, you can browse through the fonts in the sans serif category.

Click on a classification for definition

1 Old Style   2 Transitional   3 Moderns

4 Slab Serif   5 Sans Serif   6 Display

7 Scripts   8 Blackletter   9 Pi

Quit   Return

Figure 13.9 shows the first of two Pi Font sample pages printed for Dubl-Click Software's Frankfurt Ultra typeface. (The *Pi Font* in this case means all of the characters you can display and print when you hold down the Option key or the Shift-Option key combination as you strike a key on your keyboard.) Of course, none of the typefaces on these sample pages are shown here in their actual sizes, since the pages had to be reduced so they would fit into this book.

Incidentally, Frankfurt Ultra is a Dubl-Click adaptation of Frankfurter, which was designed by Letraset's Bob Newman. The typeface's combination of boldness and informality make it ideal for contemporary headings.

Letraset's Character Chooser lets you display the characters in any font in the Adobe Type 1 format and select any single character for copying through the Clipboard into any document within any application. Figure 13.10 demonstrates the selection of an accented character.

Figure 13.11 shows the result of clicking the utility's Font Info option, which will display a brief description and history of the typeface if the font file is from Letraset.

FIGURE 13.7

Text sizes of Goudy
Old Style Regular,
printed with Vari-
typer's Type
Specimen utility

Varityper Type Specimen

Text Sizes

GoudyOldStyle-Regular-DTC

A B C D E F G H I J K L M N O P
Q R S T U V W X Y Z
Æ Œ Ø
Á È Ï Ô Ù Ç
a b c d e f g h i j k l m n o p
q r s t u v w x y z
æ œ ø fi fl
1 2 3 4 5 6 7 8 9 0
( ) ~ ' ! @ # $ % ^ &
[ ] * _ + { } " " ' ' ; : ' " , . < > / ?

18-Pt. Headline

Typefaces are the tools by which human i
deas are rendered with the finest degree o
f precision. The exact emotion, the proper
emphasis, the perfect weight of a statemen
t can be conveyed only through use of the
correct typeface. In fact, a world without a
wide variety of typefaces would be as impo
verished as one without birdsong or a cha
nging sky. Typefaces are the tools by whic
h human ideas are rendered with the fine
st degree of precision. The exact emotion,
the proper emphasis, the perfect weight of
a statement can be conveyed only through
use of the correct typeface. In fact, a world
without a wide variety of typefaces would b
e as impoverished as one without birdson
g or a changing sky. Typefaces are the too
ls by which human ideas are rendered wit
h the finest degree of precision. The exact
emotion, the proper emphasis, the perfect
weight of a statement can be conveyed on
ly through use of the correct typeface. In f

9/10 on 12-pica measure

7/8

Typefaces are the tools by which human ideas are rendered with the finest degree of precision. The exact emotion, the proper emphasis, the perfect weight of a statement can be conveyed only through use of the correct typeface. In fact, a world without a wide variety of typefaces would be as impoverished as one without birdsong or a changing sky. Typefaces are the tools by which human ideas are rendered with the finest degree of precision. The exact emotion, the proper emphasis, the perfect weight of a statement can be conveyed only through use of the correct typeface. In fact, a world without a wide

8/9.5

Typefaces are the tools by which human ideas are rendered with the finest degree of precision. The exact emotion, the proper emphasis, the perfect weight of a statement can be conveyed only through use of the correct typeface. In fact, a world without a wide variety of typefaces would be as impoverished as one without birdsong or a changing sky. Typefaces are the tools by which human ideas are rendered with the finest degree of precision.

9/11

Typefaces are the tools by which human ideas are rendered with the finest degree of precision. The exact emotion, the proper emphasis, the perfect weight of a statement can be conveyed only through use of the correct typeface. In fact, a world without a wide variety of typefaces would be as impoverished as one without birdsong or a changing sky. Typefaces are the tools by which human ideas are rendered with the finest degree of precision. The exact emotion, the

10/12

Typefaces are the tools by which human ideas are rendered with the finest degree of precision. The exact emotion, the proper emphasis, the perfect weight of a statement can be conveyed only through use of the correct typeface. In fact, a world without a wide variety of typefaces would be as impoverished as one without birdsong or a changing sky. Typefaces are the tools by which human ideas are rendered

11/13

Typefaces are the tools by which human ideas are rendered with the finest degree of precision. The exact emotion, the proper emphasis, the perfect weight of a statement can be conveyed only through use of the correct typeface. In fact, a world without a wide variety of typefaces would be as impoverished as one without birdsong or a changing sky.

12/15

Typefaces are the tools by which human ideas are rendered with the finest degree of precision. The exact emotion, the proper emphasis, the perfect weight of a statement can be conveyed only through use of the correct typeface. In fact, a world without a wide variety of typefaces would be as

FIGURE 13.8

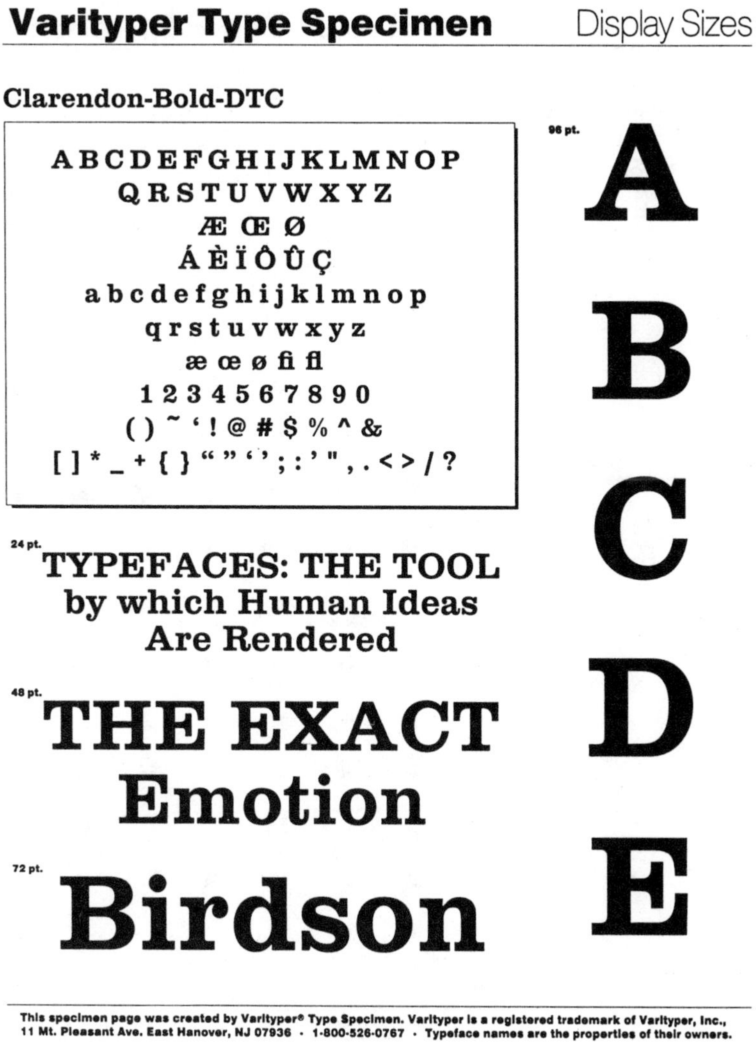

Display sizes of Clarendon Bold as printed by Type Specimen

Varityper Type Specimen   Display Sizes

Clarendon-Bold-DTC

A B C D E F G H I J K L M N O P
Q R S T U V W X Y Z
Æ Œ Ø
Á È Ï Ô Û Ç
a b c d e f g h i j k l m n o p
q r s t u v w x y z
æ œ ø fi fl
1 2 3 4 5 6 7 8 9 0
( ) ~ ' ! @ # $ % ^ &
[ ] * _ + { } " " ' ; : ' " , . < > / ?

96 pt. **A**

24 pt. **TYPEFACES: THE TOOL
by which Human Ideas
Are Rendered**

B

48 pt. **THE EXACT
Emotion**

C

D

72 pt. **Birdson**

E

FIGURE 13.9

The hidden Pi Font characters in Dubl-Click's Frankfurt Ultra, printed through Type Specimen

Varityper Type Specimen — Pi Font

FrankfurtUltraLaser

⌘ ✓ ◆

! " #

$ % & ' ( ) * + , - . /

O 1 2 3 4 5 6 7 8 9 : ;

‹ = › ? @ A B C D E F G

H I J K L M N O P Q R S

T U V W X Y Z [\ ] ^ _

` a b c d e f g h i j k

l m n o p q r s t u v w

x y z { | } ~ Ä Å Ç É

Ñ Ö Ü á à â ä å ã ç é è

ê ë í ì î ï ñ ó ò ô ö õ

ú ù û ü † ° ¢ £ ® • ß

® © TM ´ ¨ Æ Ø

¥ ª º Œ ø

This specimen page was created by Varityper® Type Specimen. Varityper is a registered trademark of Varityper, Inc., 11 Mt. Pleasant Ave. East Hanover, NJ 07936 · 1-800-526-0767 · Typeface names are the properties of their owners.

FIGURE 13.10

Selecting an
accented character
in Letraset's
Character Chooser
for pasting into a
document

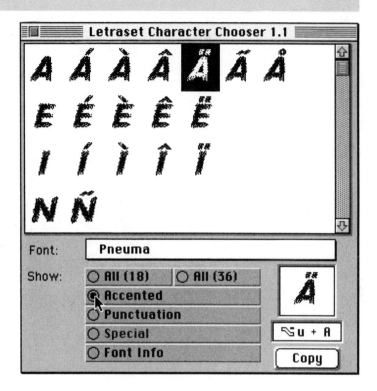

FREE FONTS YOU DIDN'T KNOW YOU HAVE

If your Mac is running under System 7, you may not be aware that the Fonts disk included with the operating system contains several fonts that are not installed automatically when you install System 7. To use these additional fonts, you can either drag them from the Fonts disk into your closed System folder or install them with a utility such as Suitcase (described in Chapter 6) or MasterJuggler (a rival product from ALSoft, Inc.).

The list of extra fonts provided varies according to the version of System 7 you're using. For example, these fonts were shipped with System 7.1: Athens, Cairo, London, Los Angeles, Mobile, San Francisco, and Venice; they're contained in a folder named Apple Classic Fonts, as shown in Figure 13.12.

FIGURE 13.11

Character Chooser
can display
background infor-
mation on any
Letraset typeface

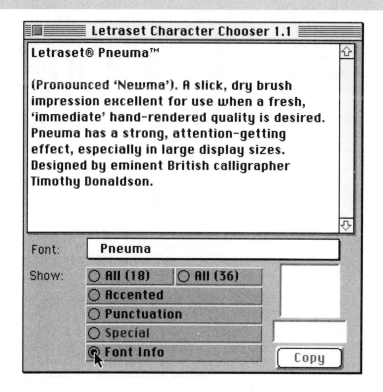

FIGURE 13.12

The Apple Classic
Fonts folder
included with
System 7.1

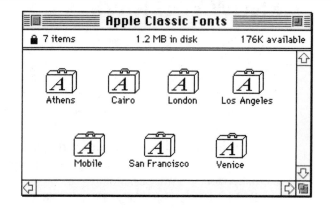

The reason the name "Classic" is applied is that these are bitmapped fonts that were supplied with the early Macintoshes. In those days, all of the Apple faces bore the names of cities.

TIP

Since the Apple Classic Fonts are bitmaps not accompanied by Adobe Type 1 or TrueType outline files for printing, the fonts may appear fuzzy if you print them in a size other than the ones furnished on the Fonts disk. You'll have to experiment to see if the quality is acceptable to you.

However, the printer drivers included with System 7 do a much better job than older drivers of smoothing rough edges as they print bitmaps in sizes that are extrapolated from actual sizes stored on disk.

Figure 13.13 shows samples of the bitmapped fonts in the Apple Classic Fonts folder, along with the font sizes available. Two of the fonts (Cairo and Mobile) are actually collections of small, useful drawings. You can see all of the drawings and the keys assigned to them by using System 7's Key Caps utility or BigCaps (both described in Chapter 6).

U SING THE STANDARD LASERWRITER TYPEFACES

If you have a printer using the PostScript language (a LaserWriter or compatible), it probably has 35 standard typefaces permanently installed (counting regular, italic, bold, and bold italic members of a family as separate typefaces, which they are).

The typical PostScript laser printer offers these Adobe Type 1 designs: Avant Garde, Bookman, Courier, Helvetica, Helvetica Narrow, New Century School-book, Palatino, Symbol, Times Roman, Zapf Chancery, and Zapf Dingbats. (*Dingbats* are symbols you can use for special emphasis—such as arrows, scissors, and check marks—or ornaments such as stars and flowers you can use to divide sections of a page or to form borders.) In addition, with the operating system you'll get Chicago, Geneva, Monaco, and New York.

Figure 13.14 shows all of these typefaces, with the exception of Geneva and New York, which the LaserWriter printer driver normally does not use.

FIGURE 13.13

The "Classic" fonts included with System 7.1

Athens comes only in an 18-point size, and may be fuzzy in other sizes such as this 20-point.

🦂✂🖌🧹🗿 (Cairo—18-point only)

𝕷𝖔𝖓𝖉𝖔𝖓 𝖎𝖘 18-𝖕𝖔𝖎𝖓𝖙 𝖆𝖓𝖉 𝖌𝖔𝖔𝖉 𝖆𝖘 𝖆 𝖍𝖊𝖆𝖉𝖎𝖓𝖌 𝖋𝖔𝖗 𝖆 𝖙𝖗𝖆𝖉𝖎𝖙𝖎𝖔𝖓𝖆𝖑 𝖊𝖛𝖊𝖓𝖙.

Los Angeles is casual, **can be bold,** *12- and 24-point.*

➡💾🔌🎵✳ (Mobile—18-point only)

San Francisco—like a random note and only in 18-point.

Venice is 14-point only and elegant.

Unless you change a Page Setup option, the driver will substitute Helvetica when you've specified Geneva in a document and will substitute Times Roman when you've specified New York. (Geneva is an old Apple sans-serif design that resembles Helvetica; New York is an old Apple serif design that resembles Times Roman, except with wider characters.) Therefore, there is no reason to use either Geneva or New York on a laser printer if they won't be printed. (Geneva is used to display all file and folder names on the Macintosh screen, unless you've changed this default under System 7 by using the Views control panel to select a different typeface.)

FIGURE 13.14

Typefaces
included with
most PostScript
laser printers

Avant Garde

Bookman

Chicago

Courier

Helvetica

Helvetica Narrow

Monaco

New Century Schoolbook

Palatino

Σψμβολ

Times Roman

Zapf Chancery

Chicago and Monaco are old nonproportional designs from Apple. Use these typefaces only if you're striving for a special effect, since their equally-spaced characters make for awkward reading. (The Macintosh menus use a proportional version of Chicago.)

Charles Bigelow designed the major Apple bitmapped typefaces for the Macintosh and was joined by Kris Holmes in creating TrueType versions that are shipped with System 7.

Courier is a nonproportional design originally developed for IBM electric typewriters. The design is clever, since narrow characters such as the lowercase i were made as wide as possible in an attempt to fill up the gaps that would otherwise appear on each side of them. Nevertheless, since Courier makes your documents appear as if they've been typed instead of produced on a computer, don't use this typeface unless this is exactly the effect you want.

Now we'll provide specific comments on the remaining typefaces included with PostScript printers. Bear in mind though that all of these designs have been overused because they're available on so many printers. If your budget will let you acquire other typefaces, do so.

Avant Garde is the sans-serif predecessor to ITC Lubalin Graph. The full name is ITC Avant Garde Gothic. (*Gothic* is another word sometimes used for sans-serif typefaces.) This family was inspired by a logo Herb Lubalin designed for *Avant Garde* magazine and was introduced in 1970 in conjunction with the founding of ITC. Its large x-height and geometric shapes still make it appear modern (in the chronological sense, not in the type-category connotation!) after all of these years. However, it's used far too often.

Bookman was designed by C. F. Griffith in 1936, but the version installed in laser printers was created by Ed Benguiat in 1975 for ITC. ITC Bookman adds readability to documents because of its large x-height and open characters and adds sophistication because of its simple but beautiful letterforms. Still, use a less familiar substitute if you have it available.

Helvetica was designed by Max Miedinger in 1957. This sans-serif design is the most frequently used throughout the world. Fortunately, because the characters are so regular and the design so neutral (it doesn't impart any noticeable style to a document), it can be used over and over without being detected. Even so, if you select some other inconspicuous typeface instead, your documents will appear fresher, and no one will know why.

Helvetica Narrow was created on a computer by simply narrowing the width of the Helvetica characters. Printing professionals consider such tampering with a design inexcusable. If it's the only sans-serif typeface you have available for squeezing many characters into a minimum space, use it. However, Helvetica Condensed is a much better typeface for the same purpose because it was designed to have narrow characters.

Century Schoolbook was designed in 1915 by Morris Fuller Benton specifically for use in children's schoolbooks. It was a modification of an 1895 design created by Theodore L. De Vinne for The Century magazine. ITC New Century Schoolbook is the version installed in laser printers. Century Schoolbook is highly readable but "typecast," if you'll pardon the pun. It's hard to look at this sturdy design with its wide characters and large x-height without thinking of children's schoolbooks.

Palatino was designed in 1950 by the noted Hermann Zapf. The characters are somewhat condensed but exquisitely formed. This is a deservedly popular family, but seen far too often because of being bundled with so many PostScript printers. Palatino is a superior face for text use.

The Symbol typeface contains useful Greek and mathematical symbols. In Figure 13.14, directly under the name Palatino, you can see the symbols you'll get if you type the characters SYMBOL with the Symbol typeface selected.

Times Roman was designed by Stanley Morison in 1932 for the London Times newspaper. Readable on newsprint or any other kind of paper and slightly condensed to conserve space, Times is the world's most popular serif typeface. Like Helvetica, it's unobtrusive and can be used frequently without calling much attention to itself. That doesn't mean you should follow the herd and use it if you have another versatile serif design you can choose in its place.

ITC Zapf Chancery is installed in PostScript printers only in its medium italic variation, although it's a complete family designed in 1979 by Hermann Zapf. Apple co-founder Steve Jobs has stated that Zapf Chancery was selected for the early LaserWriters "so people could have a typeface they could use for wedding invitations." This highly decorative design is appropriate for such uses but too busy for extended paragraphs of text. Since it's overused and easily recognizable, avoid it when you can.

ITC Zapf Dingbats is a collection of useful symbols and ornaments, designed by Hermann Zapf in 1978. Insert these symbols sparingly since they're seen very often.

ⓕ INDING THE RIGHT TYPEFACES

The remainder of this chapter deals with points to consider in selecting typefaces and introduces some interesting typefaces you might like. Since many typefaces have been used and identified in the earlier chapters, the ones shown here will—for the most part—be designs not discussed previously.

We've already mentioned that you should buy typefaces you can use again and again if your budget allows you to purchase only a few. Once you've decided on those you want, you should still proceed cautiously if the same design is available from several vendors.

The reason is that when a type vendor licenses the right to sell a typeface from the company that owns the trademark, it's usually up to the licensee to digitize the design—in other words, to turn it into a computer typeface file that you can use on your Macintosh. Some licensees digitize a design very expertly; others do it very badly. Compare samples from different vendors before you buy.

Here's a case in point: One well-known vendor digitized many typefaces at a considerable expense, only to discover too late that—through a mathematical error—each PostScript outline file would create fonts that were about 10 percent larger than the user would specify. The result was that lines of text would be too close together in an application—requiring readjustment of line spacing—and some applications would cut off part of the extremities of certain display characters. We're not going to tell you the name of the vendor, because that company is planning to correct this honest error as this chapter is being written and, hopefully, by the time you read these words, the problem will no longer exist.

Consider another example: In 1957 the Univers sans-serif typefaces were introduced—a comprehensive family designed by Adrian Frutiger. Figure 13.15 shows two different versions of his Univers Condensed Roman, *reproduced in exactly the same point size.*

Note the dramatic differences between these two unkerned specimens of, presumably, the same typeface. In the bottom rendering of the word Washington, the characters are taller than in the top version. However, the major difference is in the width and shape of the characters. For instance, the lowercase g in the bottom sample is far wider than in the top sample, and the bowl of the letter (the enclosed oval) is much more rounded—even though the weight of both samples appears to be exactly the same.

FIGURE 13.15

Two versions of
the same typeface
compared, using
the same point size
and no kerning

Washington
Washington

You could use either version of Univers without any difficulty—unless you had to match existing type in a document. Both samples are of excellent quality and would be suitable for many kinds of jobs. They're just not the same! The top specimen is Univers Condensed as sold by Digital Typeface Corporation. The bottom specimen is Zurich Condensed, the Bitstream version of Univers Condensed.

BUYING SERIF TYPEFACES

Most of the typefaces displayed in the previous chapters are serif designs, so we won't spend a lot of time discussing other serif families you might want to buy. Nevertheless, we'll call attention to a few more in order to point out some of the ramifications of purchasing type in this category.

First, take a look at Ellington, showcased in Figure 13.16. This beautiful family was designed for Monotype in 1990 by Michael Harvey and named in honor of the famous composer/pianist/bandleader Duke Ellington. Ellington is a condensed design available in four weights ranging from light through extra bold, each with italics. The characters feature variations in stroke width at unexpected points (look at the lowercase a), which mimic the hand-lettering effect of drawing with a broad-edged pen. Since Ellington is highly readable and fresh in appearance, it makes a fine substitute for the too-familiar Times and Palatino.

Another modern design we recommend highly is Italia, created in 1977 by Colin Brignall, who heads the type development operation at Esselte Letraset Ltd. This is the British company that owns both International Typeface Corporation (ITC), which creates and licenses typeface designs to other parties who then market them, and Esselte Pendaflex, which sells Letraset typefaces directly to the public as Fontek Digital Fonts.

FIGURE 13.16

Two typefaces from Monotype's Ellington family

The light that lies
In woman's eyes
Has been my heart's undoing.

—*Thomas Moore*

Italia is a modified Venetian Old Style design that uses square serifs in some instances and diagonal or sloped serifs in others. The lowercase e has a sloping crossbar reminiscent of typical Venetian fonts. Somehow Italia manages to appear both traditional and contemporary at the same time, as demonstrated in Figure 13.17.

FIGURE 13.17

Italia, a modified
Venetian design

He who sups with the devil should use a long spoon.

Italia is available in three weights, but there are no italics.

TIP

Frequently, popular serif and sans-serif families do not include italic or oblique faces. If you feel that you must have these variations, make sure that a family includes them before you buy.

One way to make your documents stand out from the crowd is to use a typeface that has only recently become available and, therefore, is rarely seen. Dante was first shown to the public in 1955, having been used in a short treatise on the life of Dante. This treatise was published by a small printshop named Officina Bodoni, established by the designer of the Dante type family, Giovanni Mardersteig.

The original metal-type version of Dante was expanded and adapted for use on the Monotype typesetting machines of the time. However, as late as 1985, John Dreyfus, a former typographical advisor to Monotype, wrote wistfully in an article for Fine Print magazine, "…I believe that by sensitive interpretation Dante could be successfully adapted for photocomposition." Fortunately, by 1992 Monotype had done considerable "sensitive interpretation" and even released a digital version of Dante for use on the Macintosh.

Figure 13.18 shows this fine design at work. Note that the strokes vary gracefully in weight, but always with great legibility. The serifs on the lowercase ascenders are angled. Dante is available in three weights, including matching italics.

FIGURE 13.18

Monotype's Dante,
long unavailable

It is better to live rich than to die rich.

—Samuel Johnson

Linotype (Linotype-Hell Company) recently released two classic typeface families previously not available for the Macintosh. One is Didot, introduced in France in 1784 by Firmin Didot, one of the sons of the man who invented the Didot point system used even today to measure type in Europe (1 Didot point = .3759 millimeters). Firmin Didot is credited with the creation of the first typefaces in the Modern classification (defined earlier in this chapter), the style later popularized by the Italian designer Bodoni. The Didot typefaces are still the book faces most often used in France. The Linotype version was designed by the famous typographer Adrian Frutiger—based on Didot's original work—and released in 1992. The new family includes a special headline version for larger sizes, as well as lowercase numerals (see Chapter 6), small capitals, and special ornaments.

Linotype's Fairfield—also released in a Macintosh version in 1992—is a larger family that offers lowercase numerals, small capitals, and swash italics. The family has four weights: light, medium, bold, and heavy. An unusual innovation is the addition of *caption* versions—typefaces that fall between the regular and italic variants in style and are intended for use in captions that will stand out from the main text of a document but be reminiscent of it. Fairfield was designed by Rudolph Rudzicka; the first typeface in the family was released in 1940, and Linotype added the remaining members over a period of many years. Fairfield is a slightly decorative design based on Old Style precepts.

In Figure 13.19, the first sample exhibits the medium and medium italic Didot typefaces. The second sample shows the medium and medium italic Fairfield typefaces, with swash italic capital letters added in the title *Through the Looking Glass*. The entire bottom sample is in the Fairfield caption variant; as you can see, it is an interpolation between the regular and italic typefaces in the family, displaying characteristics from each.

ITC Cheltenham is the work of designer Tony Stan, who in 1975 brought a distinguished old family up to date that had been introduced shortly after the turn of

Didot (Linotype):

"It's a poor sort of memory that only works backwards," the Queen remarked.

—*Through the Looking Glass* by Lewis Carroll

Fairfield (Linotype):

"It's a poor sort of memory that only works backwards," the Queen remarked.

—*Through the Looking Glass* by Lewis Carroll

Fairfield Caption (Linotype):

"It's a poor sort of memory that only works backwards," the Queen remarked.

—*Through the Looking Glass by Lewis Carroll*

the century. ITC Cheltenham Condensed features characters that are narrower than those found in many condensed typefaces. Still, Stan's version is readable even in small sizes, since it has a large x-height and thin strokes that are heavy enough to print well even under difficult conditions. You can use it to good effect in business forms that require that a large amount of material be included on a single page.

Figure 13.20 illustrates this point; it shows a portion of a speech-and-language evaluation form used by speech therapists in a public school system. ITC Cheltenham Condensed makes the form authoritative, attractive, and legible.

FIGURE 13.20

A portion of a
public-school
student evaluation
form printed in
ITC Cheltenham
Condensed

Linguistic Concepts	____ ____	Oral Direc
Sentence Structure	____ ____	Word Clas
Oral Directions	____ ____	Semantic /
RECEPTIVE LANG. SCORE	____ ____	RECEPTIV
Word Structure	____ ____	Formulate
Formulated Sentences	____ ____	Recall Sen.
Recall Sentences	____ ____	Sentence A
EXPRESSIVE LANG. SCORE	____ ____	EXPRESSI

ASSET	Raw	%ile	S.S.	WORL
Identify Labels	____	____	____	Associati.
Identify Categories				Synonym

BUYING SANS-SERIF TYPEFACES

Earlier in the book you saw several samples of sans-serif typefaces. It's easy to assume that—since these typefaces have no serifs—their clean, uncluttered lines offer little opportunity for variety and the expression of mood and character. This is not the case.

Look at Figure 13.21. Here you see an interesting quotation printed in three different typefaces. The top sample uses Helvetica. Here, indeed, you can find little character. The type is completely neutral. It presents the words without "editorializing."

The second and third samples, however, each add unique style and atmosphere to the quotation.

The second typeface in the sample is Gill Sans, designed by the renowned Eric Gill for Monotype in 1929. Gill based the typeface on geometric principles and made the design lively by including some slightly irregular characters, such as the lowercase a. There is only a subtle difference between thick and thin strokes; both are strong and will stand up under difficult printing conditions. You can use members of the Gill Sans family either for headings or for paragraphs of text. It imparts a slight aura of another era—specifically, the 1920s.

The third typeface is Image Club's Fina Heavy—basically, a display face with a definite Art Deco feeling. The contrast found in the sizes and shapes of various characters produces a continuous flow that leads the eye effortlessly from word to word and line to line. It's a beautiful typeface that must be used sparingly for two reasons: because people will remember seeing it and because its intricacies make it too difficult to read to be suitable for lengthy paragraphs of text.

FIGURE 13.21

Three different
sans-serif typefaces

Helvetica Regular:

The past is a foreign country;
they do things differently
there.

—Lesley Poles Hartley

Gill Sans Regular (Monotype):

The past is a foreign country;
they do things differently
there.

—Lesley Poles Hartley

Fina Heavy (Image Club):

The past is a foreign country;
they do things differently
there.

—Lesley Poles Hartley

The bottom line is that even those uncluttered sans-serif typefaces have personalities all their own—which must be considered when you're building a library.

T I P

A typeface is probably a sans-serif design if its name includes one of these words: Geometric, Gothic, Grotesque, or the German spelling—Grotesk.

BUYING DISPLAY TYPEFACES

Display typefaces come in so many variations that it's hard to make recommendations. What you'll want will depend largely upon the kinds of documents you produce and the amount of money you have to spend on type. If cost is not a consideration, it pays to have a large variety of display designs on hand, so that you have one that's exactly right for each situation.

Figure 13.22 shows nine examples of display typefaces that are very different from one another. They range from the casual and contemporary to formal treatments, remind you of both ethnic origins and periods of history, and feature character width that varies from ultra condensed to ultra wide. We could have shown you hundreds more.

N O T E

Remember that a display typeface can be serif, sans-serif, or script, but is assigned to the display category because it's too distinctive, intricate, or hard to read in small sizes to be considered for any use other than headings or very short paragraphs.

BUYING SCRIPT TYPEFACES

How many ways are there to imitate handwriting? As it turns out, quite a few. Figure 13.23 shows 13 different kinds of script typefaces.

Snell Black, for example, is the Bitstream version of Snell Roundhand, which was designed by Bitstream co-founder Matthew Carter. A *roundhand* is a script typeface with characters designed so they actually join one another and form continuous groups of letters when printed. A *calligraphic* typeface looks like broad-pen lettering; Vivante is an example (also known as Vivaldi). A *brush* script resembles brush lettering; in Figure 13.23, examples are Brush Script, Reporter, Salto, and Staccato 555.

FIGURE 13.22

Samples of
display typefaces

ITC BEESKNEES

Image Club Neon

IMAGE CLUB ULTRA CONDENSED SANS ONE

Croissant (URW)

BINNER (URW)

Letraset Hadfield (DTC)

Frutiger Ultra BLACK

ADOBE MESQUITE

Letraset Shamrock (DTC)

Two of the typefaces in this figure were derived from the personal handwriting of individuals. Tekton (designed by David Siegel) is based on the letterforms of Francis Ching, a Seattle architect. Nevison Casual carries the name of its designer, who based the typeface on his own handwriting.

FIGURE 13.23

Samples of script typefaces

Snell Black (Bitstream)

Cabarga Cursiva (Image Club)

Einhorn (Image Club)

Tekton (Adobe)

Nevison Casual (Image Club, etc.)

Harlow Solid (DTC, URW)

Brush Script (many vendors)

Reporter (many vendors)

Salto (Image Club)

Staccato 555 (Bitstream's Choc)

Vivante (Digital Typeface Corp.)

Biffo (Monotype)

Aritus Extra Bold Inline (URW)

BUYING BLACKLETTER TYPEFACES

The type category many people call Old English is usually referred to by professionals as blackletter. (You can buy an individual typeface named Old English too.) The blackletter classification originated from the hand-lettered manuscripts of the monasteries of northern Europe in the 15th century and is still considered appropriate for religious use, although it's also used for such very different applications as the masthead (the main logotype) of daily newspapers, including the New York Times and the Los Angeles Times. The characters are usually intricate and heavy, although there are now variations created for the express purpose of making them more suitable for non-religious purposes.

The top sample in Figure 13.24 is Cloister Black, a traditional blackletter face that exemplifies the average person's idea of an "Old English" typeface. Cloister Black belongs to the basic blackletter sub-classification called *Text* or *Textura—also known as Gotisch.* This group is characterized by angular lowercase characters that terminate top and bottom in oblique rectangles.

A typeface that has the word Text as part of its name usually belongs to the Text group. The last sample in Figure 13.24 is Goudy Text (another design by

FIGURE 13.24

Samples
of blackletter
typefaces

Cloister Black (Bitstream)

Fette Fraktur (Adobe)

American Text (Bitstream)

Mariage Drop Shadow (URW)

Blackletter 686 (Bitstream's London)

Alte Schwabacher (URW)

Goudy Text Lombardic (Monotype)

Frederic Goudy), shown here with an alternate set of capital letters drawn by Goudy in a style called *Lombardic*. This typeface, like American Text in the same figure, has design characteristics that take blackletter away from a religious feeling. In fact, you could easily envision Goudy Text with these Lombardic capital letters in the title of a book of children's fairy tales or of a book recounting the stories of King Arthur and his knights of the round table.

The second sample in Figure 13.24 is Fette Fraktur. *Fraktur* is a type of blackletter face that incorporates baroque flourishes. (The *baroque* period in Europe during the 17th and 18th centuries was characterized by extravagant ornamentation.) The next-to-last sample in this figure is Alte Schwabacher. *Schwabacher* is a blackletter variant based on cursive writing. So, again you see that the names of typefaces can often give you clues as to their appearance.

As far as the remaining samples in Figure 13.24 are concerned, URW's drop shadow version of Mariage is only one of several variations available in the company's CD-ROM typeface collection. Blackletter 686 is Bitstream's version of an elegant typeface named London (not the London included on the System 7 Fonts disk). This typeface would be perfect for a formal wedding announcement.

BUYING NON-LATIN TYPEFACES

Typefaces that aren't based on the Roman alphabet are categorized as *non-Latin*. In this classification you'll find Cyrillic (Russian), Greek, Hebrew, and Kanji (both Chinese and Japanese). Most major vendors of type for the Macintosh now offer typefaces in one or more of these alternative alphabets.

CHECKING OUT THE TYPEFACE VENDORS

If you want to buy a particular typeface, first decide if you're willing to accept a version of that typeface carrying a different name. Many so-called clone typefaces are equal in quality or better than the original; the digital type house selling the clone was simply not able to work out a licensing agreement with the owner of the trademarked name. However, other clones are of poor quality and have been produced hastily, with only a quick profit in mind.

For that matter, many licensed typefaces have been digitized by the vendor in a very unsatisfactory way. "Let the buyer beware," as the old saying goes. If you're not dealing with one of the top reputable type vendors, learn as much as you can about the characteristics of the genuine typeface and then inspect the clone carefully before you buy, to be sure it measures up.

Many type houses cross-license their libraries. This means, for example, that you can buy the entire Bitstream library on a CD-ROM disk from Varityper that also includes the Varityper library. Monotype and Adobe each sell the other's library in addition to their own. Adobe also sells typefaces from Linotype, Berthold, and Agfa. Nearly all vendors have licensed typefaces from ITC, which licenses its designs but does not sell typefaces directly.

Therefore, you have several sources for many of the typefaces shown in this book. A major exception would be original typefaces developed by Image Club; these are available only from Image Club.

If you have a CD-ROM drive and a little extra cash, buying an entire unlocked CD-ROM disk of typefaces can save you money. Those quantity discounts, you know! The least-expensive quality typeface library known to the writer that's available on a CD-ROM disk is URW's. The price of this disk is $895, which buys you 3,000 typefaces ready to use, at a cost of 30 cents per typeface.

As mentioned earlier in the book, most major companies now sell locked CD-ROM disks for a minor service charge. Once you have such a disk, you can provide your credit-card number by telephone to have specific typefaces unlocked for instant use.

If you don't have a CD-ROM drive or hundreds or thousands of dollars to spend on typefaces in a single transaction, you can buy individual typefaces from most vendors and receive them by mail or through an express delivery service.

You can also find free and shareware typefaces on computer bulletin boards—provided you have the modem and communications software required to log on to the bulletin board. Remember, shareware products are those you receive free but are expected to pay for if you like and use them. These products are usually developed by talented hobbyists or the operators of small software businesses who use this method of distribution and sales because it's inexpensive. You're on the honor system here.

L EARNING MORE ABOUT TYPEFACES AND THEIR DESIGNERS

If you'd like to know more about particular typefaces and their designers and you don't have a Monotype CD-ROM disk containing the company's Browser utility described earlier in the chapter, you still have many other options. For example, if you have a CD-ROM drive and the popular Grolier Multimedia Encyclopedia

CD-ROM disk, you'll find several articles there on related subjects. Figure 13.25 shows this disk's biography of type designer John Baskerville. An article on typefaces explains the style classifications we've defined. Another article discusses type as an element in book design.

Apple is now selling inexpensive Macintoshes with a CD-ROM drive built in. Nevertheless, if you don't have a CD-ROM drive for your Mac nor the extra money required to add one, you can obtain good information free of charge or for a very minor cost. Letraset offers an excellent booklet called The Typeface Selector that displays many of its Fontek typefaces along with comments on each face and information about its designer. Agfa has published a helpful booklet named The Art & Technology of Typography. In addition, your public library may have one or more of the following full-length books, which can also be purchased through any bookstore:

- *Anatomy of a Typeface* by Alexander Lawson

- *The Encyclopaedia of Type Faces* by Berry, Johnson, and Jaspers

FIGURE 13.25

The Grolier Multimedia Encyclopedia discusses type designer John Baskerville.

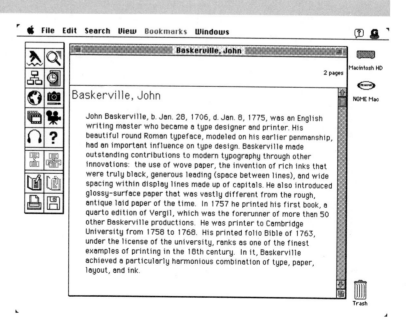

- *Modern Encyclopedia of Typefaces* by Lawrence W. Wallis
- *The Thames and Hudson Manual of Typography* by Ruari McLean

On the back cover of *Anatomy of a Typeface*, you'll find this perceptive statement, which could well serve as a commentary on our chapter:

> "To the layman, all printing types look the same. But for typographers, graphic artists, and others of that lunatic fringe who believe that the letters we look at daily (and take entirely for granted) are of profound importance, the question of how letters are formed, what shape they assume, and how they have evolved remains one of passionate concern."

S UMMARY

You can buy typefaces today for use on your Macintosh that simply could not be found a few years ago. These choices range from famous typefaces that were available originally only in metal fonts or through the use of an expensive typesetting machine to exciting new designs specifically created for use in electronic type composition on a computer. However, if you have no money to buy any of these, never forget that you can make a few typefaces look like many through the careful application of style attributes such as boldface and shadow.

When you do buy typefaces, make sure that you'll be able to use your selections frequently enough to justify the purchase price. Use key words in typeface names such as Old Style, Modern, and Text to help you find the styles you want. As you become familiar with the work of certain designers, use their names as clues to design factors and periods of history that may be reflected in their typefaces.

Buy in quantity if you can, since you'll usually obtain substantial discounts by buying several type families at a time or by purchasing an unlocked CD-ROM disk.

Creating Your Own Typefaces

CHAPTER 14

F EATURING

Using multiple master typefaces

Creating new typefaces with Kernus

Designing typefaces with Fontographer, FontStudio, and Ikarus M

Converting a typeface to a different format

Why would you want to create your own typefaces? There are several possible answers to this question. Of course, you may want to design a new typeface to fulfill an artistic urge or to sell for strictly a profit motive. On the other hand, you may have a more modest objective—perhaps a need for a slightly different version of an existing typeface that will fit better into a specific area of one of your documents.

Creating your own typefaces can be simple and almost automatic, or tedious and demanding—depending upon the software you're using and the goals you have in mind. You'll experience one of the semiautomatic methods if you use *multiple master* typefaces; these products incorporate a new technology created by Adobe that lets you vary font weight, character width, and spacing to suit your own needs. Other products have capabilities that range from changing only character spacing to providing sophisticated tools for modifying characters or designing and creating new characters and complete original typefaces. This chapter explains all of these ways of enhancing your MacWrite Pro documents.

U SING MULTIPLE MASTER TYPEFACES

Fortunately, MacWrite Pro does support the use of multiple masters. (Some applications do not, including QuarkXPress—except for version 3.1 or higher with a special multiple master extension.) Adobe is sharing the multiple master technology with other vendors, so you'll see many more of these typefaces in the near future. In fact, right now you can create your own multiple master typefaces by using the Fontographer type-design program discussed later in the chapter.

REASONS FOR MODIFYING A TYPEFACE

Why would you want to change the boldness, character width, or spacing of a perfectly good, professional typeface? As suggested above, one obvious answer would be to expand or condense type so that it will fit precisely into a specific area of a document without changing the point size. Such an area might be a text frame you've set up to contain a headline or the interior of a decorative box border you've purchased as clip art.

You might also want to change a typeface so that it will print better under difficult conditions. For example, if you're using an inkjet printer such as the

StyleWriter with very porous paper, you may want to make the characters lighter (less bold) because they will appear bolder when printed due to the way the ink will spread and be absorbed as it's sprayed onto the paper.

Another, less-apparent reason for change is to improve the appearance of a font generated from a typeface designed for a different point size.

For example, a text typeface in the Adobe Type 1 format is usually designed so that it's optimized for a 12-point size—on the theory that the purchasers of a typeface intended primarily for paragraphs of text will use a 12-point size (or close to it) much more often than any other. If you decide to use that typeface in a 72-point size as a heading or in a 6-point size as a footnote, your Macintosh will obligingly use the outline file to create the 72-point or 6-point font you've specified. However, the characters in the 72-point font may appear too heavy and spaced too far apart; the characters in the 6-point font may appear too light and too close together.

Multiple masters can correct these problems in ways far more comprehensive than merely adjusting the spacing between characters (a linear solution). First, the technology creates a new version by employing non-linear interpolation along the optical size axis between large and small master versions of the design. Letter-spacing and kerning are varied according to the size wanted. In addition, you can specify the width and weight of the characters of new fonts, within the limits set by the designer.

WHAT YOU NEED TO USE MULTIPLE MASTERS

To use multiple master typefaces, you need a Mac with at least 4 MB of RAM (random-access memory) if you're running System 7. If you're running System 6, it must be version 6.0.4 or later, with Finder 6.1 or later, Font / DA Mover 3.8 or later, and a minimum of 2 MB of RAM.

Your Mac must have both a hard disk and one floppy drive. For output, you can use any printer, typesetter, or film recorder with genuine PostScript, or non-PostScript printers such as an ImageWriter or StyleWriter that use the QuickDraw language for printing.

DANGER

Many printers are advertised as supporting PostScript that are actually using a clone of the PostScript language. These printers will usually print simple documents correctly, but will occasionally have problems with more intricate documents. When you try to use multiple master typefaces with a PostScript clone printer, the problems may become more serious. Some of these clones will not print the typefaces at all; others will print them incorrectly—for example, ignoring weight settings such as boldface or introducing unwanted spaces when you switch fonts within a document.

If multiple master typefaces are important to you, be sure to print tests using them on any PostScript clone printer you're considering buying.

To use multiple masters, you need certain utility software, some of which is provided with your purchase of a multiple master typeface. One product is not provided that is necessary if you're printing to a PostScript printer: version 5.2 or later of the LaserWriter driver. If you use a PostScript printer such as a LaserWriter, you probably have this driver already. Bear in mind though that the current version when this book was written was 7.1.1. If you're using an older version, it would be a good idea to ask your Apple dealer for an update.

TIP

You can find the version number of your LaserWriter driver in the upper-right corner of your Print dialog box.

The utility disk supplied with all Adobe multiple master typefaces includes these utilities either required or helpful in working with multiple masters: Adobe Type Manager, Adobe Type Reunion, the Font Creator, the Multiple Master INIT, and the Font Downloader. Here's what they'll do for you:

- *Adobe Type Manager* (version 3.0 or later). Lets you display type without jagged edges in any size you select and also print these PostScript typefaces on non-PostScript printers.

- *Adobe Type Reunion* (version 1.0.3 or later). Groups and displays the typefaces on your Font menu in the families to which they belong. This convenient reorganization of the menu means that you don't have to scroll through a long menu to determine which family members are available for selection. The use of Type Reunion is essential when you work with these typefaces because (as explained in a later section) the name of an individual multiple master typeface or font consists primarily of numbers and does not tell you to which typeface family it belongs.

- *The Font Creator.* The utility through which you actually create new multiple master fonts.

- *Multiple Master INIT.* A file that is loaded automatically when you turn on your Mac; this INIT is required in running the Font Creator.

- *The Font Downloader* (version 5.03 or later). A utility you can use for copying outline typefaces to your printer memory or to a hard disk attached to your printer. Although the operating system downloads typefaces to the printer memory automatically when you print a document through MacWrite Pro or another application, you may want to use this utility to store frequently used typefaces in the printer and/or its hard disk in order to avoid downloading and thereby speed up the printing process. Don't use the Font Downloader unless you have extra printer memory or a printer hard disk.

We recommended earlier in the book that you buy Adobe Type Manager and Adobe Type Reunion. As the above list indicates, you'll get both utilities free with your purchase of an Adobe multiple master typeface.

INSTALLING THE UTILITIES

The first requirement in installing a multiple master typeface is to install the utilities. Of course, you need to do this only once. When you install your second or third multiple master typeface, you can ignore this section of the chapter.

Incidentally, you can't install a new version of a utility currently being used by your system by simply copying the new version into the System folder and having it overwrite the old version. The reason is that the operating system won't let you overwrite a utility currently in use.

Follow these steps to install the utilities:

1 Locate the Multiple Master Utilities disk. (It should be one of three disks provided in the typeface package.)

2 If your system includes previously installed, earlier versions of Adobe Type Manager and/or Adobe Type Reunion and you're running under System 7, double-click your System folder to open it and drag any of these files out of the folder into the Trash: ~ATM (in the Control Panels sub-folder), ~ATM 68000, ~ATM 68020/030, and Type Reunion (in the Extensions sub-folder); you'll have to empty the Trash later, after you complete the installation and restart your Macintosh.

3 If your system includes previously installed, earlier versions of Adobe Type Manager and/or Adobe Type Reunion and you're running under System 6, follow the instructions in step 2, with these exceptions: you should find all of the files in the main System folder rather than in subfolders, and you must drag the files out of the folder onto the desktop instead of into the Trash. (System 6 won't let you drag files currently in use into the Trash.)

4 Click the close box in the upper-right corner of the System folder window to close the folder.

5 Insert the Utilities disk into a floppy drive and double-click the disk icon to open it. The disk contents should resemble Figure 14.1.

6 Double-click the Read Me file on the disk, which will start the Teach Text utility also included on the disk and display the Read Me file so you can read it. This file will contain the latest information about installation and about incompatibilities that may exist between the multiple master files and other applications, so read the file carefully. It would be a good idea to print the file too, so you can have it handy for future reference.

7 If your computer is a Mac Plus, Classic, Portable, SE, or PowerBook 100, drag the icon named ~ATM 68000 from the Utilities disk into your *closed* System folder.

FIGURE 14.1

The contents of a typical multiple master Utilities Disk

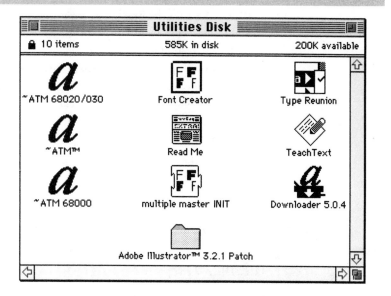

8 If your computer is any other Macintosh model, drag the icon named ~ATM 68020/030 from the Utilities disk into your *closed* System folder.

9 Regardless of the type of Mac you have, drag the icon named ~ATM from the Utilities disk into your *closed* System folder. If you're running under System 7, an Alert message will ask your permission to place this file where it belongs (which is in the Control Panels sub-folder). Click OK to give your approval.

10 Drag the following additional files from the Utilities disk into your *closed* System folder: Type Reunion and the Multiple Master INIT. If you're running under System 7, click OK in response to Alert messages.

11 Drag the icons for the Font Creator and the Downloader into any folder where you normally keep utility programs. *Do not store these files in the System folder.*

12 Restart your Mac so the newly installed files will be recognized by the operating system.

13 If your Mac is running under System 7 and you dragged old utility files into the Trash, you can now empty the Trash to delete these files from your hard disk. (This version of the operating system won't let you delete files that are currently in use, although you can move them into the Trash. Since restarting your Mac makes the system use the new utility files you placed in the System folder, you can now empty the Trash containing the old files.)

14 If your Mac is running under System 6, drag into the Trash any old utility files you moved to the desktop, then empty the Trash.

Figure 14.1 also shows an Adobe Illustrator patch, required to update older versions of Illustrator so they will support multiple masters.

INSTALLING THE TYPEFACES

Your multiple master typeface package should contain three disks: the Utilities disk you've already used, plus two typeface disks—one labeled Supplemental Disk (shown as containing Primary Fonts) and the other carrying the names of the typefaces (such as Minion and Minion Italic) and also listing AFM files as included. *AFM files* are Adobe Font Metrics files, used by very few applications and by some typeface design and modification utilities. Unless you know that you'll be needing AFM files, don't install them; they take up a lot of disk space.

The so-called Primary Fonts are the bitmapped fonts you need to install as starting points for creating new multiple master fonts; they're stored in a suitcase within a folder named Primary Fonts on the Supplemental Disk. (Bitmapped fonts on a Macintosh are always stored in special files with icons in the form of suitcases—unless the fonts have been installed into the System folder under a version of the operating system earlier than version 7.1, in which case the fonts are stored instead inside the System file itself.)

Since typefaces in the Adobe Type 1 format require outline printing files in addition to the bitmapped versions, the outlines to be installed are stored in a folder named Outline Fonts on the other typeface disk. The AFM files are stored in a separate folder on this disk.

N O T E

The following sections refer both to Macintosh suitcase files, which store bitmapped fonts, and to the Suitcase utility for managing typefaces; the utility is explained in Chapter 6 and is published by Fifth Generation Systems. Be careful not to confuse the files with the utility. When the word Suitcase begins with a capital letter in the text that follows, the reference is to the utility.

Installing the Typefaces under System 7 without Suitcase

If your Mac is running under System 7 and you're not using a utility such as Suitcase to manage your typefaces (see Chapter 6), follow these steps to install the typefaces:

1 Insert the Supplemental Disk into your floppy drive and double-click to open the disk. Then drag the Primary Fonts folder to the *closed* System folder on your hard disk.

2 When you see an Alert message, click OK to continue. The bitmapped fonts will be copied to the System folder and stored within the System file itself—or, under System 7.1 or later, stored in a special Fonts folder within the System folder. The Primary Fonts folder used for installation and the suitcase inside it that contained the fonts on the floppy disk will both disappear.

3 Click the close box to close the Supplemental Disk and drag the disk into the Trash to eject it.

4 Insert the other typeface disk into your floppy drive.

5 Double-click to open the disk and drag the Outline Fonts folder to the *closed* System folder on your hard disk.

6 When you see an Alert message, click OK to continue. The outline typefaces will be copied into the Extensions folder within your System folder (or into the Fonts folder within the System folder under System 7.1 or later), and the Outline Fonts folder that contained the typefaces will disappear.

7 If you'll be using a program that requires AFM files, follow the directions that came with that program as to where to store these files.

8 Click the close box to close the floppy disk and drag the disk into the Trash to eject it.

Installing the Typefaces under System 6 or 7 With Suitcase

If you're using the Suitcase utility for managing your typefaces, you install a multiple master typeface in the same way as other typefaces to be used with Suitcase. Follow these steps:

1 Create a new folder on your hard disk (with the New Folder command on the Finder File menu) to store the bitmapped fonts and the printer outlines that make up the multiple master typeface. We suggest that you give the folder a name such as Myriad Multiple Masters (if you're installing the Myriad typeface). If you normally store all of your typefaces within a special folder (called Fonts, perhaps), you can drag this new folder into your existing typeface folder.

2 Insert the Supplemental Disk into your floppy drive and double-click to open the disk. Then double-click to open the Primary Fonts folder, and drag the font suitcase into the new folder you created on your hard disk.

3 Click the close box to close the Supplemental Disk and drag the disk into the Trash to eject it.

4 Insert the other typeface disk into your floppy drive and double-click to open the disk. Then double-click to open the Outline Fonts folder, and drag the icons for the printer outline files into your new folder on the hard disk.

5 If you'll be using a program that requires AFM files, follow the directions that came with that program as to where to store these files.

6 Click the close box to close the floppy disk and drag the disk into the Trash to eject it.

The contents of your new multiple master typeface folder should now resemble Figure 14.2. *You must store the suitcase containing the bitmapped fonts at the same level as the typeface printer outline files*, as shown in this figure, in order for any Adobe Type 1 or Type 3 typeface to work with the Suitcase utility. You can't store the suitcase and the outline files in separate folders.

Finally, follow the instructions in your Suitcase manual to add the multiple master typeface to the list of active typefaces so that the operating system will recognize it.

FIGURE 14.2

To use the Suitcase utility, store suitcase and printer outline files in the same folder.

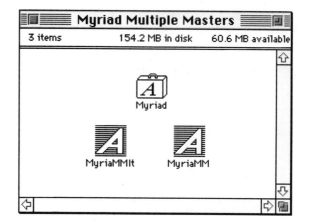

Installing the Typefaces under System 6 without Suitcase

If your Mac is running under some version of System 6 and you're not using a utility such as Suitcase, you must use the Font/DA Mover provided with the operating system in order to install your typefaces. Follow these steps:

1. If you're using MultiFinder, switch back to the Finder before starting the installation.

2. Insert the Supplemental Disk into your floppy drive.

3. Open the Font/DA Mover. Its dialog box will automatically show on the left a list of the fonts currently installed in your

System file.

4 Click the Open... button. The name on the button will change to Close, and you'll see the Open dialog box.

5 Change disks and folders in this dialog box until you locate the Primary Fonts folder on the Supplemental Disk, and click the Open button.

6 Select the suitcase file, and click Open again to open the suitcase. The right list box in the main Font/DA Mover dialog box will now display a list of the bitmapped fonts stored in the suitcase.

7 Hold down the Shift key and click to select all of the font names shown in the right list box, then click Copy. The fonts will be copied into the System file within your System folder.

8 Close the Font/DA Mover, and eject the Supplemental Disk by dragging it into the Trash.

9 Insert the other typeface disk, and open the Outline Fonts folder.

10 Drag the icons for the printer outline files into your *closed* System folder.

11 If you'll be using a program that requires AFM files, follow the directions that came with that program as to where to store these files.

12 Click the close box to close the floppy disk and drag the disk into the Trash to eject it.

If You're Printing with an Apple Personal LaserWriter NT

You may have difficulties in printing multiple master typefaces from some applications if you're using an Apple Personal LaserWriter NT printer. Apple provides an upgrade kit that will upgrade a Personal LaserWriter NT to the Personal LaserWriter NTR, which does not have this compatibility problem.

To print multiple master typefaces with a Personal LaserWriter NT, you must create a new folder named Other Fonts and store the printer outline files in that folder.

CREATING A MULTIPLE MASTER TYPEFACE

Once you have all of the necessary components installed, you're ready to create new multiple master typefaces. These new typefaces are created by using an existing primary font as a starting point and then building a new font by interpolating between the characteristics of this primary font and another primary font with characteristics at the other end of the scales used. These scale characteristics are identified by numbers that represent positions along a design axis. All current multiple master typefaces have at least three design axes: weight, width, and optical size (roughly related to point size).

For example, the default primary font in the Minion multiple master typeface has a weight of 367 (based on a range specified by the designer of 345 to 620), a width of 585 (based on a range of 450 to 600), and an optical size of 11 (based on a range of 6 to 72). Because of these characteristics, this typeface is identified as regular (as distinguished from condensed, semi-bold, or bold). If you wanted to create a similar typeface that was semi-bold, you would drag the weight slider to the right in the Font Creator dialog box, changing the weight of 367 to a higher number. (See the example later in the chapter.)

Naming Multiple Master Typefaces

The primary fonts included with a multiple master typeface are named in an unusual fashion:

- Each name starts with a number representing its weight setting on the sliding scale, followed by a two-letter code placing that setting into a category such as light, regular, or bold.

- Next in the name you'll see a number representing its width setting, followed by a two-letter code placing the font into a width category such as condensed, normal, or extended.

- Finally, the name will include a number representing the optical size of the font, followed by the code OP for optical; this number might be 11 (for an optical size corresponding to 11-point) or 72 (for an optical size corresponding to 72-point).

Thus, the name of the default primary font described in the previous section is *367 RG 585 NO 11 OP*. When you see a name like this on your Font menu, it's quite different from seeing a name like Minion Regular!

Fortunately, thanks to the use of Adobe Type Reunion, these strange primary-font names appear only on a submenu that will pop up when you highlight a name like *Minio MM* (for Minion multiple master) on the regular Font menu. So you can readily detect to which typeface family these strange coded names belong.

When you create your own typefaces, the two-letter code for weight changes to *wt* and the two-letter code for width changes to *wd*. This is how you can quickly differentiate the typefaces you've created from the standard primary fonts on the sub-menu.

In addition to the weight, width, and optical size axes, some multiple master typefaces have a fourth axis: style. The function of this axis depends upon the typeface design. Moving the slider on this axis could change a four-axis typeface from a style with prominent serifs to a style with subtle serifs and, finally, to a sans-serif style with no serifs at all; another option would be to use a style axis to vary the direction and size of a shadow for each character, as demonstrated in Figure 14.3.

The table below lists the two-letter codes used in the names of multiple master typefaces, with their meanings. Of course, a single typeface will probably not offer all of the variations shown because the artist who created the typeface has not considered some of them appropriate for the design. The lowercase codes shown in the table at the left within parentheses will appear in the names of the new custom typefaces you generate yourself. The codes in capital letters appear in the names of the primary fonts from which your versions are generated.

NAME CODES FOR MULTIPLE MASTER TYPEFACES

weight (wt)	XL	Extra Light
	LT	Light
	RG	Regular

NAME CODES FOR MULTIPLE MASTER TYPEFACES

weight (wt)	XL	Extra Light
	LT	Light
	RG	Regular
	SB	Semi-bold
	BD	Bold
	BL	Black
	XB	Extra Black
width (wd)	XC	Extra Condensed
	CN	Condensed
	SC	Semicondensed
	NO	Normal
	SE	Semiextended
	EX	Extended
	XE	Extra Extended
optical size (op)	OP	Optical size
Style (st)	Dependent upon the individual typeface.	Listed in the specimen book for the typeface.

Using the Font Creator

To create a new typeface from a multiple master, follow these steps:

1 Locate the Font Creator utility in the folder in which you've stored it.

2 Double-click the Font Creator icon to load the utility. You'll see the Font Creator dialog box shown in Figure 14.3.

3 Press the downward-pointing arrow at the left-center position in the dialog box to reveal the names of the typeface designs available, highlight the one you want, and release the mouse button. Figure 14.3 shows Adobe Minion as selected.

FIGURE 14.3

The Font Creator
dialog box with its
default settings,
ready to generate
new typefaces
from the Adobe
Minion multiple
master

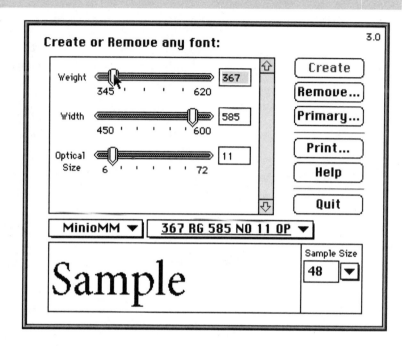

④ Press the downward-pointing arrow to the right of the selection box showing the typeface names to reveal the names of the primary fonts available for the design you've selected. Highlight the name of the font you want to use as a starting point for your new typeface, and release the mouse button. Figure 14.3 displays the default primary font, 367 RG 585 NO 11 OP; the default font name is always underlined on the pop-up list. As soon as you've made a selection, the sliders at the top of the dialog box will move to the positions specified for the font axes in the name of the primary font.

⑤ Drag the sliders to make the changes you want for your new typeface in the weight, width, optical size, and style (if available) axes. You'll want the optical size to be the same as the point size in which you'll most often use the new typeface. The sample box at the bottom of the dialog box will show the effect of your changes. The default font size in the sample box is 48 pt.

6 To change the default sample point size, press the downward-pointing arrow in the Sample Size box to pop up a menu of the sizes you can use for this display, in the range 9 pt. to 48 pt. Simply highlight a different size and release the mouse button to see the sample in a size that may be closer to the size of the typeface variation you plan to create. In addition, you can click in the area containing the sample text itself and type different text, which will thereafter be displayed instead of the default word Sample.

7 When you've completed the selections for your new typeface, you can click Print... to print a sample page before actually creating the typeface with these settings. However, the sample page will show the result of your choices displayed only in sizes ranging from 7.9 pt. to 13.17 pt.

8 At any time you can click the Help button to view a help screen.

9 Click the Create button to generate the new typeface, then click Quit to close the Font Creator utility.

The Font Creator does not create a new printer outline file for any of your new typefaces. It creates only a new bitmapped font that will be stored within the System file in your System folder if you're not using Suitcase. If you *are* using Suitcase, this new bitmapped font will be stored instead within the font suitcase for the original multiple master typeface (such as Minion MM or Myriad MM) — wherever you have that suitcase stored on your hard disk. When you use your new typeface, your system will generate it for printing from the existing multiple master printing outline, using the new bitmapped font for guidance as to the changes to be made.

Figure 14.4 shows the settings and the resulting typeface name for a new typeface based on the Adobe Minion multiple master. As you can determine from looking at the settings, this variant is to be bold (a high weight setting—582), as condensed as possible (with narrow characters, determined by the low width setting—450), and as large as possible (using the maximum optical size setting—72).

Figure 14.5 shows the sample page the Font Creator printed using the settings in Figure 14.4. A text sample from an essay by Ralph Waldo Emerson is reproduced in seven different sizes, preceded by a sample alphabet. Seeing this 8.5- by 11-inch page reduced as it must be to fit in this book makes it difficult to

FIGURE 14.4

The settings and name for a new bold, condensed, 72 pt. typeface to be generated from Adobe's Minion multiple master

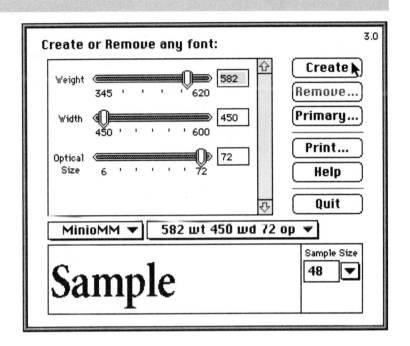

judge the quality of the samples reproduced. So you'll have to take our word for it that they don't look good. Of course, the reason is that the new typeface was generated for a 72-pt. size but that the sample page shows only sizes ranging from 7.9 pt. to 13.17 pt. Therefore, the type looks too heavy with insufficient spacing between the characters.

You can delete any typeface generated or even any primary font by clicking the Remove... button and then selecting its name from the list that will appear. You can regenerate any primary font deleted by clicking the Primary... button and then selecting its name from the list that will appear.

Why would you want to delete a primary font? Since the Font Creator can regenerate them, you might want to delete primary fonts you don't need at the moment in order to save space on a crowded hard disk.

If you delete typefaces you've created, you can restore them through the Font Creator only by recreating them again from scratch. However, a few applications (including Adobe Illustrator) have the ability to restore typefaces you've created, used in a document within the application, and later deleted from your system through the Font Creator. Most applications will simply replace the missing typefaces with Chicago.

Figure 14.6 shows the Alert message you'll see after issuing the command within the Font Creator to delete either a primary font or a typeface you've created

---

FIGURE 14.5

A sample page generated for a 72-pt. typeface from the Minion

MinioMM_582 wt 450 wd 72 op Specimen

ABCDEFGHIJKLMNOPQRSTUVWXYZ
abcdefghijklmnopqrstuvwxyz&0123456789
ÆÁÂÀÄÅÃÇÉÊËÈÍÎÏÌÑŒÓÔÒÖÕØÚÛÙÜŸæáâàäåãçéêëèíîïìñ
œóôòöõøßúûùüÿ£¥ƒ$¢¤™©®@ªº†‡§¶*!¡?¿.,:;„"""' ‚‚,,…'"<>
«»()[]{}|/\‐‒—–·'´`^¨˜°~¯˘,·o#%‰=-+*~<‡>+¬°∧/·|

Character set
12.16

At the gates of the forest, the surprised man of the world is forced to leave his city estimates of great and small, wise and foolish. The knapsack of custom falls off his back with the first step he makes into these precincts. Here is sanctity which shames our religions, and reality which discredits our heroes. Here we find nature to be the circumstance which dwarfs every other circumstance, and judges like a god all men that come to her. We have crept out of our close and crowded houses into the night and morning, and we see what majestic beauties daily wrap us in their bosom. How

7.9

At the gates of the forest, the surprised man of the world is forced to leave his city estimates of great and small, wise and foolish. The knapsack of custom falls off his back with the first step he makes into these precincts. Here is sanctity which shames our religions, and reality which discredits our heroes. Here we find nature to be the circumstance which dwarfs every other circumstance, and judges like a god all men that come to her. We have crept out of our close and crowded houses into the night

8.10

At the gates of the forest, the surprised man of the world is forced to leave his city estimates of great and small, wise and foolish. The knapsack of custom falls off his back with the first step he makes into these precincts. Here is sanctity which shames our religions, and reality which discredits our heroes. Here we find nature to be the circumstance which dwarfs every other circumstance, and judges like a god all men that come to her. We have

9.12

At the gates of the forest, the surprised man of the world is forced to leave his city estimates of great and small, wise and foolish. The knapsack of custom falls off his back with the first step he makes into these precincts. Here is sanctity which shames our religions, and reality which discredits our heroes. Here we find nature to be the circumstance which dwarfs every other circumstance, and judges like a

10.13

At the gates of the forest, the surprised man of the world is forced to leave his city estimates of great and small, wise and foolish. The knapsack of custom falls off his back with the first step he makes into these precincts. Here is sanctity which shames our religions, and reality which discredits our heroes. Here we find nature to be the circumstance which dwarfs every

11.14

At the gates of the forest, the surprised man of the world is forced to leave his city estimates of great and small, wise and foolish. The knapsack of custom falls off his back with the first step he makes into these precincts. Here is sanctity which shames our religions, and reality which discredits our heroes. Here we find nature to be the

12.16

At the gates of the forest, the surprised man of the world is forced to leave his city estimates of great and small, wise and foolish. The knapsack of custom falls off his back with the first step he makes into these precincts. Here is sanctity which shames our religions, and reality which discredits our heroes.

13.17

Quotation from an essay by Ralph Waldo Emerson (1803-1882), entitled "Nature", published in 1844.

FIGURE 14.6

The Alert
message seen
before deletion
of a multiple
master font

with the utility. The name of the primary font or typeface will be shown within the quotation marks. You can click the Remove button to proceed with the deletion of the item, click the Remove More... button to see a list of other primary fonts and typefaces you could remove, or click Cancel to abort the removal command.

Once your new typeface has been created, you'll find it on your Font menu (displayed with the help of Adobe Type Reunion), as shown in Figure 14.7.

TIP

Remember that you can always print a multiple master primary font in any size, as you would a standard Type 1 typeface without using the Font Creator to generate a variation.

Figure 14.8 shows the result of creating and printing the new typeface specified with the settings shown in Figure 14.4. The new typeface is shown on the first line of Figure 14.8. In contrast, the typeface on the second line was generated from the standard Minion semi-bold primary font with an 11-point optical size.

In creating the figure, we printed both lines in a 72-point size. This figure demonstrates the advantages of using a multiple master typeface. The bottom line could be any text typeface that you might choose to print in a 72-point size. Since the typeface was probably designed for an 11- or 12-point size, the result may be characters that are too far apart and otherwise spaced poorly. (Note how far the capital M in Multiple is from the lowercase u that follows it.) On the other hand, the characters in the top line are spaced perfectly—without kerning. The characters are also narrower and bolder because of the settings used in the Font Creator to create this new typeface—an advantage only if you happen to want these particular characteristics but indicative of the versatility of a multiple master.

FIGURE 14.7

A new multiple master typeface displayed at the bottom of a Font submenu created through Type Reunion

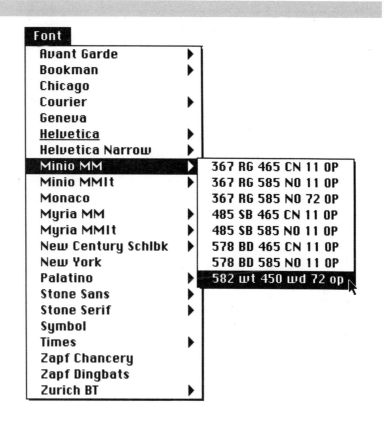

Font
Avant Garde ▶
Bookman ▶
Chicago
Courier ▶
Geneva
Helvetica ▶
Helvetica Narrow ▶
Minio MM ▶
Minio MMIt ▶
Monaco
Myria MM ▶
Myria MMIt ▶
New Century Schlbk ▶
New York
Palatino ▶
Stone Sans ▶
Stone Serif ▶
Symbol
Times ▶
Zapf Chancery
Zapf Dingbats
Zurich BT ▶

367 RG 465 CN 11 OP
367 RG 585 NO 11 OP
367 RG 585 NO 72 OP
485 SB 465 CN 11 OP
485 SB 585 NO 11 OP
578 BD 465 CN 11 OP
578 BD 585 NO 11 OP
582 wt 450 wd 72 op

FIGURE 14.8

A typeface created for use in a large point size (top line), contrasted with another designed for use in an 11-point size

Minion Multiple

Minion Multiple

TIP

A rival to multiple masters—FontChameleon (from Ares Software)—lets you create new typefaces by varying several characteristics simultaneously, including x-height and the style of serifs.

USING THE FONT DOWNLOADER

MacWrite Pro (and most other applications) will automatically download to the printer the outlines for the fonts you've selected. However, you may want to save that downloading time during the actual printing by storing in the printer's memory the typefaces you'll use frequently—*before* you start your day's work. Some printer outlines are permanently stored in the ROM (read-only memory) of your printer. For example, (as discussed in Chapter 13) a LaserWriter usually stores outlines for such typefaces as Helvetica, Times Roman, Bookman, Avant Garde, and Palatino—including italic and bold variations, 35 typefaces in all. You don't need to download any such typeface already in ROM.

DANGER

Don't download typefaces manually if your printer memory is limited. The reason is that typefaces are normally downloaded automatically by an application as they're needed for each document and flushed from the printer memory when they're no longer needed, in order to make room for the next batch. Typefaces you download manually will stay in the printer memory until the printer is turned off or restarted, regardless of the printer-memory requirements of other typefaces you may have specified in your documents.

To use the Font Downloader, follow these steps:

1 Make sure your printer is on and selected in the Chooser.

2 Locate the Font Downloader utility in the folder where you've stored it on your hard disk.

3 Double-click the Downloader icon to load the utility. A small Downloader menu bar will replace the normal Finder menu bar. This menu bar contains only File and Special menus. (The name is displayed for an Edit menu, since the Edit menu usually appears just to the right of the File menu on the Macintosh; however, the name is dimmed in this case because the Font Downloader has no Edit menu.)

4 Pull down the Downloader File menu, and select Download Font.... You'll see the dialog box shown in Figure 14.9.

5 If you don't have a hard disk for your printer (you probably have only one or more hard disks attached to your computer, not to your printer), the Device box at the right side of the dialog box will read Memory. You can then download typefaces only into the printer memory and can't change the Device setting.

- If the printer does have its own hard disk, you can change the setting in the Device box to download typefaces to the printer hard disk instead if you wish. To do this, press on the word Memory. A list will pop up showing Disk 1 and other options if they're available. Highlight the device name you want and release the mouse button.

FIGURE 14.9

The Download Font dialog box for the Font Downloader utility

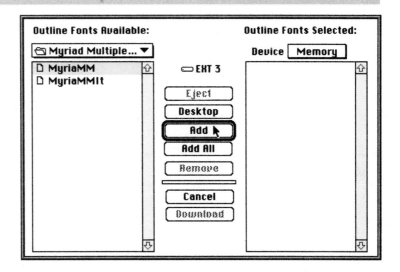

6 Change folders for the left list box until you locate the multiple master typefaces you want to download.

7 Select a single typeface by clicking to highlight its name, or Shift-click to select more than one typeface, then click the Add button. The typeface names will appear in the right list box, which shows those typefaces currently selected for downloading. If you want to download all of the typefaces in the current folder, click the Add All button instead.

8 Change the folder for the left list box again if you also want to download typefaces from a different folder, select those typefaces, and add them, following the instructions in step 5.

9 When the names appear in the right list box for all of the typefaces you want to download (from several folders, if necessary), click the Download button to complete the process of actually downloading the typefaces into the printer memory or to a selected printer hard disk.

10 Pull down the Downloader File menu again, and select Quit to close the utility.

Another command option on the Downloader File menu lets you download to the printer a file written in the PostScript language that contains PostScript language fonts and thereby print that file. Before you select this *Download POSTSCRIPT File...* option, you must have manually downloaded the specified outline typefaces and you must have saved the PostScript file in a text-only format. Then you can merely select the file name from the Open dialog box displayed by issuing the command and click OK; the file will be printed.

N O T E

After using the Font Downloader utility, don't forget to close it. As long as it remains in the memory of your Mac, it will control your printer and keep you from printing files through MacWrite Pro or other applications.

USING THE DOWNLOADER SPECIAL MENU

Typefaces you download to a printer hard disk will remain on this disk after you've shut down your Macintosh, ready for use when you start up the computer again. To remove typefaces you've downloaded to a printer hard disk, use the Font Downloader Special menu, shown in Figure 14.10.

Follow these steps to remove a typeface from the printer hard disk:

1 Make sure the printer is turned on and selected in the Chooser.

2 Pull down the Special menu and select Printer Font Directory.... You'll see a directory of the typefaces currently downloaded to the printer memory (unless someone has previously changed the Device setting from Memory to Disk 1 or some other printer-disk name).

3 If the Device setting does not show the name of the printer hard disk containing the typeface you want to remove, press the name in the Device box to display the list of available devices and select the correct printer disk. You'll now see a list of the typefaces currently stored on the printer hard disk.

4 Click to highlight the name of a typeface you want to remove, as demonstrated in Figure 14.11 (or Shift-click to select more than one name), then click Delete, followed by OK. (Click only OK if your goal is merely to examine the list of typefaces on the printer disk rather than to remove any.)

FIGURE 14.10

The Font
Downloader
Special menu

```
 ⌐  🍎  File   Edit  [Special]
                    ┌─────────────────────────────┐
                    │ Printer Status        ⌘S    │
                    │ Printer Font Directory ...  ⌘F │
                    ├─────────────────────────────┤
                    │ Clear Font Cache ...        │
                    │ Restart Printer! ...   ⌘R   │
                    │ Use Different Password ...  │
                    └─────────────────────────────┘
```

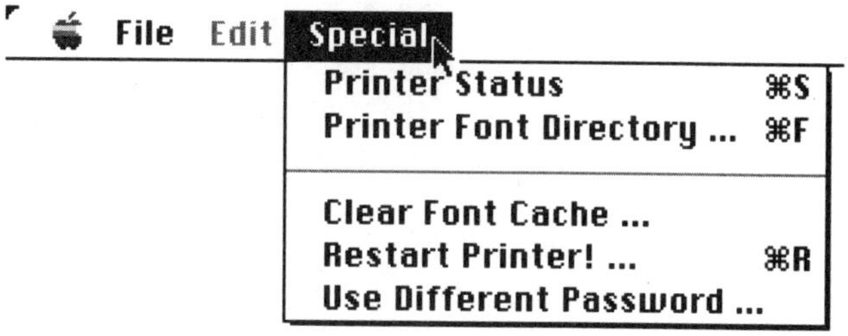

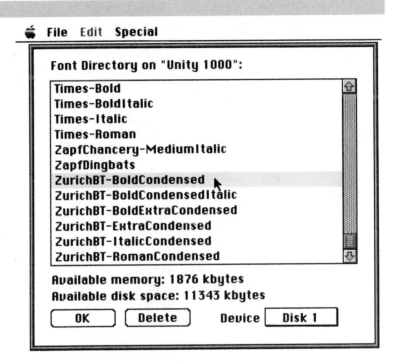

FIGURE 14.11

Selecting a typeface for deletion from the printer font directory

File   Edit   **Special**

Font Directory on "Unity 1000":

Times-Bold
Times-BoldItalic
Times-Italic
Times-Roman
ZapfChancery-MediumItalic
ZapfDingbats
ZurichBT-BoldCondensed
ZurichBT-BoldCondensedItalic
ZurichBT-BoldExtraCondensed
ZurichBT-ExtraCondensed
ZurichBT-ItalicCondensed
ZurichBT-RomanCondensed

Available memory: 1876 kbytes
Available disk space: 11343 kbytes

[OK]   [Delete]   Device [Disk 1]

The Printer Status option on the Downloader Special menu gives you the name of the printer currently selected in the Chooser and tells you whether that printer is idle or busy; the printer must be idle in order to accept downloaded typefaces.

The Clear Font Cache... command removes information from a printer memory regarding the font sizes in use; select this option if the downloading of many typefaces has filled up the printer font cache storing font-size information so that performance suffers on a PostScript Level 1 printer. Issuing this command causes the display of the warning message shown in Figure 14.12. If you click OK in response to the message, the printer will be restarted and the font cache will be cleared.

The Restart Printer!... command has the same effect as manually turning off the printer and then turning it on again; a restart will remove typefaces that have been stored in the printer's memory.

FIGURE 14.12

The warning
message seen
after issuing the
Clear Font
Cache... command

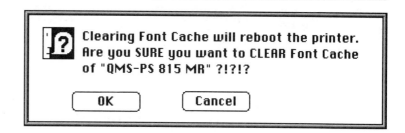

The Use Different Password... command is used only on a network when a printer password has been assigned and has subsequently been changed by the network administrator. The new password must be entered with this command before you can download typefaces or PostScript files.

USING KERNUS TO CREATE NEW TYPEFACES

URW has developed Kernus, a utility which can automatically create new typefaces from any existing typeface in the Adobe Type 1 format. These new typefaces will have individual character spacing based on a selected point size and can be accompanied by kerning tables containing up to 1,000 kerning pairs. Since some applications cannot recognize that many kerning pairs for a typeface, you have the option in using Kernus of limiting kerning pairs to a number smaller than 1,000. If you select a smaller number, the utility will automatically select the most important kerning pairs from its usual list of 1,000 up to the limit you've specified.

Kernus options include the ability to change the spacing of any two-character combination and also to add your own combinations to the kerning tables, a feature that could increase the number of kerning pairs well above 1,000.

The main dialog box for Kernus is shown in Figure 14.13. Note that you can set the point size you want to create by measuring either in *pica points* (the font measurement standard used in the United States and Great Britain) or in *Didot points* (the font measurement standard that predominates throughout most of Europe). You can also specify the *kernstrength* (the general spacing you want, ranging from .05 for wide spacing to 2 for narrow spacing) and the *designsize* (the size

FIGURE 14.13

The main Kernus
dialog box

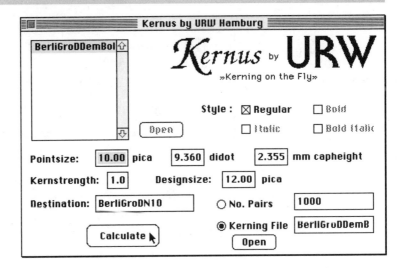

for which the typeface to be altered was originally designed, if you know this in-formation). *Capheight* is measured in millimeters and is based on the measurements of a capital H.

You can select boxes to create regular, italic, bold, and bold italic typefaces in the same size at the same time. The utility takes about 30 seconds to generate one new typeface.

Kernus is included free of charge on URW's TypeWorks typeface-library CD-ROM disk.

USING FONTOGRAPHER

To most Macintosh users, Altsys Corporation's Fontographer is the best-known program for modifying typefaces or designing new ones, although some professional type designers have other preferences. At this writing, Fontographer is the only program known to the author with which you can create typefaces in the multiple master format.

Fontographer is versatile and relatively user-friendly. It can create typefaces from Adobe Illustrator or Aldus FreeHand artwork, automatically trace scanned images to create typeface outlines, create multiple designs by interpolating between existing typefaces, and instantly generate typefaces with varying degrees of boldness (changing the weight). In addition, it has drawing tools, including one that automatically mimics the effect of using a calligraphic pen and another that lets you create script typefaces by using a pressure-sensitive drawing tablet. (However, your Mac needs only a mouse in order for you to use most Fontographer features.)

The program works with Bézier curves, generates kerning tables, and lets you import and/or save fonts in TrueType or Adobe Type 1 and Type 3 formats.

TIP

Remember that creating new typefaces from scratch is an intricate, demanding process. Unless you have plenty of patience and a little artistic ability, start using a typeface design program with a modest goal in mind—such as creating a single new character for a special purpose.

Ⓤ SING FONTSTUDIO

FontStudio offers capabilities similar to those found in Fontographer, except that it doesn't offer a calligraphic pen tool or multiple-master support, and you can't use a pressure-sensitive tablet to create script typefaces. FontStudio was developed by Letraset, (Esselte Letraset, Ltd.) a company that has been creating famous typefaces and related products for more than 30 years. It's an excellent program.

Ⓤ SING IKARUS M

Ikarus M is the Macintosh version of URW's Ikarus, a standard system for the creation of digital typefaces that has been used by nearly all digital type foundries since its introduction in 1972. This is a powerful program geared for the needs of the professional designer. Ikarus M was developed with the Aristotab 0304 digitizing tablet in mind, but also works with other tablets such as those manufactured by Wacom. You cannot use Ikarus M satisfactorily with a mouse alone.

The Ikarus M workspace is based on a high-resolution em- square of 15,000 by 15,000 units. Each unit of the em-square is mapped to 0.01 millimeters on the tablet.

Instead of using Bézier curves, which are modified by using control points located outside a character contour, the Ikarus format places the control points exactly on the contour. An on-screen values table shows the exact coordinates for each Ikarus control point, and you can make precise numerical changes in these points from the keyboard if you prefer.

One of the unique Ikarus features is the ability to modify contours automatically to create different degrees of aging. In other words, you can use parameter settings to make a typeface resemble the worn letters of a centuries-old hot-metal font.

You can save individual characters and logos as EPSF images, as well as creating TrueType and PostScript Type 1 and Type 3 typefaces. There is no support for multiple masters, and you must buy an additional URW program called Linus M in order to do auto-tracing. URW offers a package price when both products are purchased at the same time.

C ONVERTING A TYPEFACE TO A DIFFERENT FORMAT

If you merely want to convert an existing typeface (TrueType, Type 1 or Type 3) into another of these three formats, you can use FontStudio (described above), Metamorphosis from Altsys, FontMonger from Ares Software Corporation, or Image Club's Evolution (available as an individual product or included free on the company's typeface CD-ROM disks).

S UMMARY

Remember, it's relatively easy to create a new typeface from a multiple master or by using a utility such as Kernus. In either case, the entire process is almost automatic, and you're only generating a new version of an existing design.

However, actually designing a new typeface from scratch is a matter of laboriously creating dozens of original drawings. These drawings must not only be of excellent quality if your design is to be successful, but each character must fit smoothly between or adjacent to any other characters in the typeface that it will ever encounter in the language to be used.

As indicated earlier, it's wise to undertake a small project, such as the design of a single character or logo, before trying to compete with the work of designers like Bodoni, Goudy, or Zapf.

Installing
Macwrite Pro

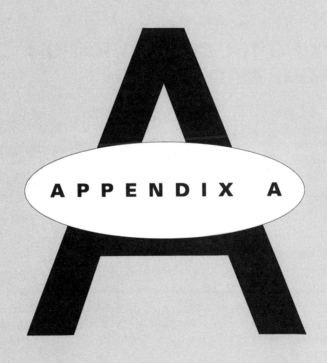

APPENDIX A

You can install MacWrite Pro on a Mac Plus, an SE, or any newer-model Macintosh, running under System 6.0.5 or later, including any version of System 7. Your Mac must have at least one 800K floppy drive (or a SuperDrive or compatible) and a hard disk. The computer must have at least 1,500K of free memory (1.5 MB of RAM) available in order to run MacWrite Pro; by this, we mean 1,500K of memory not already used by the operating system and utility files (INITs) that load automatically with the operating system.

C HECKING THE CONFIGURATION OF YOUR MAC

If you're not sure if your Mac meets all of these requirements, ask your Apple dealer. If you have no dealer nearby who is familiar with your system, you can check several of these requirements yourself through the Apple menu. Follow these steps:

1 Start your Mac, but don't open any programs.

2 Pull down the Apple menu (the menu in the upper-left corner of your screen that is represented by a small drawing—or *icon*—in the shape of an apple).

N O T E

 If you're new to the Macintosh, note that you "pull down" a menu by placing the mouse pointer on its title or icon, then holding down the mouse button. The menu will drop down, revealing its contents.

---

3 Still holding down the mouse button, move the pointer so that the first item on the menu is highlighted. This item reads *About This Macintosh....*

4 Release the mouse button. You'll see a small information window similar to the one shown in Figure A.1. This window will display the name of your Macintosh model, the version of the

System software in use, the total amount of memory installed, and the size of the largest block of memory not currently in use.

FIGURE A.1

The About This Macintosh window for a Quadra model 700

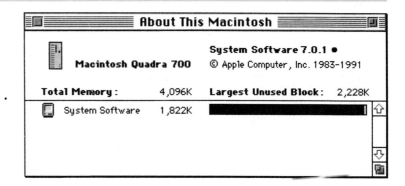

As you can see, the Macintosh in Figure A.1 is a Quadra 700 with a total of 4,096K of memory installed—or about 4 megabytes (MB). (This kind of memory is also called *RAM*—for Random-Access Memory.) Of this total amount of memory, System software version 7.0.1 is currently occupying 1,822K, leaving 2,228K available for use by programs.

This information tells you that the Mac is a recent model, running under a version of the operating system supported by MacWrite Pro, and with enough free memory available to run the program even if you allocate it 1,500K or more.

Remove the About This Macintosh window from your screen (close the window) by clicking the *close box*—the small square in the upper-left corner of the window.

TIP

If your Mac doesn't have enough memory to run the operating system plus MacWrite Pro, you have two possible solutions to this problem.

First, of course, you can have your dealer install additional memory; the cost can run as little as $200, depending upon the pricing policies of the dealer and the amount of memory you add.

The other alternative—available only if your Mac is running under System 7—is to replace System 7 with an earlier version of the operating system, which will require less memory. Use this second alternative only if you can't add more memory— because System 7 has many advantages which you would then have to do without.

MacWrite Pro has very modest memory and hardware requirements, so most Mac systems can run the program without difficulty.

ℝUNNING THE INSTALLER

MacWrite Pro is shipped in a compressed form on a series of disks stored in a sealed envelope inside the software package. To install the program on your hard disk, you must run the Installer—a utility program included on the first disk in this series. The Installer will decompress the files automatically and store them on whatever hard disk you specify that is attached to your Macintosh. Follow these steps to accomplish the installation:

1 Deactivate any virus-detection program you may have installed in your system. Such programs usually interfere with software installation.

2 Restart your Mac by switching it off and on or using the Restart command on the Special menu, holding down the Shift key as it restarts. This action will start the computer with extensions off—meaning that utility files that would normally load into your Mac's memory automatically (those INIT files) will not load. These utility programs too may interfere with software installation.

3 Insert the first disk of the MacWrite Pro installation software into your floppy drive. An icon for the disk will appear on your screen.

4 *Double-click* this icon. (Place the pointer on the icon, and depress the mouse button twice in quick succession.) A window will open showing the contents of the floppy disk.

(The window will resemble Figure A.2 but may not match it exactly, since Claris occasionally changes the files included with MacWrite Pro and its other programs.)

5 Double-click the Installer icon to start the installation program. An opening screen will be displayed, telling you that you're in the Installer. As soon as you click the OK button to acknowledge this message, you'll see the Easy Install window shown in Figure A.3.

6 If the hard disk named is not where you want MacWrite Pro installed, click the Switch Disk button in the window until the name appears of the hard disk you want.

7 For an automatic, complete installation of the program and its related files such as a dictionary for spell-checking, simply click the Install button once. The installation program will keep you informed as to its actions as it completes the installation and will prompt you to insert the other disks in the installation series as they're needed.

8 If you're an experienced Mac user and you want to install only selected files (perhaps because your hard-disk storage space is limited) click the Customize button instead of Install. You'll display a different screen containing a complete list of the files

FIGURE A.2

The contents of the first installation disk

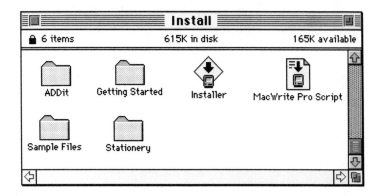

The Easy Install
window

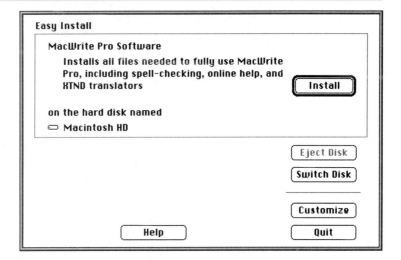

you can choose. Click any file name to see an explanation of
the purpose of the file, which will appear at the bottom of the
installation window. Then click the name of the first file you
want to install and hold down the Shift key as you click the
names of the other files you want. (Holding down the Shift key
keeps each new selection from canceling out the previous selection.) When you've completed your choices, click the Install
button in this window and follow the directions you'll see on
your screen. If you install all files, you'll need 3 MB of hard
disk space.

9 After completing either the Easy or Custom installation, reactivate
any virus-detection software and restart your Mac so it will recognize the new files required for support of MacWrite Pro.

10 To start MacWrite Pro, double-click the icon for the folder containing the program, then double-click the icon named Mac-
Write Pro, shown on the following page.

MacWrite Pro

CHANGING THE MEMORY ALLOCATION

Your Macintosh may have a few megabytes of extra memory not required for running the operating system and MacWrite Pro plus any other applications you'd like to have loaded simultaneously. If you're in this fortunate position, you may want to allocate additional memory to MacWrite Pro. Doing so will let you handle very large or intricate files more easily.

However, when you allocate more memory to an application than its minimum requirements, remember that this additional memory will thereafter be reserved for the application any time that program is open—whether or not the memory is needed. Figure A.4 illustrates this point. In this view of the About This Macintosh window, 1,500K memory has been allocated. Only MacWrite Pro and the operating system are loaded, and MacWrite Pro is using less than half of its assigned memory because no work is being done in the program at the moment. (The amount of memory actually in use is indicated by the black portion of the MacWrite Pro bar in the window.) Nevertheless, the entire 1,500K is still reserved for MacWrite Pro.

FIGURE A.4

MacWrite Pro
retains its full
memory allocation,
even when some
of the memory is
not in use

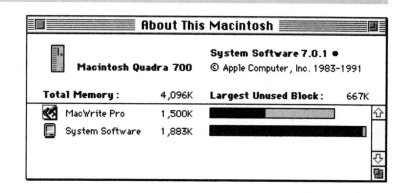

To change the amount of memory reserved for MacWrite Pro, follow these steps:

1 Quit MacWrite Pro, if the program is currently open.

2 Click once on the MacWrite Pro program icon to highlight it. (Don't double-click or you'll open the program again.)

3 Pull down the File menu, and select the Get Info option. (Shortcut: hold down the ⌘ key and press the letter I.) You'll see an Info window similar to the one shown in Figure A.5, providing you with statistics about MacWrite Pro.

FIGURE A.5

The Info window
for MacWrite Pro

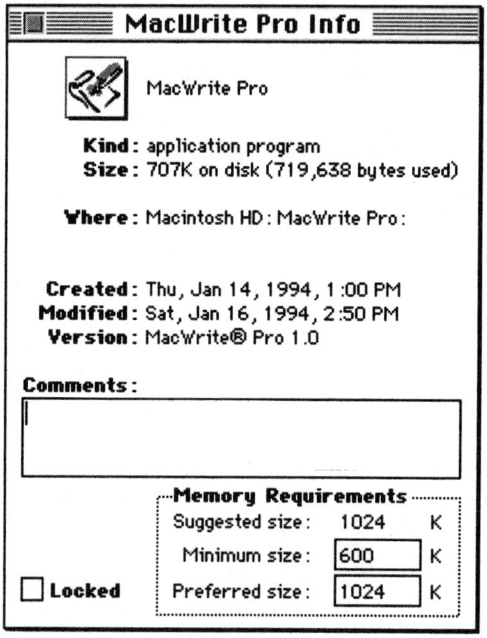

```
┌─────────────────────────────────────────┐
│ ▤▦▥▥▥    MacWrite Pro Info    ▥▥▥▥▥       │
├─────────────────────────────────────────┤
│   ┌──────┐                                │
│   │ ✎▨   │   MacWrite Pro                 │
│   └──────┘                                │
│                                           │
│      Kind : application program           │
│      Size : 707K on disk (719,638 bytes used) │
│                                           │
│     Where : Macintosh HD : MacWrite Pro : │
│                                           │
│                                           │
│   Created : Thu, Jan 14, 1994, 1:00 PM    │
│  Modified : Sat, Jan 16, 1994, 2:50 PM    │
│   Version : MacWrite® Pro 1.0             │
│                                           │
│  Comments :                               │
│  ┌─────────────────────────────────────┐ │
│  │                                     │ │
│  │                                     │ │
│  └─────────────────────────────────────┘ │
│            ┌─Memory Requirements──────┐   │
│            Suggested size :   1024   K    │
│            Minimum size : │ 600  │   K    │
│ ☐ Locked   Preferred size : │1024  │  K   │
└─────────────────────────────────────────┘
```

4 In the Memory section at the bottom of the window, change the number in the Current Size box from 1500 (for 1,500K) to any larger number you wish (provided, of course, that you have enough free memory available to allow the use of the larger number).

5 Click the close box to close the window. The next time you start MacWrite Pro, its new memory allocation will be in effect.

Product Sources

APPENDIX B

For your convenience, the following directory lists addresses and phone numbers for the manufacturers of products mentioned in this book. The information was current at the time of publication.

Adobe Systems
1585 Charleston Road
P.O. Box 7900
Mountain View, CA 94039
(800) 833-6687

Agfa
Division of Miles Inc.
200 Ballardvale St.
Wilmington, MA 01887
(800) 424-8973

Altsys Corporation
269 W. Renner Rd.
Richardson, TX 75080
(214) 680-2060

Apple Computer
20525 Mariani Ave.
Cupertino, CA 95014
(408) 996-1010

Ares Software Corporation
561 Pilgrim Drive, Suite D
Foster City, CA 94404
(415) 578-9090

Baseline Publishing
1770 Moriah Woods Blvd., Suite 14
Memphis, TN 38117-7118
(901) 682-9676

Bitstream
215 First St.
Cambridge, MA 02142
(617) 497-6222

Broderbund Software
500 Redwood Blvd.
Novato, CA 94948
(415) 382-4400

Casady & Greene
22734 Portola Drive
Salinas, CA 93908
(408) 484-9228

Claris Corporation
5201 Patrick Henry Dr.
Santa Clara, CA 95052
(408) 727-8227

Dataproducts Corporation
6219 De Soto Ave.
Woodland Hills, CA 91365-0746
(818) 887-8000

Digital Typeface Corporation
9955 W. 69th St.
Eden Prairie, MN 55344
(800) 947-8880

Dubl-Click Software
22521 Styles St.
Woodland Hills, CA 91367
(818) 888-2068

Dynamic Graphics
6000 N. Forest Park Dr.
Peoria, IL 61614-3592
(309) 688-8800

Epson America
20770 Madrona Ave.
Torrance, CA 90503
(800) 922-8911

Fifth Generation Systems
10049 N. Reiger Rd.
Baton Rouge, LA 70809
(504) 291-7221

The Font Company
7850 E. Evans Rd., Suite 111
Scottsdale, AZ 85260
(602) 998-9711

Grolier Electronic Publishing, Inc.
Sherman Turnpike
Danbury, CT 06816
(800) 356-5590

Image Club Graphics
1902 Eleventh St. S.E., Suite 5
Calgary, Alberta T2G 3G2 Canada
(800) 661-9410

Kensington Microware
2855 Campus Dr.
San Mateo, CA 94403
(800) 535-4242

LaserMaster Corporation
6900 Shady Oak Road
Eden Prairie, MN 55344
(800) 950-6868

Letraset (Fontek)
40 Eisenhower Drive
Paramus, NJ 07653
(800) 343-TYPE

Linotype-Hell Company
425 Oser Avenue
Hauppauge, New York 11788
(800) 633-1900
Canada: (800) 285-8973 + '3'
United Kingdom:
(0242) 222-333
Germany: (06196) 98-2640
Continent: (06196) 98-2754
Japan: 0120-396-839

Metro Image Base
18623 Ventura Blvd., Suite 210
Tarzana, CA 91356
(800) 525-1552

Monotype Typography
53 W. Jackson Blvd., Suite 504
Chicago, IL 60604
(312) 855-1440

Portfolio Systems
10062 Miller Ave., Suite 201
Cupertino, CA 95014
(408) 252-0420

QMS
One Magnum Pass
Mobile, AL 36618
(800) 631-2692

Silicon Valley Bus Co.
22546 Summit Rd.
Los Gatos, CA 95030
(408) 353-6000

URW
4 Manchester St.
Nashua, NH 03060
(800) 229-8791

Varityper, Inc.
11 Mt. Pleasant Avenue
East Hanover, NJ 07936
(201) 887-8000

 **NDEX**

Boldfaced page numbers indicate definitions and the principal discussions of primary topics and subtopics. *Italic* page numbers indicate illustrations.

Symbols

<< >> (angle brackets), in mail-merge letters, 226
* (asterisk), in searches, 29
{ } (curly brackets), in mail-merge letters, 226
… …(ellipsis), in menu commands, 4
— (em dash), 147–148, *147*
– (en dash), 147–148, *147*
= (equals), 235
> (greater than), 235
>= (greater than or equal to), 235
- (hyphen), 147–148, *147*
< (less than), 235
<= (less than or equal to), 235
< > (not equal to), 235
? (question mark), in searches, 29
" " (quotation marks), straight versus curly, 132–133, 146–147, *147*, 210–211, 244
[ ] (square brackets), in mail-merge letters, 226
[(left bracket key), for "curly quotes," 147

A

Abadi Extra Bold Condensed typeface, 121, *122*
About This Macintosh window, 346–347, 351–353
access privileges
At Ease program and, 261–262
to folders and hard disks, 190–193
saving, 188, *188*, 194, *194*
for users and groups, 187–188
accessing other computers, **194–199**. *See also* file sharing
choosing computers to access, 195

choosing items to share, 196–198, *196*, *197*
logging on, 196
added character sets, 148–150, *148*, *149*, *150*
Adobe Font Metrics (AFM) files, **320**
Adobe Systems, 356. *See also* multiple master typefaces
Adobe Illustrator, 95, 139, 320, 341
Adobe Photoshop,
creating gray images with, 73
for scanned images, 101–102, *102*, *103*
Adobe Type Manager, 152, 316, 317–320
Adobe Type Reunion,
Character dialog box and, 206–207, *208*
Font menu and, 32, *34*
installing, **316–320**
multiple master typefaces and, 326
and showing actual typefaces on Font menu, 213–214
PostScript fonts, **152–153**
purchasing typefaces, 308
Type 1 typeface format,
Apple Classic Fonts and, 291
availability of, 153
converting, 342
creating, 341–342
explained, **152**
Fontgrapher and, 341
Image Club typefaces and, 139
installing typefaces in, 320
modifying, 315
Type 3 typeface format,
creating, 341–342
explained, **152**
Fontgrapher and, 341

Image Club typefaces and, 139
typefaces,
Abadi Extra Bold Condensed, 121, *122*
Antique Olive Bold Condensed, *249*, 250
Arrighi, *123*, 124
Blackoak, 132, *132*
Cantoria, 124, *125*
Caslon, *280*, 282
Caslon Expert Collection, 148–149, *149*
Centaur, *123*, 124
Expert Collections, 148–149, *149*
Fette Fraktur typeface, *306*, 307
Garth Graphic, 138, *138*
Helvetica Inserat, 252, *253*
Ironwood, 252, *253*
ITC Kabel, 142, *142*
Joanna, 135, *136*
Juniper, 88, *89*
Mesquite, 90, *91*, 160, *161*, *304*
Monotype Script Bold, 90, *92*, 138, *138*
Pepita, 132, *132*
Perpetua Bold, *247*, 248
Photina Bold, 146, *147*
Plantin family, 121–122, *122*
Popular, 132, *132*
Shannon, 138, *138*
Stencil, 112, *113*, 130, *131*
Stone Phonetic, 150, *150*
Tekton, 304, *305*
AFM files, **320**
AG Old Face Shaded typeface, 90, *92*
Agfa, 356
The Art & Technology of Typography, 309
typefaces,
CG Omega, 140
Garth Graphic, 138, *138*

F REE COMPANION DISK FROM
⋮ IMAGE CLUB GRAPHICS

If you want to use the sample envelope, report, announcement, invitation, newsletter, and notice stationery files presented in this book without keying them in yourself, you can send for a free companion disk containing all the templates, and Image Club typefaces and clip art. You can use these files to speed your learning (less typing), or as modifiable applications that you can refine to suit your needs. You must already have access to MacWrite Pro to use these files.

To receive the free companion disk, please complete the order form below and return it with $10.00 for shipping and handling. Please send check, international money order, or credit card number to the address shown on the coupon. Sorry, only one disk per coupon.

When you return the coupon, you will also receive free catalogues about other Image Club products.

. . . .

Image Club Graphics, Inc.
Attn: Disk Offer
1902 Eleventh Street, S.E.
Calgary, Alberta
T2G 3G2
Phone (403) 262-8008   FAX (403) 261-7013

_____ Please send the free companion disk for *The MacWrite Pro Book*. *
_____ Please send me a catalog of Image Club products.

Name: _____

Company: _____

Street:_____

City, State, Zip: _____

Country: _____

P.O. Box Number (if applicable) _____

* There is a $10 shipping and handling charge.

Method of Payment. Check one:

_____ Check or Money Order
_____ Credit Card (VISA, MasterCard, American Express)

Credit Card Number:_____

Expiration Date:_____

SYBEX is not affiliated with Image Club Graphics and assumes no responsibility for any defect in the disk or files.

SYBEX

FREE BROCHURE!

Complete this form today, and we'll send you a full-color brochure of Sybex bestsellers.

Please supply the name of the Sybex book purchased.

_____

How would you rate it?

_____ Excellent   _____ Very Good   _____ Average   _____ Poor

Why did you select this particular book?

_____ Recommended to me by a friend

_____ Recommended to me by store personnel

_____ Saw an advertisement in _____

_____ Author's reputation

_____ Saw in Sybex catalog

_____ Required textbook

_____ Sybex reputation

_____ Read book review in _____

_____ In-store display

_____ Other _____

Where did you buy it?

_____ Bookstore

_____ Computer Store or Software Store

_____ Catalog (name: _____)

_____ Direct from Sybex

_____ Other: _____

Did you buy this book with your personal funds?

_____ Yes   _____ No

About how many computer books do you buy each year?

_____ 1-3   _____ 3-5   _____ 5-7   _____ 7-9   _____ 10+

About how many Sybex books do you own?

_____ 1-3   _____ 3-5   _____ 5-7   _____ 7-9   _____ 10+

Please indicate your level of experience with the software covered in this book:

_____ Beginner   _____ Intermediate   _____ Advanced

Which types of software packages do you use regularly?

_____ Accounting	_____ Databases	_____ Networks
_____ Amiga	_____ Desktop Publishing	_____ Operating Systems
_____ Apple/Mac	_____ File Utilities	_____ Spreadsheets
_____ CAD	_____ Money Management	_____ Word Processing
_____ Communications	_____ Languages	_____ Other _____
		(please specify)

Which of the following best describes your job title?

_____ Administrative/Secretarial _____ President/CEO

_____ Director _____ Manager/Supervisor

_____ Engineer/Technician _____ Other _____
(please specify)

Comments on the weaknesses/strengths of this book: _____

_____

_____

_____

_____

Name _____

Street _____

City/State/Zip _____

Phone _____

PLEASE FOLD, SEAL, AND MAIL TO SYBEX

SYBEX, INC.
Department M
2021 CHALLENGER DR.
ALAMEDA, CALIFORNIA USA
94501

SYBEX

Ⓜ️OVING THE POINTER

Beginning of document	⌘-↑
Beginning of line	⌘-←
End of document	⌘-↓
End of line	⌘-→
Main text from header, footer, footnote, or frame	⌘-Return
Next character	Right arrow or Control-]
Next line	↓
Next paragraph	Option-↓
Next word	Option-→
Previous character	←
Previous line	↑
Previous paragraph	Option-↑
Previous word	Option-←

Ⓜ️OVING TO AREAS WITHOUT MOVING POINTER

Beginning of document	Control-A or Home
End of document	Control-D or End
Next page	Shift-Control-L or Shift-Page Down
Next screen	Control-L or Page Down
Previous page	Shift-Control-K or Shift-Page Up
Previous screen	Control-K or Page Up